P9-BII-744

DESERT MAP & AERIAL PHOTO
73-612 HWY. 111
PALM DESERT, CA 92260-4022
(619) 346-1101

MIGRANTS WEST

Toward the Southern California Frontier

by Ronald C. Woolsey

Foreword by
Gordon Morris Bakken

GRIZZLY BEAR PUBLISHING COMPANY
P. O. BOX 1266
CLAREMONT, CA 91711-1266

COPYRIGHT 1996
ALL RIGHTS RESERVED,
INCLUDING THE RIGHT OF REPRODUCTION
IN WHOLE OR IN PART IN ANY FORM
LIBRARY OF CONGRESS CATALOG CARD NUMBER
96-76750

WOOLSEY, RONALD C./1949-
MIGRANTS WEST,
TOWARD THE SOUTHERN CALIFORNIA FRONTIER/
WOOLSEY, RONALD C./ 1ST ED.
FOREWORD
BY GORDON MORRIS BAKKEN
DUST JACKET PAINTING
BY ANDREW DAGOSTA
MAP DRAWING
BY MICHAEL SANDOVAL
BOOK & DUST JACKET DESIGN
BY MARSHA E. BANAS
INCLUDES FOOTNOTES, BIBLIOGRAPHY, INDEX
FIRST TRADE EDITION
ISBN 1-881591-14-X

CONTENTS

MAP

PHOTOGRAPHS

Acknowledgment

I am indebted to many scholars, librarians and research professionals who have provided commentary and insight into various aspects of Southern California history, critiqued portions of this manuscript and inspired my overall research and writing.

Gordon M. Bakken and Doyce B. Nunis Jr. have been friends and mentors for two decades, encouraging my earliest research of the court cases and manuscripts available at the Seaver Center for Western History and Los Angeles Law Archives. Robert Blew, Abraham Hoffman and Thomas Tefft have provided important readings of the text. Over the years, several conversations with scholars at the Huntington Library have been helpful in the formation of my approach to this study, including discussions with Judson Grenier, Wilbur Jacobs, Donald Pflueger, Martin Ridge and Andrew Rolle. The California History Group at the Huntington Library, co-founded by Michael Engh and Howard Shorr, has provided a forum for some aspects of this work, and the group members have always been supportive in my research.

The staffs at the Bancroft Library, California State Library, Honnold Library, Seaver Center for Western History and Huntington Library graciously offered their help and expertise in my research of manuscript and photograph collections at their respective institutions.

My thanks go to the many editors who have published monographs by the author related to this study. Those journals and magazines include the *Southern California Quarterly, California History, The Californians, True West Magazine, The Missouri Historical Reivew* and the Los Angeles *Westerners Branding Iron Quarterly*.

Professional editing of the manuscript has been generously provided by Paul Hawley and Jean Sherrell, while artists Andrew Dagosta and Michael Sandoval have graciously applied their talents to the map design and dust jacket cover.

Financial sponsorship through grants and fellowships were provided by the National Endowment for the Humanities, National Council for Basic Education, the Andrew W. Mellon and the John Randolph and Dora Haynes Foundations through the Huntington Library, and Michael Milken Teaching and Research Grants from the Los Angeles Archdiocese. The Historical Society of Southern California and Thomas F. Andrews, HSSC Executive Director, deserve a special thanks for their support, financial assistance and recognition as a teacher-scholar through my receipt of a 1994 O'Flaherty Teaching Award.

Most important, I am indebted to my family: wife of 25 years, Patricia, and children Colleen and Andrew. Their unselfish spirit, patience and understanding provided me with the perseverance necessary to complete this work.

My good wishes go to all of the above individuals, organizations and institutions for their contributions to this study, although any shortcomings of this publication are the responsibility of the author alone.

Ronald C. Woolsey
La Verne, California
August 1996

In Memory of

Donald H. Pflueger
a teacher, a scholar,
and friend

Foreword

Southern California's early history has been portrayed as a Hispanic Eden of benevolent priests and happy Indians that gave way to another idyllic era of ranchos managed by gentle dons who supervised skillful vaqueros and industrious natives only to be lost in a wave of Anglo migration that, in turn, brought a self-governing dominion of democracy despite the machinations of a violent underclass. By other lights, the missions were concentration camps, the dons exploited native labor, and the Anglos were mere capitalistic opportunists who mined the mountains, fields, and streams leaving the environment and culture hopelessly polluted. Often lost in these debates about the covering thesis of California's early history are the lives of the people that lived Southern California's early period. Lost too is an appreciation of history as lives in a local environment that was both cultural and spatial. Southern California was a place in the West where the Hispanic culture confronted native cultures and both were changed. Anglos arrived to go through a similar process. But the particulars of change were personal and can be teased out of lives, not abstractions.

Southern California was an evolving multi-cultural, gendered landscape with all of the stereotypes common to the land. In the study of particular lives in this particular place, *Migrants West: Toward The Southern California Frontier* has put people and personality into the history of the region in its early days. Drawing upon extensive archival sources and a growing literature questioning stereotypes and grand generalizations, this book allows each of us to find people in their place and to allow there lives to illuminate our own. This is no small excursion into the history of Southern California and we are all beneficiaries of Ron Woolsey's years of dedicated research and writing.

One of the many themes running through this book that deserves early notice is the role of law in the society. Readers will quickly note that many of the persons explored in the text were lawyers or judges. Many of the people had occasion to be a part of the legal process. Their view of the society was colored by the lens of law. As John Phillip Reid has taught us, the migrants of the overland trail were lawminded. The law was the taught, learned and accepted customs of the people in a community centered on the law of the sovereign. People respected private property and in so doing, adhered to a morality of law. David Langum has demonstrated that in Mexican California the common-law tradition of the migrants came into conflict with the shared customs of its Hispanic residents. Hispanic conflict resolution was bargained in a personal set of arrangements rather than in the adversary context of judicial trial. Ron Woolsey adds to this text by recounting the personalized texturing participants gave to events grounded in their legally formed lens. The commingling of law and community from multiple perspectives gives yet another insight into the lives of those who shaped our early history.

Early Southern California molded an emerging American experience in a multi-cultural context. Those that lived it give us new glimpses of the experience passed on to us in history further textured by Ron Woolsey's *Migrants West, Toward The Southern California Frontier.*

Gordon Morris Bakken
California State University, Fullerton

Introduction

M*igrants West: Toward The Southern California Frontier* is a collection of pioneer vignettes about men and women with diverse skills, varying degrees of ambition and different cultural backgrounds. All of them complemented the development of the community, spanning several decades, from the Rancho period to the post-Civil War years, and highlighting major issues in frontier settlement like vigilantism, race, and commercial growth. Historian Jackson Putnam observed that the "symbolic frontier," or the impact of the Westward Movement on the American psyche, could be better understood by focusing on the "conflicts which raged within each frontiersman."[1] These pioneers represent separate points on a horizon, which together make a colorful panorama of frontier experiences, providing an open window to Southern California's past.

In the 1830s and 1840s, commercial opportunities attracted Abel Stearns and other New England traders. Ambitious opportunists took advantage of new trade routes with the Orient and Latin America, sold and traded abundant supplies of California timber and hides, exploited new markets and traded finished goods fashioned by local artisans and metalworkers. Abel Stearns led this Anglo migration, as a trader and landowner who soon became influential in politics, then found himself caught between competing nations with different cultures.

Stearns, like many Yankee expatriates, assimilated within Hispanic society, married within a ranchero family, adopted native customs and embraced an agrarian lifestyle typical of California's pastoral period.

Even as the American conquest tested Stearns' loyalties, Native Americans were also caught between Mexican to Anglo rule. Mexico's secularization of the missions left many Indians homeless, working at subsistence level for themselves or for the Californio hacienderos who had so eagerly taken over church lands; some sought refuge on deteriorating mission properties. Hugo Reid, a Scot immigrant who married an aborigine, Victoria, was the lone voice raised among the mute pleas of the Indians. Alarmed at the dilapidated condition of the rancherias, Reid wrote a series of newspaper articles that detailed Gabrieleño customs, thereby educating an Anglo audience as to the civilized qualities of the Gabrieleño tribes. While Yankee abolitionists were demanding an end to slavery, Reid was calling for a reservation to protect the Native American from the hardships that followed their liberation from the missions.

Southern California commerce expanded during the 1850s, displacing the ranchero while asserting Anglo influence in law and politics. Charles Ducommun and Joseph Lancaster Brent were at the forefront of an expanding settlement. Ducommun, a Swiss immigrant, became an active leader in civic and financial affairs as a vigilante, entrepreneur, financial lender and watchmaker. Brent represented the ambivalence most Westerners felt having left their birthplace, a dilemma evident with the Civil War. He was a Southerner, Democratic political kingmaker and legal advisor to the Californios, who had vigorously opposed any covert movement to force California's secession, but left the state to fight for the Confederacy, never to return to the West.

Other travelers had little choice in the decision to migrate. A desperate and destitute Margaret Wilson migrated to Southern California with her family, hoping to benefit from the cattle demand created by the gold rush. Judah was brought to Southern California by John Evertson, a South Carolinian slaveholder who had moved to Southern California to begin anew, perhaps acquire a plantation, grow cotton and purchase more slaves like Judah.

During the 1850s, land title disputes, the decline of cattle ranching and the differences between Hispanic customs and Anglo jurisprudence accelerated cultural tensions, creating a perception of Anglo injustice or indifference toward Hispanic rights. Open defiance sometimes found expression in the form of social banditry, which was a label for frontier-styled Robin Hoods. Juan Flores and other bandidos symbolized defiance for Hispanics who had little faith in frontier justice. The Anglo community, alarmed by such lawlessness, granted extralegal powers to Sheriff James Barton and other peace officers. Law enforcement officials assumed the authority to enlist posses, hold vigilante trials and administer public executions. Most Hispanics, however, tried to work within the system to improve the community in the post-conquest era. Don Antonio Coronel, a ranchero from the bygone days of Mexican rule, vainly attempted to maintain the fading prestige and power of a once elite class. It was like trying to bottle the wind.

Southern California also reflected the sectional divisions of America at mid-century, including the issues of slavery, states rights and secession. Newspaperman Henry Hamilton and firebrand Edward John Cage Kewen articulated the Confederate cause, defended Southern rights and opposed unfair Union policies. For Kewen and Hamilton, the Southerners' bid for independence spoke to an independent frontier community, and they believed themselves spokesmen of Western sympathy for the Southern cause.

Anglo immigration steadily increased during the post- Civil War years, spurred by real estate speculation, the introduction of the Southern Pacific Railroad and the growth of the citrus industry. Don Antonio Coronel met writer Helen Hunt Jackson during this period of new settlement, acting as mentor and guide while she toured Southern California for research on her novel, *Ramona*. The book idealized Mexican Southern California, focused national attention on the plight of Native Americans and forever defined the mythic romance of the rancho days, an era that Coronel had fought so hard to preserve in his lifetime.

Finally, the Southern California frontier had its chroniclers, a literary entourage that brought thematic sense to the everyday deeds of Western settlement. Benjamin Hayes and Horace Bell posed contrasting views on law and community, which represented the very essence of frontier settlement. Outspoken, controversial and only sometimes interested in the truth, Bell wrote a collection of reminiscences that were a metaphor for his own life: an unforgiving land, filled with danger, providing a stage for society's struggle to remain civilized. Judge Hayes' diaries show a less combative spirit. He believed that Western settlement was a principled quest to establish American democracy. Where Bell saw a frontier to be conquered, Hayes found an Eden to be cultivated -perceptions that laid the basis for their opposing attitudes toward society and justice.

If individuals are representative of ideas larger than themselves, then historical biography can offer new meaning to the frontier era. As Western writer Wallace Stegner once observed, "(T)here is something about exposure to that big country that not only tells an individual how small he is, but steadily tells him who he is."[2] The pioneers in *Migrants West: Towards The Southern California Frontier* speak to us in the same way, telling us who we were, and how significant that era was to our region's past.

Judge Benjamin Hayes' residence

 Pico House (circa 1870) built during the apex of Southern California's first land boom

 Ignacio Coronel's residence

 Ignacio del Valle's townhouse

 Plaza Center (circa 1825)

 Plaza Church (circa 1822)

 Pelanconi House (circa 1855)

 Avila Adobe (circa 1818)

 Benjamin D. Wilson's house

 Early location of the Los Angeles Star, bought and operated by Henry Hamilton in 1856

 Benjamin and Margaret Wilson's General Store

 Charles Ducommun's Hardware Store

 The Bella Union Hotel served as a temporary residence of early settlers

 Bell Row (later Mellus Row), which James Barton helped construct in 1850

 Abel Stearns' Arcadia Block

 Abel Stearns' adobe home, El Palacio

 The Montgomery Saloon, a meeting place for Confederate sympatizers

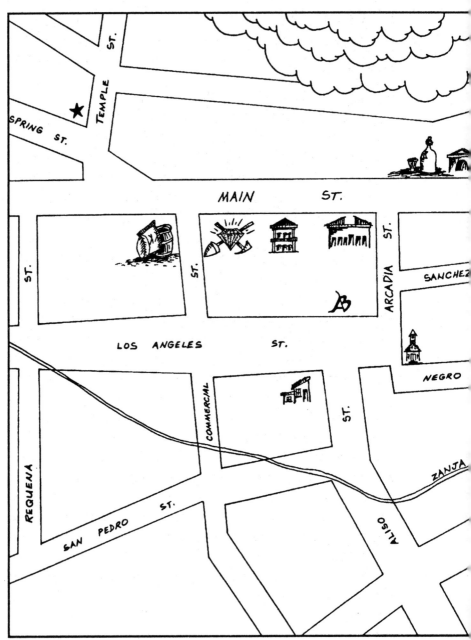

Legend of Selected Locations page XV

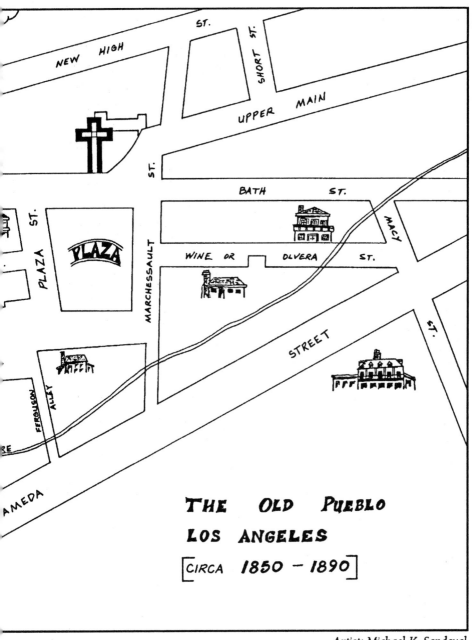

THE OLD PUEBLO
LOS ANGELES
[CIRCA 1850 – 1890]

Artist: Michael K. Sandoval

"The people of the United States
have never in the least realized
that the taking possession of
California was not only a conquering
of Mexico, but a conquering of
California as well."

quoted from *Ramona*
Helen Hunt Jackson

CHAPTER ONE

Abel Stearns
and an
Adopted Land

I n 1829, Abel Stearns came to California in search of a new life which would be rich in promise, leaving behind his early years in Massachusetts where personal tragedy and misfortune had dogged him. Orphaned before his teenage years and widowed by his mid-twenties, Stearns sought tranquility at sea as well as mercantile opportunities, following the trade winds along the Pacific routes, visiting Mexico, and eventually landing in the Mexican province of California. Stearns was only one of those early Yankee migrants who rose to prominence in Southern California, but would soon stand out and be remembered as "the richest" man of his era.[1]

Stearns' first venture was an attempt to acquire land on the Sacramento River. He loved the water, and his commercial instincts suggested that Northern California was ripe for river commerce in new markets for lumber, cowhides, beaver and otter pelts. Trader Alpheus Thompson encouraged him to pursue the trade in sea otters, a business free of regulation and competition. "No time should be lost," wrote Thompson, "as a fortune can soon be acquired with good luck and good management."[2] Like other Yankee expatriates, Stearns saw California as an untapped resource, a pristine land inhabited by a blithe people described by Robert Glass Cleland as being "free from the pressure of economic competition, ignorant of the wretchedness and poverty indigenous to other lands, amply supplied with the means of satisfying their ample wants."[3] Stearns' writings to fellow Anglo traders extolled the country's virtues, and believing, as one of his acquaintances proclaimed, that California was "the most delightful country in the world."[4]

Unfortunately, however, the cumbersome workings of the Mexican government dampened Stearns' ambitious plans for establishing a trade and land title. Local authorities rejected his initial efforts to acquire land because of political considerations. Officials generally were wary of the Anglo motives in coming west, fearing that the foreigners' intent was to undermine Mexican authority. Governor Manuel Victoria in particular, threatened by rivals within as well as without the territory, was unsympathetic to Stearns' appeals and suspicious of the Yankee's loyalty to his own leadership.

By 1832, Stearns had failed to purchase land in Northern California; his prospects of establishing residency seemed remote. Despite the suspicions and political obstacles to acquiring land, Stearns was determined to make a new life in California. He declared his resolve in a letter to one business acquaintance: "I [Stearns] still have the right to remain in this Territory or in any other part of the Republic."[5] Looking southward, he turned to San Pedro, favorably situated between the maritime centers of San Diego and San Francisco yet removed from the political intrigues at Monterey. Traders had considered the San Pedro harbor an inferior port, little more than an "expansive mud flat" until Phineas Banning developed the area nearly two decades later.[6] Stearns believed that Southern California had potential, it's strong hide and tallow trade outweighing any liabilities, even the ruinous drought underway since he'd first come to California: "We have an envious [enviable] advantage owing to the great productivity of the region."[7]

In 1834, Stearns opened a trading post at San Pedro and quickly established contacts at Monterey, thus positioning himself as a liaison between Northern California merchants and local rancheros.[8] Stearns' *Casa de San Pedro* represented Californias first link in a commercial network extending toward the Orient, south to La Paz and around Cape Horn to the Atlantic seaboard. His tiny outpost, supported by local rancheros and a coastline trade in hides, lumber, and otter, capitalized on these routes. "The future of the Pueblo," Stearns predicted, "is towards the sea."[9]

As it happened, however, Stearns had been overly optimistic about the strength of the Southern California economy. Almost entirely agrarian, it was vulnerable to uncertain weather and sensitive market conditions. Cattle, a "moving wealth," dominated Hispanic life, creating both social and economic fabric to such an extent that it retarded commercial diversification.[10] Inclement weather disrupted breeding and limited grazing, resulting in smaller numbers of cattle for slaughter. In 1829, the year Stearns landed in California, a severe drought destroyed nearly 40,000 cattle in the southern region. "Business has not been so good," wrote Stearns, hoping that a wet winter would bring brighter days with "a good harvest of Tallow, probably better than we have had for some years."[11] But economic downturns continued to plague Southern California throughout the Mexican period, eroding that trade on which Stearns had pinned so much of his hopes.[12] In 1840, the San Pedro trading post handled 1326 hides; in 1844, only 863.[13] During one bad stretch, Stearns lamented that "If I could put my property into cash or hides I might possibly return to the U.S."[14]

But Stearns probably never seriously intended to return to his birthplace because the depressed economy was nationwide. Credit was tight and money scarce in the Jackson and Van Buren years, and local residents received pessimistic reports of adversity elsewhere. Missourian David Waldo wrote John Rowland, a Stearns acquaintance, about hard times back East, mounting public anxiety, "and the want of all confidence

Abel Stearns

through the United States."[15] There was turmoil even closer to home. One correspondant, William Keith, reported to Stearns that political instability in Sonora, Mexico, had led to rebellion and depression with "nothing but famine staring us in the face."[16] These widespread economic difficulties so slowed the pace of migration that by 1840, less than two dozen Anglos were living in Los Angeles, with only five new emigrants recorded between 1835 and 1840.[17]

The ability to survive difficult times required ingenuity, resourcefulness, and flexibility to respond to a changing marketplace. So Stearns wore many hats throughout the 1830s: surveyor, marketing agent, alleged smuggler, and trusted member of the *Ayuntamiento*, a city council which consisted of the wealthy elites. He altered his dependence on the hide trade, instead catering to larger demands within the locale. His day book at San Pedro reflected the pueblo's needs for textiles, porcelain, wine, dry goods and lumber. By 184U, the retail operation showed consistent sales and a profit despite a tough market.[18]

Stearns' financial prospects mirrored larger economic trends, as the one-note rancho economy was forced to gradually shift toward a diversified marketplace. Surplus Indian labor created by secularization as well as the growth of an overland trade both produced a new dynamic within the pueblo, and the commercial economy added a variety of goods and artisan trades. By 1844, Los Angeles had made adjustments to volatile weather patterns and a sensitive business climate. According to historian Howard J. Nelson, the city "had many typical commercial establishments; the services of scores of urban craftsmen and a full third of the residents of the town were engaged in non-agricultural pursuits."[19]

Stearns also typified a migrant wave of Yankee merchants: men driven by capitalist instincts that demanded judgment based on a ledger. Success was an ethical standard unto itself, centered on the old Puritan precepts of tireless work and thrift.[20] Stearns' writings reveal an industrious and pragmatic personality. Succinct and forthright, he was not inclined to casual correspondence or effusive descriptions: "We have no news here worth noting," he once wrote.[21] For Stearns, the Southern California frontier meant lean years with urgent imperatives. He once, for example, conducted business correspondence on Christmas day without even mentioning the season.[22] He was a fair man but also a recalcitrant one, particularly if he sensed someone was trying to take advantage of him. "I (Stearns) am very stubborn in such matters and if it is just to pay I will pay what is just."[23]

Sentimentality had no place in Stearns' world of business, as illustrated by his attitude upon the sale of the San Pedro trading post, which also signaled the end to his longtime professional association with trader, John Forster. Their working relationship had lasted a decade, during which Forster represented Stearns in a variety of roles as a marketing agent and confidant on policy matters. Forster had been a good soldier, and both men had shared promising visions and bitter disappointments. With the sale of *Casa de San Pedro*, Forster bid adieu in sentimental language, expressing his indebtedness to his friend for being a "competent" entrepreneur and because of "the many benefits received and kindness shown."[24] Stearns, in contrast, couched his feelings in unsentimental advice, wishing his companion good fortune through "industry, economy and perseverance."[25]

Unlike the future gold-seekers who would be lured by the prospect of quick riches, Stearns participated in a more orderly pioneer movement. These merchants, retailers, craftsmen and skilled tradesmen believed in commercial ownership and free markets, and looked to the West as a place where they could settle and build a new future. Stearns personified what scholar Ray Allen Billington identified as "the thousands of small-propertied farmers, ranchers, and entrepreneurs who formed the bulk of the westward-moving population."[26] He was a businessman rather than a gambler, always weighing the consequences of his investments and loans to associates, rancheros and government officials, and though he took measured risks it was "not without the knowledge that there is risk in so doing at least in the delay of payments."[27]

Throughout the 1840s, Stearns acquired sprawling ranches and entered the social circles of the Californio elite. His network of acquaintances included the upper tier of politicos and dons among the landed gentry such as Sepulveda, Avila and Bandini. Thomas Larkin, Monterey's most influential businessman, consulted with Stearns on matters of government and commerce.[28] "He (Stearns) had been in the country so long that he was rather considered as belonging to it," recalled Stearns' longtime friend and business acquaintance, William Heath Davis.[29] Alfred Robinson, a trader and customer of Stearns,

Able Stearns adobe on Main St. (mule team in front) Circa 1876

considered the Yankee expatriate to be a mentor to many Anglos and Hispanics, a man for all seasons, and "they (residents) looked upon him as the man of the village."[30]

Stearns lived the best of the archetypal pioneer experience in achieving personal success and influence in a foreign land. His fluent Spanish enabled him to move freely between the Anglo and Hispanic worlds, finding common interests in business dealings, while minimizing cultural obstacles by adopting native traits. He bartered, haggled over price, traded news and eventually shook hands with a *compadre* in order to cement a simple business transaction. He accepted the Roman Catholic faith, became a citizen, and attended fandangos and parish services with other residents. Social interaction not only strengthened personal bonds with governors, dons and merchants but also led to a widower's romance joining his interests with the influential Bandini family.[31]

In 1841, the 43-year-old Yankee expatriate married 14-year-old Doña Maria Arcadia Bandini. Stearns, embarrassed by the age discrepancy, tried to minimize it by having his own age altered on the marriage certificate. A comely girl with a whimsical quality, Arcadia Bandini Stearns made an ideal hostess with the social graces necessary to entertain and converse with her husband's business contacts. She softened her spouse's frank, pensive New England demeanor with grace and charm. "She was very beautiful," remarked an admiring William Heath Davis.[32] Other contemporaries frequently rated her as the "handsomest" girl in the pueblo, while a few companions even chided Don Abel for his good fortune. Arcadia indeed proved the ideal foil to a husband engagingly known as "Horseface."[33]

Marriage into the Hispanic Californio upper class increased Don Abel's entree into the world of the ranchero, offereing still greater opportunities to acquire land and influence. In 1842, Stearns purchased the *Rancho Los Alamitos*, which included 900 cattle, 1,000 sheep, and 240 horses. The "little cottonwoods" stretched across present-day Orange and Los Angeles counties and approximated 28,000 acres, representing the cornerstone of Stearns' empire.[34] The dearth of rainfall and desire to expand his ranching concerns led to new land purchases in San Francisco and San Diego. By 1845, Stearns had become disenchanted with his trading outpost and sold the San Pedro operation that year in order to devote himself full time to running his ranchos.[35]

Many local residents skeptically looked at Stearns' marriage as just another Anglo attempt to usurp Californio lands since foreigners could aquire property only through intermarriage and conversion to the Catholic faith. Horace Bell noted that a ranchero's daughter made "a rich catch for one of those matrimonial sharks."[36] In Stearns' case, the general populace were particularly cruel in their comments on his pending marriage and relationship with Arcadia. Stearns wanted a shortened engagement with Arcadia in order to diffuse criticism, second-guessing, and any outside pressures which could derail the couples wedding plans, thus shielding her from the undeserved ridicule "of thoughtless young people which might be caused by difference in our ages."[37] He knew that some skeptical Californios would always consider him an outsider to the rancheros' world where *la familia* was essential to social acceptance. "The world will always be the world as long as it exists," mused a reflective Don Abel. That world would "ascribe weaknesses he has never had, accuse him of works he has never done and vituperate against him in terms he does not deserve."[38]

Stearns' earlier feuds with the Mexican government further invited criticism and suspicion of his motives. During the 1830s, for example, local officials had accused him of smuggling and otherwise covertly supporting insurgent opposition. One Mexican official admitted that he had received "bad information" about Stearns, while others "remained silent when he had made inquiries respecting me (Stearns)."[39] John Forster defended his friend's reputation to suspicious residents at San Luis Rey.[40] Stearns' unpopularity reflected a natural mistrust between Anglos and Hispanics throughout the province, and particularly in Los Angeles where he had been a visible figure in local affairs. Associate John Marsh had observed that Stearns' relations with the Mexican populace were better in Yerba Buena than in the old pueblo, believing that "a kinder spirit exists here (Yerba Buena) and less prejudice & dislike for foreigners than in the City of Angels."[41]

Stearns and other expatriates faced obstacles inherent in Mexican rule that further divided foreigners and locals. Southern California was in transition even before the Mexican-American War, a time when social dislocations in Mexico herself undermined foreign confidence in Mexican ability to govern such a remote province as California. Secularization of the missions in 1834 had disrupted the balance between church and state, uprooted the native tribes and produced a surplus labor pool. Without the protective umbrella of the mission padres, the Native American fell prey to the temporal world of low wages and unwritten servitude. "Soon commenced a work of destruction, under the name of reform," recalled Alfred Robinson.[42]

Indian frustrations often led to armed resistance. Paiute and

Mojave tribes raided southern towns, prompting the formation of vigilante groups to protect their property.[43] The church, symbol of a failed as well as resented past, was a target of vandalism and theft. Angry Indians accosted a mission administrator at San Juan Capistrano, burglarizing the church altar and sacristy.[44] Explained Alfred Robinson, "These flourishing institutions, as they had been, were in danger of immediate subversion and ruin."[45]

A worsening economic environment, high unemployment after secularization, and unrestricted access to taverns and parlors led to increased crime, which further eroded Anglo confidence in Mexican authority.[46] The aggregate number of general assaults, murders and thefts more than doubled in the decade after secularization.[47] Stearns himself was even a victim of violence. In 1835, a local resident, William Day, claimed that the wine he had purchased at Stearns' San Pedro trading post was sour. Stearns disagreed about the quality of the wine at the time of the purchase and refused to compensate the unhappy customer. The men argued and Day stabbed Stearns across the face during the heated exchange.[48]

Not only crime troubled the pueblo. By 1844, only a handful of Mexican soldiers stayed in Los Angeles, while a confusingly rapid succession of governors in the years just before the Mexican-American War led to further instability.[49] At Los Angeles, four abortive coup attempts, one desertion and three assaults upon soldiers occurred between 1835 and 1845.[50] For all intents and purposes, Mexico left the California province to self-rule in the revolutionary traditions of the mid-19th century.[51]

Stearns, a member of the Los Angeles city council, probably felt partly responsible for the deteriorating situation. He strongly believed in participatory government, being active in civic affairs since his earliest days in the pueblo. Ever since 1833, when the city council granted him a license to practice law, Stearns tallied election results, chronicled minutes of the city council, and arbitrated disputes.[52] In 1836, he also became an early member of the *Ayuntamiento*, the city council, where he focused on civic reform, road improvements and better harbor facilities. For Stearns, a man committed to progressive government and a safe economic environment, found that lawlessness and a displaced Indian population threatened both Anglo business interests and community reform.[53]

Although political intrigue was commonplace in Mexican California, Anglos had become increasingly alarmed by the region's instability, particularly after the Texas question increasingly strained Mexican-United States relations in the 1830s. The hide and tallow trade had tied the Far West to American interests, thus making a stable California a top priority to foreign entrepreneurs. "Uncle Sam," declared one Santa Barbara resident, "will have something to say on this coast before long."[54] One zealous Missourian hoped that Texas would annex California. If that scenario developed, he quite expected to "be a Ranchero in some part of your romantic and beautiful and healthy country."[55]

Stearns was especially irritated with the constant changes in leadership, policy shifts and disagreements with the governor that disrupted commerce in general and affected his business in particular.[56] He expressed relief after order was restored following one of the many small rebellions so "that we can proceed to business with some confidence."[57] Stearns who had rejected vigilantism as a legitimate method of reform also found revolutions were "not at all pleasing," so it is not surprising that when Texas' independence inspired several of his acquaintances to suggest a similar movement for California, he was conspicuously subdued.[58] Even by 1846, with relations strained between Mexico and the United States, a revolt still seemed unrealistic to Stearns and, in his words, "a wild scheme as there is neither people nor means to support it."[59]

United States Consul Thomas Larkin, Stearns' close friend

at Monterey, had disdainfully watched the volatile changes in Mexican rule, believing this political vulnerability was an opportunity for United States to acquire California. By late 1845, Larkin cautiously initiated diplomatic overtures for a "peaceful conquest" of California. A consummate manipulator, sensitive to Mexican interests, Larkin had contact with the Polk Administration about the potential for war with Mexico, while also trying to assuage the fears of General José Castro and Pío Pico about any potential American annexation of California. The situation was precarious since diplomatic failure could signal a call to arms. Relations between the United States and Mexico had steadily deteriorated under the Polk Administration, and talk of war which accelerated within the United States sharpened tensions among Anglo residents. By the spring of 1846 Larkin's efforts appeared to be all the more urgent in the interest of peace.

The pace of military events moved far too quickly for Stearns' systematic and prudent nature. The Bear Flag Revolt of 1846 dimmed any hope for diplomatic resolution of the differences between Californios and Anglo-Americans. Mexico and the United States were not at war, and the Bear Flaggers use of force eliminated the possibility of moving toward reasoned solutions. Military figures such as John C. Frémont, Robert F. Stockton, Archibald H. Gillespie and Stephen Watts Kearny carried out the United States military campaign in California. The brief war had sweeping movements of men and ships, unexpected skirmishes and decisive battles as well as heroes and casualties on both sides.

The advent of Mexican-American hostilities placed Stearns in a quandary: did his loyalties belong to his Anglo heritage or to his adopted Mexican homeland? Thomas Larkin wanted Stearns' evaluation of the Mexican will to fight since the seat of government had been moved to the Pueblo.[60] But when Larkin, anxious to bring the region under United States control, pressed his old friend for an opinion on American annexation

Adobe remains of Abel Stearns Hide House – circa 1870

and sentiment in Los Angeles, Stearns hesitated, unwilling to offer any opinion that would encourage hostilities. He was a Mexican citizen with close ties to the Californio as well as the Mexican political leadership. Larkin's request, Stearns believed put him in an awkward situation in his diplomatic communication with Pio Pico and General José Castro. Larkin grew impatient with his friend's noncommittal attitude and eventually supported Fremont's military expedition southward.[61] Don Abel never actively opposed the conquest, but he certainly did not support a military takeover of Mexican territory. Benjamin Wilson, a pioneer who also had established familial as well as commercial ties with the Californios, nevertheless chose to support the United States, intimating that Stearns' "mere calculating" was self-serving, in contrast to the "patriots" who actively supported the American war effort.[62]

Stearns certainly had a vested interest in Mexican California through property, family and social position and so, from the vantage point of the ranchero, annexation posed several questions beyond the issue of conquest and settlement. The question of United States citizenship for the Californio required clarification, not to mention the question of property rights and civil liberties.

It would be unfair to characterize Stearns' intentions as less than sincere; note his use of the word "us," as he wonders whether the United States would "admit us to become yankees."[63] Another consideration involved American military intervention, an option that Larkin favored only as a last resort. Stearns believed that most Southern Californians would risk an uprising "if they were sure of immmediate protection against the Mexican government."[64] Finally, any conquest required empathy with the vanquished, and an understanding of Hispanic needs. Stearns urged Frémont, for example, "to send a number of Catholic clergymen who understand the Castilian language, men of liberal principles and good moral character."[65]

If anything, Stearns is best understood as a Westerner moved by the Frontiersman's sentiment that often valued provincial needs above all else. His allegiance to California went beyond the interests of either foreign power, Mexico or America. Stearns had lived in the territory for nearly two decades and never returned to his former country; for him, the bond between settler and frontier at least equaled his allegiance to birthplace. Mexican rule indeed had its flaws, creating unnecessary tensions between foreigner and government and thereby eventually influencing many American settlers to support independence or conquest. Stearns, however, was committed to political reform within the context of Hispanic rule, so in his eyes, military force was neither viable nor necessary. Stearns, the pragmatic Westerner and, as writer Doris M. Wright observed, he "was working for California, and he did what he believed to be best for it and for himself."[66] In 1846, he found himself caught at a political crossroads with no retreat possible; moderation in the interest of California was no asset.

Stearns' years in Mexican Southern California offered economic opportunities against a backdrop of social and political conflicts. He benefited as a Jacksonian man, coming to the West in search of free markets and unlimited natural resources. The Yankee expatriate's tenacious Puritan character helped him overcome difficult times, and his frugality and pragmatism enhanced his fortunes on the Western frontier. The absence of both centralized authority and established economic entrenchments allowed entrepreneurs the freedom to succeed in an open marketplace. *Casa de San Pedro* serviced a variety of consumer needs that mirrored the region's increasingly a diverse economy. For Stearns, financial survival resulted from an ability to capitalize on these divergent interests, but the basis of his fortune would come from acculturation with the Californio elite. Land was power. By 1846, Stearns had become a don, a prominent figure who highlighted all that was powerful among the upper class.

Nevertheless, advantages of doing business during the pre-conquest period were matched by distinct problems for the Yankee merchant in the same period. For example, the same laissez-faire atmosphere that proved so economically propitious also contributed to the political uncertainty that fostered antagonisms between expatriates and the Hispanic populace. To compound difficulties, the absence of federal control and the adverse effects of secularization coincided with a rise in crime. Most Yankee expatriates were so frustrated with local affairs that they were all but ready to welcome annexation or independence. Don Abel also weighed the vexations of his locale against the bonds of family and land. By 1846, the impending conquest had crystallized the problem of divided loyalties, and Stearns' ambivalence seemed an honest expression of those sentiments.

Although events rendered Stearns' judgments moot, his years in Mexican Southern California embraced larger issues. His experiences highlighted the problem of Anglo-Hispanic relations within the context of opportunity, growth and capitalist designs. Southern California offered a future to the Yankee merchants, a future that would encroach on the Hispanic culture and heritage even as the Hispanics had drastically changed the world of the Native Americans. For Abel Stearns and his times, cultural tensions posed dilemmas between the need to preserve traditions and the desire for change.

CHAPTER TWO

Hugo Reid and the Native Americans: A Voice in the Wilderness

Hugo Reid and Abel Stearns settled in Southern California during the twilight stages of the mission era, a time when only a handful of Anglo-Americans lived in the region. They had common interests in Mexican California, their paths frequently crossing in friendship and business and, above all, their shared ambitions rested on a hopeful note on the Western frontier. California presented new opportunities, a fresh start away from the crowded East Coast, from the nationalist and class rivalries fracturing Europe.

A Scot born in the British Isles in 1811, Hugo Reid displayed a restless spirit in the wake of a divided Europe, ravaged by years of Napoleonic wars. In 1829, he left home and traveled throughout Latin America and Mexico. Three years later, he sailed from Mexico to California to participate in the Pacific coast trade.

Reid, like Stearns, married in Southern California and quickly adopted the ranchero lifestyle. Both men were foreigners, separated from Hispanic culture by language and religion, who befriended each other from mutual economic interests. Reid depended on Stearns' San Pedro trading post for goods and everyday necessities. He purchased an array of items to stock his own rancheria, including household tea, coffee, kitchen utensils, tools and building materials. "I think with the above & what is already in the house that the king, queen & young princess will be able to make out," he jested after one lengthy request for items.[1] Reid, in turn, entertained Stearns at his San Gabriel adobe, even offering the casa as a getaway vacation for Don Abel and his young wife, Arcadia. Like his New England counterpart, Reid became involved in local affairs during Mexican rule and in the later transition to Anglo-American rule. In the words of Harris Newmark, "Reid was a cultured Scotsman who had a part, as a member of the convention, in making the first Constitution for California."[2]

Yet Reid and Stearns had different attitudes towards fame and fortune. Stearns enjoyed the game politics, the cajoling, social posturing and intrigue associated with influence and power. He entertained the ranchero elites, intermarried with the Bandini clan and built a wealthy empire of cattle and land. Reid, however, never enjoyed wealth or popularity. He was an entrepreneur of many faces: a viticulturist and farmer who oversaw a meager crop of barley and wheat, and a trader of assorted domestic items, including monkey sackets, pots, kettles, and brooms –hardly wares for the rich and famous.

Reid was never successful, partly because his marriage to a Native American limited his social standing within Hispanic society. He married into an impoverished Indian rancheria and lived in humble surroundings at his *Rancho Via Espina*. While Stearns pondered new land acquisitions, Reid constantly fell into debt for basic necessities. Reid, often bedridden with various maladies, frequently borrowed items from his *compadre's* San Pedro store with little prospect of repayment. "All my life I am (a) bother (to) you," he once apologized in a rare admission of vulnerability.[3] But Reid justified his dependency as a noble reminder of his *compadre's* own good fortune. Stearns, he felt,

The Indian Village and the Hugo Reid Adobe at the Los Angeles Arboretum

"should sacrifice a little to friendship & charity."[4]

Reid and Stearns' personalities were as different as their life circumstances. Stearns, somber and dry, must have blushed at his friend's mordant wit and biting tongue. Reid enjoyed poking fun at pretensions, especially the incongruities that went with the frontier lifestyle. The crusty Scot never missed an opportunity to needle his Yankee friend. "You being in fact little better than the Boston magistrate," he once reminded Stearns, "who gave an order to hang lanterns to the doors of shops at night without expressing whether they were expected to contain candles."[5] He chided the 43-year-old Stearns about marrying a teenager and the ironic possibility of becoming a godfather to the Stearns' offspring. Reid offered sardonic advice to his taciturn friend on how to speed the process (Stearns would never have children). "May God keep you in good health and may he send you a baby soon," Reid encouraged his friend, "to wet your trousers when you are all dressed up to remind you that you are the father of a family and that your friend esteems you."[6]

While Stearns jousted for position to influence local affairs, Reid remained aloof from the political intrigue that governed the *ayuntamiento*. Reid was devoted to his family and a rancheria steeped in mysticism, tied to ritual forever alien from his own cultural roots. He was, after all, a foreigner in a alien land, and his own sense of isolation fueled his interest in the Gabrieleño tribes, who were a local symbol of Native American isolation throughout the frontier. These experiences transcended the Scot's personal relationships.

A bedridden Reid, too ill to participate in an August harvest, complained when his family left for the laborious task so necessary to their winter survival. The family's all- consuming toil left him helpless, frustrated and lonely. "They will end by driving me crazy," he groused.[7] Reid, however, frequently abandoned his family for weeks to live as a hermit among the Gabrieleño tribes located in the surrounding hills. These abrupt and unexpected separations exasperated his poor wife, Victoria. Reid even missed his daughter's funeral leaving his devoted friend Stearns to make the necessary arrangements – a misdeed Victoria would never quite forgive.[8]

Reid's life was a blend of Hispanic customs with the traditions of a seemingly timeless aboriginal culture. He was a man of riddles in a world of rhyme.

> Better late than never
> Better never than late
> Late better than never
> Never better than late
> Never late than better
> Take your change out of that[9]

If Stearns symbolized a merging of Anglo and Hispanic traditions, then Reid's life highlighted the sad legacy of those conquests on the Native American. His writings on the Southern California Indians became a manifest of reform, calling for separation of native cultures from the unending tide of migrating peoples. Reid's essays decribed the aborigines in the aftermath of the mission era as a people displaced from their land, thus presenting a strong argument for the establishment of a reservation in Southern California.

In 1852, the Los Angeles *Star* published Reid's 22 essays on native customs, economy and government -an informative treatise on Indian culture and mission life. The articles established Reid as the foremost expert on local tribes, and increased his chances for a appointment as Indian agent for the southern district. He had a unique understanding of Indian affairs. Marriage gave Reid entry into a rancheria family, access to tribal elders and insight into secularization's adverse effects on the native inhabitants.[10]

Reid took his writing seriously, something that could not always be said for this free-spirited adventurer's attitude to his other pursuits, a meandering list including gold prospecting and sailing. In the instance of his writings, however, Reid had spent months in seclusion until he completed the final drafts of his essays. He wanted to educate a public that assumed the Native American was a savage yet also did not want to sway them to the romantic, Rousseauean equally inaccurate notion of the "noble savage", and so he avoided an idealized view of local tribes. "I flatter myself," he noted, "on being able to furnish facts, not falsehoods hatched up to satisfy the curiosity of a chance traveller."[11]

Reid's observations gained instant notoriety and became a resource for Helen Hunt Jackson's novel, *Ramona*. The articles preserved anthropological data on aboriginal language, idioms and traits. More important, Reid's letters were a social comment that crystalized the Indians' plight for an Anglo readership. It was the era of *Uncle Tom's Cabin*, a period when morality assumed new meaning among Americans, and Hugo Reid's letters on the Indian's hardships are best understood within that context of reform.

The essays underscored the complexity of native culture, revealing a sophisticated people, complex in language and literature. He drew analogies with European societal traits when possible. One essay categorized common nouns and verbs used in the native tongue, which matched standard English usage. Reid noted that "their language is simple, rich, and abounding in compound expressive terms." He catalogued an extensive vocabulary list of Indian words, equated their phonetic usage in the native tongue with similar sounds in the Romance languages, and asserted that Indian literature followed an epic scheme similar to that of the Greek and Roman classics. The natives told legends "of incredible length and containing more metamorphoses than Ovid could have engendered in his brain had he lived a thousand years."[12]

In many ways, Reid acted as gadfly to the conscience of his Anglo readership, subtly admonishing them for their arrogant, myopic perspective on Indian cultures. With the same pointed sense of humor that he displayed toward Stearns, Reid chided the sanctimonious aims of Christian missionaries, emphasizing the similarities between Roman Catholic doctrine and ritual with local customs and beliefs. Pagans were not pagans at all; rather, they had comparable fables, legends and their own religious stories about miraculous virgin births and ascensions. One essay compared elements of the Apostles' Creed, Old Testament commandments and the Our Father, rituals rooted in the belief of one God as a "giver of life," a faith in a resurrection of the soul and the avoidance of using the deity's name in vain. So too, the eagle had a separate feast day, while the crow and owl were revered as sacred animals.[13]

Reid provided a meticulous account of all the tribes and their locales, accentuating the complex political organization and hierarchy within the tribes. He listed nearly 30 rancherias and noted that almost 40 additional villages existed. Unity prevailed throughout the region, and all tribes were "one great Family under distinct Chiefs." Chiefs ruled a lodge, and each lodge, not unlike Congress, retained the power to declare war. Traditional standards of authority existed whereby elders held the most respected positions. Tribes respected marriage, granted divorce in extreme cases, and respected the solemnity of baptisms and burials.[14]

Reid contrasted the best in Indian life with deficiencies in the pueblo. The rancherias had an efficient messenger service as children relayed correspondence between tribes, a far better way than the local Anglo-American system, in which mail was dumped into a grocery barrel to languish until someone claimed it, possibly even the addressee. Reid told of a sophisticated monetary system based on shells as a measurement for legal tender, an irony not lost in a gold rush era of scarce hard currency, wild price fluctuations and upredictable demand.[15]

Reid's articles detailed a sophisticated aboriginal lifestyle that paralleled with Anglo-European traditions. His characterizations of peaceful tribes and non-threatening images of a civilized people contrasted sharply with what had become the prevailing image in an era of high tension between Indians and settlers. He brought dignity to his subject, offered empathy to his readership, and laid the basis for a humanitarian approach to aboriginal-Anglo relations. If anything, Reid put in print what George Catlin captured on canvas: a glimpse of everyday native lifestyles, at play and in work, as a people and society living in harmony with their frontier environment.

In reality, Southern California tribes were frustrated because they were being denied legal rights of land ownership and self-rule. After the secularization of the San Gabriel and Capistrano missions, the Indians were set free only to become victims in an unsympathetic world. Alfred Robinson best summarized the missions decline with his observation of circumstances at San Diego. "Here everything was prostrated -the Presidio ruined - the Mission depopulated -the town almost deserted, and its few inhabitants miserably poor."[16] Unemployment ran high, alcoholism was endemic and poverty the common condition among the rancherias. Naturally, this impoverished and hungry people soon resorted to cattle raids on the ranchos, vandalism of the missions and disorderly conduct around the pueblo. William Heath Davis observed the cruel cycle of poverty and isolation of mission Indians who "became impoverished and they returned to their former uncivilized life, making occasional visits to the different ranchos to steal horses."[17]

Reid saw the unhappy conditions at San Gabriel, a mission devastated by secularization, now surrounded by a ruined land and displaced people. "Thousands of cattle were slain, for their hides only," recalled Alfred Robinson, "whilst their carcasses remained to decompose upon the plains."[18] Helen Hunt Jackson's *Ramona* characterized the missions decline through the eyes of a proud Californio from the fading Mexican era. Senora Moreño "saw the ruin of the Missions steadily going on, their vast properties melting away, like dew before the sun."[19]

Injustice soon followed the destruction of the mission. Reid sometimes mediated Indian complaints of mistreatment by outsiders. In one instance, he wrote Stearns about a native who had "come to me crying" that he had been berated by one of Stearns' workers. "I thought it better to take him with me," wrote a diplomatic Reid.[20] Poverty led to disease. "There is no peace for the wicked -So says the writ. I have been occupied in the mission -Great cry & little wool."[21] In a letter to Stearns, he portrayed desperate conditions in quiet terms. "Request small syringe. Yglesia is dying, also requests balsam and sweet spirits."[22]

Reid portrayed the Southern California Indians as a civilized and peaceful people to an Anglo audience that regarded the natives as primitive savages. Intertribal disputes were infrequent, suggesting that a comradely atmosphere existed among the local tribes.[23] Historian George Harwood Phillips noted that Indian conflicts "developed mainly over territorial infractions and usually took place when food was scarce."[24] As a confederation of rancherias, the tribes united only when endangered by outside forces. Reid considered the Indian respect toward law a reflection of worthy values. Robbery, syphilis, alcohol abuse and murder rarely occurred on the rancheria, virtuallly the opposite of those conditions that prevailed at the ruined missions and in and around the pueblo immediately following secularization.[25]

Reid's aboriginal profile of gaiety and courage was similar in demeanor to the Californio. The bright dress, flowers, necklaces and bracelets of their costume represented a happy people in the best traditions of rancho life. Indian festivals of flowers resembled the elaborate gala of dance and games associated with the *fandangos* and *bailes* common to the pueblo. He saw a people of dignity, noble savages, generous toward friends, defiant when threatened. Reid described the hunt as a test of fortitude in the best traditions of a medieval knight. A trial by ordeal took the measure of a hunter's loyalty and included fasting and submission to nature's dangers. One challenge required a hunter to lie exposed on an ant hill and endure the suffering in silence so as "to make them watchful," according to Reid, "vigilant and clear sighted."[26]

Reid's essays were a realistic social commentary on the effects of foreign conquests, portraying Indians as a civilized people that had been victimized by settlement of the West. Native American resistance to European assimilation was evidenced by mission runaways, periodic raids on settlements, revolts and rejection of land ownership. The Indian question had confounded Spanish and Mexican officials and clergy for decades, and Reid's criticism of the mission era turned a spotlight on these policy failures that had left the aborigine destitute in the wake of secularization. Thus the neophytes, concluded historian C. Alan Hutchinson, "who supposedly owned the mission lands they worked, were eventually to lose them."[27]

Reid felt that church traditions had some impact on native customs, mixing traditional religious imagery such as heaven, hell and Satan into their native beliefs. In terms of justice, the punishment of whipping became common among tribes only after the Spanish conquest, an obvious criticism of mission disciplinary methods.[28] Reid certainly resisted the Catholic influence in his own life, passively tolerating the Mass or Benediction services that his converted wife attended. "Religion," he groused, "has hurt my nerves, having been yesterday at church."[29] During one poor financial stretch, Reid quipped "that good luck will ensue" because he had not witnessed any baptisms since a Dalton family baptism brought "all sorts of calamities."[30]

Reid's narratives on the Southern California tribes urged a new approach to Indian affairs and a reconsideration of public policy toward tribal lifestyles. His portrayal of advanced societies, pacifistic by nature and compromised by foreign settlement, put forth compelling reasons for a reservation. He articulated the intricate beauty of the native tongue, once lost over time, and a need to return to "old standards." Reid observed that most of the Southern California Indians had always resisted cultural indoctrination by the mission padres. He wrote that native runaways, called *hindas*, undertook dangerous risks to escape to the mountains because the price of freedom outweighed the consequences of capture and punishment. This expression of defiance -flight- prevailed even after secularization, as "scantily clothed and still more scantily supplied with food," Reid noted, "nearly all the Gabrieleños went north while those of San Diego, San Luis and San Juan overran this county."[31]

The Indian question had specific relevance to Southern California by the early 1850s, for friction between outlying tribes and settlers increased after the American conquest. Disparate living conditions, a steady influx of immigrants, and cultural antagonisms led to violence. Native warriors often attacked overland travelers in the mountain passes and at the outlying regions leading toward the Gila and Santa Fe trails. The Tulare Indians often raided the cattle ranches and farms in

Hugo Reid Adobe

the southern counties. Government neglect, broken treaties, and high taxation were often cited as causes for Indian rebellions. To an exasperated Los Angeles *Star*, the lack of adequate protection invited trouble, and blame rested with "the military commander in this State."[32]

Disease and suffering at the rancherias invited crime and violence, particularly at San Gabriel. Reid composed his essays while deteriorating conditions at the missions left church buildings as easy targets for theft and vandalism. One report indicated that "as many as four large dwelling houses have been constructed from the materials thus carried away."[33] Local tribes were also the victims of unsolved murders. Only a week after the publication of Reid's first essay, the Los Angeles *Star* reported that two Indian men were found dead in town, one killed by *aguardiente* while the "other was stabbed and cut in various places." The newspaper urged an investigation into violations of Indian rights. "The Indian law is badly enforced in this county," the *Star* declared, "and the reason of many inconveniences we suffer in the city."[34]

Reid believed the American conquest had worsened the Indians' lot through hostility and indifference. In 1848, he assessed the depressed conditions at San Gabriel along with his own financial woes. "The taking of the country by the Americans," Reid concluded, "is undoubtedly the curse!"[35] Native American concerns were overshadowed by the gold rush and a people more interested in settling the West than in saving souls and eventually integrating the Indian into society, as the Hispanic ideal ran. Reid never fully grasped this sad fact, but he certainly sensed that Indians were in desperate need of immediate reform. To Reid, these native depredations were a matter of American policy that demanded national solutions. "Ought not the government of the United States in consideration of those lands, hard toil & labor make them a remuneration, give them an annual supply of clothing, give schooling to their children with much more justice (since justice is the theme)."[36] A reservation, therefore, seemed as much a duty of Americans as a right of Indians. "Ought not the Indian families," Reid asked, "have a reservation made them which they could cultivate under a certain system?"[37]

Reid's essays on the Southern California tribes appeared in the Los Angeles *Star* between February and July of 1852. The

Bedroom interior of the Hugo Reid Adobe.

entries were popular and reissued in newspapers throughout the state. The *Star* hoped the articles would generate sympathy, sway public opinion, and "have a practical tendency to ameliorate the (Indians') condition."[38]

Reid's statewide notoriety would have led to his eventual appointment as Indian agent in the southern district. According to Robert F. Heizer, "If Reid had lived he might have succeeded Wilson, and in so doing would have been profitably employed in a work in which he had great interest and competence."[39] Sadly, Reid died only a few months after the publication of the Indian essays, and the work of a reservation and the ramifications of Indian policy would be left to others. Hugo Reid nevertheless had elevated the Indian question to a matter of public attention, challenging local and national leadership to address the problem, and thereby establishing the rationale behind future reforms in Southern California.

CHAPTER THREE

Margaret (Hereford) Wilson and The Westward Odyssey

Margaret Hereford Wilson is best remembered as the second wife of Benjamin D. Wilson, a noted Southern California settler, Indian agent, civic leader and entrepreneur described by biographer Midge Sherwood as "one of the most colorful figures in the development of California. No history of the State is complete without him."[1] Indeed, Margaret is nearly eclipsed by the deeds of her famous spouse, even though she is a colorful personality in her own right. A product of the Victorian mores of 19th-century America, her qualities were tested by her pioneer experiences in the Southwest. Her journey to California reflected the intoxicating allure of American expansion, a dream of a better life, perhaps quick riches, cheap land and most of all, a new start in a promising locale. Her westward trek to California was arduous, crossing unknown territory, and engaging a variety of cultures along interesting frontier topography.

Margaret Hereford Wilson spent her formative years in search of a personal identity against the backdrop of a bustling Midwest filled with rough talking, hard drinking, male opportunists and adventurers. It was a restless era, when an endless stream of hopeful settlers moved west in search of land and opportunity. Born in 1820, Margaret Hereford was raised in St. Louis, gateway to the West. Her father died in the mid-1830s, a tragedy that drew young Margaret closer to her mother and relatives. She traveled between Missouri and Tuscumbia, Alabama, visiting relatives, discovering her Southern lineage and socializing in a genteel world of slaveowners, gentlemen and ladies. She enjoyed the hospitality and carefree ambience of plantation life: picnics at nearby lakes, buggy rides and festive local dances.[2] She fantasized about living forever in this time gone by. "My friends are as kind to me as can be," she enthused, "as if I could be happy anywhere from my Mother it would be with them."[3] She adopted the perspective of the old South, and once boasted that the Hereford clan was "almost equal to Virginia."[4]

Hereford also embraced the enlightened ideas of those mid-19th-century Victorian women who valued education as the key to feminine independence and moral ascendency in a male-dominated world. "Piety," she observed, "is ever pleasing but when it is united with intelligence its beauty is as attractive as its worth is beyond calculation."[5] She had read history and admired powerful women of the past: Queen Elizabeth, who "elevated the standard of female education"; Mary Montague, for her "universal benevolence"; Madame Roland, a martyr to the Reign of Terror but "distinguished for her superior talent, discernment and fortitude"; and Madame DeStael, an intellectual committed to egalitarian ideals, including the notion that women, as well as men, should be "taught that the human mind should be enriched with the wealth of ages."[6]

Hereford displayed a progressive attitude amidst the world of slaves and prejudice. The fear of Caribbean-style slave revolts and aggressive Abolitionists put many slaveowners on the defensive: many who had begun to question both the morality and economy of their "peculiar institution" reacted to outside pressure with defiance and abandoned their own criticisms of the system to present a united front, maintaining that slavery was a positive good and necessary to the South's welfare.[7] Margaret did not share the Southern anxiety over potential slave rebellions, believing that most servants were loyal to their masters. In one instance, she noted that local authorities released nearly two dozen suspected black insurrectionists for lack of evidence. Nonetheless, citizens' groups formed nightly patrols as a precaution against slave uprisings, although Hereford scoffed that "such things are always exaggerated."[8] Although Margaret, daughter of slaveowners, was not an Abolitionist, she cared for her personal slaves in St. Louis, oversaw their daily routine, and tended their needs when they were ill. Margaret Hereford viewed slaves as being just as worthy of considerate treatment as whites. Give my "respects to all of my friends black and white," she requested during one trip away from home.[9]

The teenage Margaret was opinionated, inquisitive and optimistic; attractive qualities that were not overlooked by single men. One Southern gentleman fell in love with her charm and wit. He wrote somewhat rashly to Margaret that "though our acquaintance has been short, I have never known one of whose love I would have been proud in the character of a wife."[10] His proposal was rebuffed. In 1836, a short acquaintance was virtually out of the question since a formal courtship was required, particularly for a 16-year-old girl. In any event, Margaret was destined for a later, lasting romance. At the age of 22, she married Thomas Hereford, a distant cousin and Virginia physician of modest means, and they had one son, Edward.

The Hereford marriage was plagued by illness and personal tragedy. As Thomas' health steadily declined throughout the 1840s, he desperately searched in vain for a climate that would cure his chronic lung and stomach disorders. During these sojourns he would be away from St. Louis months at a time, traversing parts of Arkansas, Virginia, Kentucky and Kansas forcing his young wife to rearrange priorities and adapt to a solitary lifestyle. "It is a great trial to be separated," wrote the dutiful but lonely Margaret, but "I would not have you return if I could as long as you are benefited by staying."[11] When he ran out of strength, she bolstered Thomas' spirits: "You must not give way to despondency and gloom, there may be yet some bright days in store for us."[12] Her own resolve would be tested when they traveled west together.

Thomas and Margaret's eventual migration to California unfolded in uneven stages as new hardships confronted the family. Unlike the argonauts who later would be driven by the dream of quick riches, and unlike the ambitious champions of Manifest Destiny, the Herefords looked to the West for better health, opportunity and a permanent home.[13]

By 1846, the couple had become increasingly interested in the Southwest, an arid land of old world enchantments, abundant resources, different cultures with exotic customs. Mexico's borderlands also represented untapped markets rich in trading opportunities. Since the early 1840s, the Mexican government had encouraged foreign investment in New Mexico through land grants and commercial incentives. The Herefords planned to take advantage of these inducements, and tried wholesaling merchandise in New Mexico and Texas.

When Thomas Hereford left for Santa Fe with a cargo of assorted goods in late 1846, he was not alone. St. Louis was a jumping-off point for southwestern trappers headed for Taos and Santa Fe, for covered wagon families traveling northwest toward the Oregon territory, and for Mormons emigrating to the Utah territory. Not surprisingly, St. Louis had become a haven for dreamers and opportunists. On his departure from St. Louis to Oregon, Francis Parkman noted that "the gunsmiths and saddlers were kept constantly at work in providing arms and equipments for the different parties of travellers."[14]

Hereford's journey took him along the Santa Fe Trail, the route used by fur traders, merchandisers and cattle drivers since 1821.[15] It was an unpredictable trip, crossing a land of thunderstorms, drought and hostile Indian tribes. Hereford's party

The Wilson Family.
Margaret, Edward Hereford and brother-in-law John Hereford (wearing a vest)

had stopped at Bent's Fort near Cimarron, Kansas, when Comanche or Arapahoe Indians ambushed them. Fortunately, the group lost only 50 head of cattle, many recouped the next day when they captured some of the Indian band. A military detachment escorted Hereford's group to Santa Fe.[16] By then it was summer, 1847, and the arid climate proved an elixir, envigorating Hereford and sending his spirits soaring. He wrote Margaret of his improving health, cheerfully noting that the "climate is very agreeable."[17]

The next leg of the journey along the Mexican frontier provided another set of problems for Hereford as well as other travelers. Political intrigue and bureaucratic breakdowns had eroded the Mexican government's effectiveness in protecting its settlements along the northern borderlands, as that country teetered between what historian David J. Weber described as the competing forces of "centralism and federalism."[18] As the confusion increased so did lawlessness along the border. Though the local militia tried to assume a greater role in regulating of everyday affairs, stealing and banditry became commonplace occurrences in large towns with active marketplaces.

Nor was the militia thoroughly reliable at the distant edges of the frontier. Once, for example, in Santa Fe, the soldiers that had escorted Hereford became more of a nuisance than protection for the travelers. Military protocol vanished, discipline broke down, and the presence of both loose women and drunkenness created a dangerous situation, which threatened to deteriorate into a confrontation with the town's residents. Thomas Hereford found the milieu "perfectly disgusting. Almost every officer & private has their own woman."[19] So offended was Santa Fe's Mexican population that rumors began to circulate that they were going to rise against the foreigners prompting Hereford to join a citizens' guard to protect the city and compelling him to sleep in his clothes with his gun in his arms. As distasteful as it was, however, Hereford believed that staying was worth the danger. "I can see nothing to induce a person to remain," he conceded, "but the making of money & that can be done."[20]

Hereford's determination was small consolation to the lonely Margaret, separated from her husband by miles of dangerous territory and, for all she knew, facing a potential widow's fate. Margaret worried nonetheless, and she counseled Thomas in one letter that "whenever you feel tempted to do wrong, you must look at the ring I gave you, which I hope will prove a shield to guard you from temptation."[21]

By spring of 1848, Margaret resolved to go to Thomas at Santa Fe. His health improved and encouraged as to his prospects by New Mexico's potential markets, Hereford began scheming to retail merchandise throughout the St. Louis-Santa Fe-Chihuahua route. He entered a partnership with his cousin, Solomon P. Sublette.[22] If all went according to plan, Hereford hoped he would make a sizeable profit and return to St. Louis with a higher degree of social respectability. And this his pride demanded of him: "I left Saint Louis for the combined object of health and money, and without realizing one or both, I would be in a worse condition than before leaving."[23] After Margaret and Eddy joined him, they made the best of the pioneering situation; at least the family were together, and Margaret found Santa Fe's adobe-styled living "much better than I had any idea of." As ever, of course, the frontier's greatest liability was separation of families. "Need I tell you (my dear Mother) how often and how much I think of you?" she wrote. "I shall bear our separation as well as I can."[24]

Unfortunately, the Herefords' gamble did not succeed, leaving them in a desperate situation far from home. Uncertain markets, strained Mexican-American relations and frequent Indian raids along the southwestern trails had so restricted trade that the economy was deteriorating.[25] By the summer of 1849 Margaret and Thomas were broke, forced to watch their savings disappear as the market collapsed and prices fell and expensive import duties forced them to abandon their cargo on the banks of the Del Norte river.[26]

But Thomas stubbornly refused to return to the United States. He had not yet made his fortune, was determined to try again, and had heard that physicians were needed farther south, at Chihuahua, Mexico. The Herefords had become comfortable with Hispanic customs at Santa Fe. An "Old Spanish Lady" in Chihuahua took pity on the vagabonds, welcomed the family into her home, taught them Spanish and dressed Margaret in the native beads and trinkets. "I am a very great favourite with her," noted an appreciative Margaret. However compatible the Herefords were with Hispanic culture, nonetheless the move would take them further from the States, away from the protection of the American government, and more vulnerable than ever to unforeseen dangers. But they had few choices and, as Margaret reasoned, were resolved to take the risks to "extract ourselves from poverty and disease."[27]

The Herefords arrived in Chihuahua in the early summer of 1849, Margaret's second resettlement in a year. Life in northern Mexico centered on mining, farming and sprawling haciendas redolent of a pastoral lifestyle. Chihuahua had approximately

10,000 inhabitants, large in comparison to other Mexican townships, but in the estimation of historians Liliane Crete and Ruth R. Olivera, "it sank in significance when compared to the cities of the south (southern Mexico)."[28] During their stay, the Herefords gained a rich appreciation of the desert land and native customs. There was a carnival atmosphere that accentuated the gaiety and color in Mexican life. Thomas was fascinated with the exhilaration of the crowd at a bullfight, laughed at the clowns who performed at intermission, and danced to the polkas that preceded the matador's entrance into the stadium. He was awed by the danger presented by the charging bull, having once seen *El Toro* collapse part of a ring in one collision. And he pointedly observed the charm and beauty of the young señoritas dressed in the swirling, bright gowns.[29]

Mexico was a land of enchantment, a new Eden to the Herefords, filled with gracious hosts and a plentiful bounty of fruits and vegetables. The open-handed residents gave the Herefords two small hairless dogs that were indigenous to the region as loving pets for their young son, Eddy. The family enjoyed lower Mexico's abundant citrus fruits, noting the peculiar colors and shapes of the melons and vegetables. Margaret was delighted by the tasty sweets and rich jams, considering these delectibles the "most delightful preserves I ever tasted." She also marveled at the varieties of cactus and multi-colored flowers, sending an assortment of seedlings to relatives in Missouri.[30] Indeed, the Herefords found Chihuahua a new Eden, a much-needed respite from their sagging economic fortunes.

Despite the Mexican people's hospitality, the Herefords could not remain indefinitely at this oasis. Chihuahua's social mix of some wealth and much poverty supplied the American physician with plenty of work but no avenue to economic independence. Mexico's government faltered after the Treaty of Guadalupe Hidalgo, so much so that it weakened local authority and encouraged the always hostile Indians to raid along the routes leading to town. The fierce Apache and Comanche warriors were becoming increasingly bold in their attacks on travelers, threatening parties as large as 30 or 40 members along the local routes. In March of 1850, the shocked Hereford family greeted their badly wounded cousin, Rambler Hereford, his legs heavily bandaged from an encounter with Indians along the trail to El Paso. It became evident that the longer they stayed in Mexico, the less likely it was that they would safely return to the States. "The Indians had become so dangerous," wrote a somber Margaret, "that (Thomas) would be risking all of our lives" if they remained at Chihuahua. So it was that danger and economics that forced the family to look farther west in the direction of California. "Dr. Hereford has detemined to go to California, and I am going with him," Margaret declared, "as there is no other alternative."[31]

The Gila and Santa Fe routes were active transits in the rancho era, making California vital to the southwestern trade in hide and tallow. The gold rush further piqued America's interest in the Far West, as argonauts filled the overland trails along the Taos-Santa Fe-Los Angeles routes. Opportunists and adventurers risked their lives in daring schemes capitalizing on the mining phenomenon, particularly cattle driving to provide beef for the gold-hungry hordes across the overland trail.[32] One American entrepeneur offered Thomas a partnership if he would drive a herd to Southern California as cattle prices soared tenfold. The influx of prospectors to the California gold fields also increased the demand for cattle, clothing, food of any kind and equipment. With complete financial backing from a local entrepreneur, Thomas purchased nearly 200 head of cattle and mules to herd to Los Angeles by way of the southern trail, across the Colorado River and over the desolate Mojave Desert. Thomas estimated that "should I have no bad luck I hope to reach their (California) in three months. I have to travel about two thousand miles through the Indian country." For his efforts, Thomas would share half the profits from the cattle drive, perhaps realizing as much as $15,000. Considering the desparate circumstances at Chihuahua, the dangers involved with the venture seemed certain but small in comparison. "Nothing but poverty would or could make me undertake it," he reasoned in a later letter to Margaret, trying to make his wife understand why he was willing to enter into such a risky scheme.[33]

The Herefords took separate routes to California in order to minimize risk to the whole family. Thomas' route overland was arduous, slow and susceptible to Indian raids; plus far more dangerous than the route that Margaret and Eddy would take crossing the Mexican wilderness toward the coast, catching a steamer to San Francisco, traveling south and reuniting with Thomas at Los Angeles.

When she left St. Louis, Margaret never dreamed that her fortunes would carry her to the Far West, away from family for years, and with no prospect of returning soon. "I felt bad when I wrote my farewell letter from Independence, but it was nothing to this," she wrote in still another farewell note to her mother. She had no desire to settle in California despite the fantastic stories of gold strikes. To Margaret, gold fever strangely resembled the exaggerated rumors that had induced her relatives' emigration to Missouri. Gold miners would "be as much disappointed as Uncle Tom was when he went to Missouri to dig coal." Now she only hoped that they would make a sufficient profit from the cattle drive to return to Missouri.[34]

On April 1, 1850, the Herefords went their separate ways toward a common destination as planned. Margaret, Eddy and Rambler Hereford began a 270-mile trip to Mazatlan, crossing the central plateau, a landscape of uneven texture: prairie grasslands, parched desert, and barren soil dotted with cactus and scrubs. Within a week they had reached Durango, a city best known for the deadly scorpions in its environs. It was here that Rambler realized he could not continue the journey. His wounds from the Indian attack had left him too weak to tackle the next leg of the trip through the rugged Sierra Madre. The western range rose 7,000 feet, contained only a few natural passes and was infested with robbers and thieves. Travel had to be swift and light. Margaret and Eddy abandoned their carriage and rode horseback, alone over the sun-bleached hills and barren desert of northern Mexico. "I believe that I am almost the first American woman that ever crossed these Mountains," she later remarked in awe rather than boast.[35]

On April 20, three weeks after their odyssey had begun, the exhausted travelers reached the port city of Mazatlan. Margaret tearfully wrote her mother about the arduous journey. "It is needless for me to attempt to describe my feelings or to speak of them," she exclaimed, "You can well imagine what they are in this strange land separated from all that are dear to me." She purchased passage for Eddy and herself aboard a steamer destined for San Francisco. Once in California, she planned to contact relatives and regain her strength before traveling southward to meet her husband.[36]

Two months later, on June 1, a weary mother and son arrived at San Francisco in "health and safety." The Hereford's vessel was one of many clippers and steamers that jammed the dockets, abandoned at shore by passengers and crew alike, filled with hordes of naive gold seekers hoping to make a fortune in the northern mines. "Hundreds of people are moving to and fro in every direction in the City," Margaret wrote, probably as much dazed as amazed by the instant civilization springing up here at her feet. "Buildings are going up as if by magic."[37] Gold Rush San Francisco, particularly in contrast to the ageless, unchanging Mexican deserts, must have seemed incredibly chaotic to her, an indulgent city bursting with an excess of rapid urban growth. Overcrowding, unsanitary conditions, disease, unemployment and a high crime rate characterized the city's tenement problems. "San Francisco is quite a large city, notwithstanding they had two large fires there in a short time many will suffer from want before they can get employment," she sadly observed.[38] It was here, in the bustling, crudely cosmopolitan city, that Margaret Hereford felt more alone than at any time during her long and strange journey. Here, she was at least safe and had the luxury of being able to let herself be overwhelmed by the collage of lands and peoples she had been bombarded with during the past: the rugged southwestern trails, vast borderlands, defiant Apache tribes, the colorful Hispanic lifestyle and, now, the urgent, hectic pace of San Francisco. "Oh my dear Mother, you do not know how lonely and desolate I feel in this strange land."[39]

Hereford spent the summer recuperating with relatives at San Jose. For the next three months, she settled into a household routine; working at domestic chores, tutoring her son, and regaining her sense of place and purpose. Though revived, fulfilling needs that had been neglected during her years of travel and anxiety, Margaret's relief was to be shortlived. By October, she had still not heard from Thomas. Local acquaintances assumed the worst, and even a despondent Margaret resigned herself, admitting that she "had nearly despaired of ever seeing him again."[40] At age 31 she faced the tragic possibility of becoming a widow like her mother.

She again turned to her mother in an October letter, recounting her doubts about Thomas' fate, her lonely predicament in a "solitary land" and her longing to see family and friends. "I thought it was hard, when the Doctor went to Santa Fe and left me but it was nothing compared to this," she confided. But Margaret was a strong woman, able to channel her doubts into a resolution to wait and hope. Thomas finally arrived in San Jose to a relieved and grateful wife, more than six months after the family had departed in Mexico.[41]

Hereford had been fortunate during the six-month cattle drive across the barren southwestern deserts. Although several men deserted because of the severe conditions and threat of Indian raids, leaving Hereford with only a handful of men to complete the drive, the expedition had lost few animals. Thin and gaunt, Thomas told Margaret that he was cautiously optimistic about the sale of the cattle and mules. He had scaled back his expectations since Chihuahua, and now hoped to realize but a modest profit from the venture. When the Herefords began assessing California as a permanent residence, they were thankful to be alive and together again, now that the journey was complete. Unlike most settlers, their experience had taught them not to anticipate gold or riches, but only a "meager living" on the coast.[42]

The Herefords arrived in Southern California to find conditions little better than at Santa Fe and Chihuahua: a depressed economy, lack of hard currency and a volatile marketplace. As a result Thomas only broke even on his enterprise. "I realised nothing," he tersely observed, "as we offered them for cost without being able to find a purchaser."[43] Still, there were hopeful signs that Los Angeles might have a prosperous future. By 1851, the pueblo was experiencing a minor population boom, benefiting from the sensation over gold. Its cosmopolitan montage of peoples included Europeans, Anglo-Americans, Southerners, professionals, families and bachelors; all enterprising settlers who brought unique skills and talents. The Herefords could walk through Los Angeles and discover a French candy store, an English bakery, array of dry goods shops, several attorneys, five practicing physicians, a half-dozen markets, and one drug store. Los Angeles more and more took on the appearance of a store-front village displaying an urban character in its variety of fledgling retail businesses.[44]

The Herefords arrived in Los Angeles at the cutting edge of this migration, one of 50 new families that came in 1851, signaling a decade of steady migration from the slave states, particularly Texas, Louisiana and border states such as Missouri.[45]

The Herefords soon made friends with other transplanted Southerners; Henry Rice Myles, a Kentucky physician; Benjamin Wilson, a early pioneer from Tennessee; and William

G. Dryden, an attorney and future Los Angeles judge. With little capital, Myles and Hereford opened a wholesale merchan-
dising operation, and Wilson boarded the Herefords at his family home.[46] "I have been very fortunate," Thomas Hereford
noted, "in finding friends who are willing and able to aid me."[47]
By now, Thomas had entirely abandoned any hopes of finding
quick riches in Southern California, or possibly making a trek
to the California gold fields. For the Herefords, any thought of
"get rich quick" had been dashed on the banks of the Red River
and burning sands of the Southwest's deserts. Thomas would be
happy if he could regain his health, and live in "a plain way,
which is all that I desire."[48]

The Hereford family lived quietly at Los Angeles throughout
the spring and summer of 1851, touring the locale, becoming
acquainted with the environment, and planning a home. They
were in good spirits: prospects for their new life looked rosy.
Thomas thought that Margaret "look(ed) as young as ever she
did." After so much travail and uncertainties, the Herefords
began to relax, enjoy the mild climate and unscheduled pace of
the rural West and the serenity of the seascape surroundings.
They were thinking about buying property at San Pedro, about
160 acres of shoreline near the harbor perhaps, envisioning like
Abel Stearns before them, San Pedro's opportunities in mer-
chandising and trade.[49]

But the Hereford's dreams would not come to pass. Thomas'
health had never fully recovered from his past ordeals, and he
also seemed driven, unable to stop working at a frenetic pace to
build his business, unable to give his body the rest it needed
even though, as a physician himself, he should have been able
to see his folly. How Margaret felt watching her dear husband
literally working himself to death can only be speculated about.
"While I can walk I have no fear of want," he resolutely
declared, and continued to push his physical limits.[50] The
chronic tuberculosis progressively worsened, and on January 7,
1852, Thomas Hereford passed away at the home of Benjamin

Don Benito Wilson when he married
Margaret Hereford -circa 1853

D. Wilson. Dryden and Myles, along with Wilson, were with Hereford at the end, witnessing his last will, which included a few personal items and family mementos left to his family.[51]

Benjamin Wilson, a 41 year-old Angeleno, was himself a widower, taking pity on Margaret and Eddy, he helped manage their affairs in the months that followed Thomas Hereford's death. An early pioneer, Don Benito, as he was affectionately called by the Californios, came to Los Angeles with William Workman's overland expedition in 1841. He married Ramona Yorba, daughter of a respected Californio ranchero, but in 1849, Ramona died, leaving Wilson with a 5 year-old girl and 3 year-old boy. Margaret Hereford and Benjamin Wilson were brought together by their common experiences, tragedies and parental responsibilities. From this bond grew, first, a mutual respect and finally, affection.

For Margaret, Wilson represented security on a lonely frontier.[52] He was a war hero, adventurer and community leader. During the Mexican-American War, Wilson had rallied local support for the American cause, risking execution by a Mexican firing squad. His reputation had been carved on the West's plains and deserts and his education, as explained friend Joseph Lancaster Brent, came from the "rude frontiersmen and trappers who constituted the fringe of the American advance."[53]

In 1853, Margaret Hereford and Benjamin Wilson were

married at Los Angeles. The new groom respectfully wrote Margaret's mother to announce his honorable intentions. "As strange as it will seem to you," he noted, "yet to me it has appeared quite natural, that is natural that I should have loved your Daughter."[54]

During the next 20 years Wilson played a key role in Southern California's development, his career taking several twists: as an Indian agent at the Tejon reservation, a State senator, booster, and lobbyist for the introduction of the Southern Pacific Railroad. The Wilsons fashioned a genteel lifestyle at their estate in Chino Valley, reminiscent of the grace and charm Margaret had known in the South of her childhood. The rolling hills and manicured orchards located at Lake Vineyard created an enchanting setting for the Wilsons to pursue their labor of love, viticulture; and they spent their later years together nurturing citrus orchards and managing a winery. In 1878, at age 67 Benjamin Wilson passed away at Lake Vineyard.[55]

The years of Margaret's second marriage were rewarding ones, spent nurturing a family and new generation of grandchildren. She also was able to reunite with the family that meant so much to her, bringing her mother to California, She raised two stepchildren as well as Eddy, bore two girls by her second husband and proudly watched her offspring marry into prominent local families, the Pattons and De Barth Shorbs. She had her share of tragedies as well, outliving two children and two husbands. But she had endured, survived and personified the frontier woman in that historic moment in American expansion when the pioneer spirit of migration defined the nation's character and caught the public's imagination, uniting the country through settlement and growth. For Margaret Hereford Wilson, the Westward Movement offered a new life, but at cost of hardship mingled inextricably with hope and the achievement of a better future on the Southwestern frontier.

CHAPTER FOUR

Judah v. Evertson

The 1850s were a national watershed for seemingly unrelated events that, together, would change the country forever. At the beginning of that decade, the South was losing roughly 1,000 runaway slaves a year; John C. Calhoun, the ardent spokesman for Southern rights, died after a long battle with tuberculosis; President Zachary Taylor, a Virginia-born Southern sympathizer, suddenly died of an acute intestinal disorder; Texas demanded a large part of the New Mexico territory recently acquired in the 1848 Treaty of Guadalupe Hidalgo. Meanwhile, the Old Spanish Trail fell into disuse with the emergence of quicker Northern California routes to the mines; transcendentalist Nathaniel Hawthorne published *The Scarlet Letter*, attacking social conformity and rigid mores; prostitutes constituted up to 20% of California's female population; and John R. Evertson had brought his female slave, Judah, to California.

Little is known of either Evertson or Judah except for a few court records and minor references in the 1850 census. Neither person played a significant role in Southern California history. Yet, they represented issues of momentous consequence to the nation, symbolically bridging the gap between the remote West and the continental United States. The arrival of Judah and Evertson in Southern California has special meaning, reflecting as it did that region's presence in the larger context of the great mid-century upheaval that would split the nation.

Evertson, a South Carolina slaveowner, decided to move his family to the West after the Mexican-American war. He first stopped in Texas, as did many Southerners of that era, and then in 1849, came overland to Southern California with his wife, three children and two negro slaves. As it happened, the Evertson party were the only survivors of a wagon train that was ambushed by Indians in the Texas desert. It was 1850 when Evertson settled in Los Angeles and became the county's first census auditor.[1]

Evertson's arrived in Los Angeles during a time of serious sectional tensions over slavery, states' rights and secession. Within that context, California's admission as a free state focused the debate between free and slave states. Northern and Southern congressional leaders bitterly argued over the merits of expanding slavery into territories newly acquired from Mexico, particularly California, which had drafted a free state constitution and applied for statehood. Evertson, like other slaveowners, was caught between these polarized camps: his slaves were legally free pending Congressional approval of California's admission, in a legal position much like indentured servants -free without rights to citizenship, subject to the arbitrary dictates of their master.

Southern California was at the heart of this debate, for its agricultural economy and temperate climate favorable to cotton production naturally attracted Southerners. Among these emigrants were some slaveowners who thought that they had as much right to settle in the West as any U.S. citizens, despite bitter opposition from anti-slavery forces. In 1846, Northerners introduced the Wilmot Proviso to block the expansion of slavery into the territories acquired from Mexico. Although unsuccessful, the Wilmot Proviso marked the beginning of a bitter political fight to exclude slavery in the Southwest. Four years later, when California applied for statehood as a free state, the

South blocked admission and threatened to secede, setting the political stage for another major confrontation between sectional interests.[2]

John Evertson came to Southern California when not only admission but also the future of slavery in California was still in doubt. One September afternoon in 1850, Evertson returned home to find that his domestic servant, Judah, had not finished her household chores. Furious, he whipped Judah, repeatedly hitting her with a peach tree switch, then chased the hysterical young girl from the kitchen to the backyard, around a clothesline, and into the front street in full view of neighbors and pedestrians.[3]

On September 5, John R. Evertson was charged with assault in the Los Angeles Court of Sessions. One witness testified that he saw Evertson "whip and violently beat with a club or some longer weapon resembling a club a negro woman named Judah." Evertson admitted that this was true, except that it was a switch and not a club. He testified that the swelling around the victim's eyes was caused by drinking rather than any blows to the face. As an African American, Judah was not allowed to testify in court under California law, but Judge Jonathan Scott determined that enough evidence had been presented to indict Evertson, and set bail at $400. A week later, Justice Augustín Olvera presided over the court as a six-man jury determined Evertson's innocence or guilt.[4]

Judah v. Evertson was one of the first Southern California cases adjudicated under Anglo law that allowed charges to be brought against a white man for an assault on an African American. Beyond this extraordinary legal precedent, little else had changed in the life of Judah. Though a servant rather than a slave, she was still vulnerable to the violent whims of her master without any real chance for a fair trial.

Judah's desperate circumstances accentuated the bitter controversies surrounding California statehood. The Far West, though geographically remote, became one focal point of

Model of Los Angeles pueblo at the time of statehood.

national debate, and a major factor in the escalating of sectional discord during the ante-bellum era, igniting a tinder box. The *Judah v. Evertson* case also brought into sharp focus the question of whether slavery would flourish in the West considering geography, economics, and the plentitude of Asians willing to work hard for very low wages. Most important, however, the 1850 controversy cut to the heart of the pro-slavery argument. The frontier symbolized America's future, representing the hopes of many Americans, including the slaveowner. As a free state, California clouded that future for the South, creating a political majority in the Senate which favored the free states, and thus jeopardizing the possibility of future slave states being created from the western territories. The implications were dramatic. The loss of future slave states portended the eventual abolition of slavery, especially in view of increased Northern opposition.[5]

The Congressional debates over California statehood illustrated the basic antagonisms separating sectional interests. The new state was a microcosm of larger disputes about popular sovereignty: free soilers and anti-slavery proponents opposed slavery expansion into the West, and they encouraged territories such as Kansas to exclude slavery prior to statehood. Southerners, however, argued that slavery should be legalized in all territories until a state constitution was drafted and accepted by Congress. At the heart of the debate was whether slavery represented a legitimate part of American life, or as Abraham Lincoln later argued at Springfield, Illinois, upon accepting the 1858 Republican senatorial nomination: "A house divided against itself cannot stand. I believe this government cannot endure, permanently half slave and half free."[6]

Henry Clay, known with justification as "The Great Compromiser," introduced a compromise proposal that was the basis for political maneuvering throughout the Congressional debates of 1850. The Kentucky senator's idea for resolving sectional tensions and restoring national tranquility was threefold. First, he suggested, California could become a free state while Utah and New Mexico would decide, at some future date, whether they wanted slavery or abolition within their borders. Next, Clay balanced the territorial proposals with resolutions that addressed the issue of slavery as it existed, recommending that slavery be continued in the District of Columbia as long as Maryland and the District favored its existence. Finally, Clay proffered a stricter fugitive slave bill, earnestly upheld and rigidly executed by the Federal government. Clay's proposals, though not entirely his own sentiments, were designed to placate the polarized camps on both sides of the issue.[7]

Several Southerners objected to the California portion of the Clay compromise package. They reasoned that California had illegally bypassed the territorial stage and had circumvented the slaveowners opportunity to migrate there. A few slaveholders questioned the validity of the new state's constitution, considering that the area had not had enough time to develop a sizeable and legitimate electorate. Representative M.J. Wellborn of Georgia stated that California was permitted "to usurp territorial dominions confessedly not their own."[8] James A. Seddon of Virginia argued that California was being rushed into the Union by anti-slavery factions, thus violating the peoples' sovereignty. Seddon believed California's admission was a slap at the Southern states, which "would destroy the very basis of the constitutional compact."[9] One Alabama congressman, Samuel W. Inge, bluntly stated that California statehood was part of an anti-slavery plot to "exclude the people of half the States."[10]

California statehood defied the basic premise of the Missouri Compromise, which called for the simultaneous admission of a free and slave state to maintain political equality in the Senate. Some Southerners saw Southern California as the key to maintaining the compromise: Why not retain the spirit of the Missouri line by dividing California into two separate states? Representative James Mason of Virginia supported the extension of the 36° 30' line to the Pacific Ocean. The South, he claimed, would not tolerate a "law which excludes the institution of slavery in any territory below the line adopted in 1820."[11] Judge W.L. Sharkey of Mississippi maintained that Southerners were "entitled at least to have the Missouri Compromise line extended to the Pacific, which would give her a part of California."[12] Envisioning the worst case scenario, David Yulee of Florida believed that if California was lost to the ranks of the free states, the political balance between slave and free interests would be destroyed. He warned that if California were admitted without a countervailing slave state, "then it is indispensable with me that there should be a distinct recognition of her (the South's) equal rights in the remaining territories."[13]

The California issue galvanized a growing opposition to Southern rights. Anti-slavery opposition to expanding slavery previously embodied in the Wilmot Proviso, represented a tangible threat to California's admission. The West became the battleground with respect to free soil or slavery. The slaveholding argument was rooted in states' rights principles and the legal conception that slaves had no rights. African Americans, like John Evertson's servants, were commodities, property to have been purchased and exchanged like cattle or other types of merchandise. Further, African Americans, like the California Indians, had no standing in court. To some Southerners, it seemed understandable that restriction denied them of their fundamental rights. "Slave property in the Southern states should be recognized as property throughout the United States," fumed Jefferson Davis.[14] Representative Isham G. Harris of Tennessee believed that restricting the expansion of slavery not only denied Southerners their property rights but also "destroyed that principle of equality of right and of privilege upon which our whole system of Government must rest."[15] "The national flag," Robert W. Johnson of Arkansas sadly conceded, "has proved to be no protection to a southern man's property."[16]

Many paternalistic-minded slaveowners felt that slavery was a positive good rather than the evil portrayed by their opponents. Blacks were childlike, helpless, naive, unskilled and dependent on their compassionate masters. In the view of many Southerners, in that era when corporal punishment was administered commonly in "taught-to-the-tune-of-a-hickory stick" schools as well as in the home, slaveowners like John Evertson were acting in a manner similar to how a father reprimands a prodigal son.

As attacks on slavery grew, unabashed pro-slavery forces went even farther defending their "peculiar institution" on legal and moral grounds. Amidst escalating rhetoric on both extremes, Georgia's firebrand Robert Toombs asserted that slavery held a legitimate place in American history and that the Constitution had continually upheld its legality. "This is a proslavery Government," Toombs thundered, "slavery is stamped upon its heart."[17] Senator Badger looked to ancient history to make his point. Citing the Greeks, Romans and early

Manuel Dominguez, Southern California representative to the Monterey Convention that had excluded slavery from the state constitution.

Christians, Badger considered slavery "an institution among us so ancient, so sanctioned, surely it cannot be that it is, in itself, utterly unlawful."[18] Congressman William Alston of Alabama, believed that slavery in fact elevated blacks from the barbarous state that existed in Africa, and he reminded the North "that in the case of the negro, the hardship is not in the loss of freedom, as it would be with the white man, for he has always been a slave."[19] Jeff Davis considered slavery a "blessing" in relation to its alleged evils of cruelty.[20]

Although militants were now asserting that slavery was an integral part of American life, that in itself did not necessarily prove that slavery was equally viable on the frontier, though most of the Far West was more like the agrarian South than the industrial North. Southern California defied the Missouri Compromise line, with its underlying assumption that an imaginary border could realistically divide the nation into diametrically opposed sections. All the Southern California delegates to the Monterey convention voted for ratification of the state constitution, a clear indication that they were more interested in statehood than in the slavery issue.[21] James Buchanan, despite his Southern sympathies, admitted that under the circumstances, "every State which shall be carved out of California will eventually be a free State."[22]

Southern congressional leaders stubbornly refused to concede that expanding slavery was unrealistic. Thomas S. Bocock of Virginia maintained that Southern staples could be cultivated in Southern California while blacks could be used in mining.[23] In June of 1850, a convention of Southern state representatives met at Nashville and openly supported an extension of the Missouri Compromise line to the Pacific Ocean. A similar proposal was offered in a Congressional amendment written by Pierre Soule of Louisiana. All in all, declared Virginian James Mason, the South only wanted "to have the door left open, and to have it kept open."[24] To many slaveholders, settlers like John R. Evertson represented a promising future, a new era when Dixie could share equally in the settlement of the Far West. Jeff Davis pleaded that Southerners were merely asking for "the benefit of an experiment."[25]

The proposed extension of the 36° 30' line through California gained limited support in the 1850 Congressional debates. Yet State admission seemed far from certain, and pro-slavery forces wanted some assurance that the peculiar institution would be protected in western territories prior to statehood. Alabama's William Alston considered it a Northern duty "to make laws to protect the citizen in the enjoyment of all his rights in these territories."[26] Congressman Finis McLean of Kentucky wanted some assurances that California's admission as a free state would be the exception to the rule, and that no

Monterey, old capitol

"other territories may form state governments and come in upon the same principles."[27] Georgia senator John Berrien demanded federal protection of slavery in the territories until a judicial opinion could be rendered on the subject. Otherwise, Berrien concluded, free labor would "control the destiny of the territories."[28]

Not all Southerners were convinced that slavery would ever become an institution on the Western frontier, partly because its economic viability in certain types of agriculture was already being questioned in the South: who knew what economic system would eventually arise on the frontier? Many Southerners saw slaveowners who had come west, like John Evertson, as the exception rather than the rule, particularly in view of the Congressional debates over California's admission as a free state. This state of mind was expressed by the Mobile *Advertiser*, which editorialized that the South should have known what was coming when the United States acquired the Mexican territory. "They (the South) had full and fair notice of the consequences," noted the Southern newspaper, recalling the debates over Missouri, Texas and the Wilmot Proviso.[29] Henry Clay, the unrivaled leader of compromise sentiment, ruefully noted that "slavery is not likely to be introduced into any portion of that territory (the Southwest)."[30] "It is almost certain," conceded Alabama congressman W.R.W. Cobb, "that negroes will never be taken there (California) in any other than very inconsiderable numbers."[31]

At the time of California's admission there were indeed only a handful of African Americans in Los Angeles. The 1850 census recorded 15 blacks in the county, most of them brought in by former slaveowners and were registered as servants.[32] Most of these people worked inconspicuously as laborers, maids and other domestic workers; and then there was the highly visible African American Peter Biggs. He traveled to Los Angeles as a freedman following the Mexican American War. Biggs was an exception to the popular image of blacks as a docile, servile race: he, in flamboyant contrast, was a successful entrepreneur, independent, gregarious and highly visible in the community. As the city's first barber, Biggs catered to black and white alike, and thus was privy to gossip concerning numerous details of the private and public lives of many of the pueblo residents.[33]

The 1850 Congressional debates raged for nearly nine months as a tense drama unfolded in the House and Senate. Several factors eventually led to compromise, at least for a while: first, John C. Calhoun, articulate spokesman for Southern rights, died in the midst of the debates; next, the June convention at Nashville offered no solutions to the Congressional impasse but did reject the extremist alternative of secession and finally, President Zachary Taylor, Southern sympathizer and opponent of Clay's Omnibus Bill, died of a gastric disorder in midsummer. By August, there was a different set of players on the field. Two powerful adversaries of Clay's proposals were gone and the Nashville Convention, expected to be the first step toward secession, disappointed Southern radicals in that regard. Finally, through parliamentary maneuvering and the astute leadership of Stephen Douglas, the elements of the Great Compromiser's Omnibus Bill were eventually passed in separate Congressional votes.[34]

Even so, basic questions separating sectional interests remained: federal jurisdiction over fugitive slaves, slavery expansion in the territories, and as ever, the continuing delicate balancing act between sectional interests in the Senate. After California's admission all but nullified the intent of the Missouri Compromise, denying slaveowners access to land south of the 36° 30' line, the issue of slavery on the frontier depended more heavily on confusing interpretations of popular sovereignty.

More significantly, the 1850 Compromise ignored the issues of emancipation and citizenship, the fundamental question of African Americans legitimate place in the democratic process. For Judah, this meant bringing charges against her former master without having the opportunity to testify in court.

On September 9, four days after John R. Evertson was arraigned on assault charges by Judge Jonathan R. Scott, California was admitted into the Union as a non-slaveholding state. On September 13, a Los Angeles jury found Evertson not guilty of wrongfully beating his black servant, Judah.[35] California had become a free land, but a bitter war and years of political debate would pass before African Americans would gain equal rights under the law.

CHAPTER FIVE

Joseph Lancaster Brent
and
Frontier Politics

L ike the explorers, trailblazers and colonizers of earlier conquests, American settlers headed for the West for a variety of practical reasons. Adventurers blazed trails; trappers followed the trade routes between Taos and Los Angeles; poor men came for free land and merchants looked across the vast Pacific toward the Orient and beyond. But one event distinguished this mid-19th-century Westward Movement, focusing it on California and accelerating what had been a gradual migration with the discovery of gold at the American River in 1848. "In that year Argonauts from the ends of the earth converged on California," observed John Walton Caughey, "and engaged in an orgy of gold gathering that ranks as the greatest of all mining rushes."[1] Many emigrants, however, were ill-prepared for the arduous work and disappointment of the diggings. Southern California became a refuge for the displaced and forgotten: those with broken dreams who were determined to remain in the West and build a new life.

Joseph Lancaster Brent's journey west typified this circuitous migration to Southern California. He stayed for a decade, during which time he became a central figure in the political and social life of Los Angeles. As an influential politician, Brent saw the inside workings of a decade, living in a frontier struggling with problems of race, politics and commerce. His experiences reveal a diverse society, underlying the contrasts between the fading rancho era and the emerging rough-hewn character of Anglo-American frontier settlement. It was the rush for gold that brought Joseph Lancaster Brent to the West, but it was in Southern California that he would leave his imprint as a central figure in local politics.

Born in Maryland and later a resident of Louisiana, at 23 Brent was attracted by the "wonders and riches of California," and fascinated by the stories of fortunes made in the mining camps along the Kern River. For months, Louisiana had been the southern gateway to California, as gold fever raged from Shreveport to the Gulf of Mexico. The New Orleans *Daily Picayune* warned returning prospectors to hide their booty because "ravenous rogues who infest our cities are on the watch for them in almost every public place."[2]

In late spring of 1850, Brent left for California via the Panama route, which included an overland crossing of the isthmus and a final seafaring leg to San Francisco. This route was far less arduous than an overland expedition, with the prospect of favorable weather and easy access to steamers on the Pacific shore, and was faster than the long voyage around the Horn.[3]

Brent boarded a vessel at New Orleans with all of his possessions, including his father's extensive law library. Once he arrived in California, Brent thought he might practice law, perhaps join the mining camps, or start a commercial venture. In any event, the confident young man who thought himself "as good as any Englishman" sailed to Panama aboard a crowded ship filled with Europeans and Americans, artisans and unskilled laborers, speculators, gamblers and idealists. In July of 1850 Brent landed at San Francisco harbor, a crowded port filled with steamers and clippers, many of them abandoned off-shore. The discarded vessels had brought thousands of people to California, including an exhausted Margaret Hereford (Wilson) only a month before.[4]

Brent found gold rush San Francisco a disagreeable place. The rapid influx of immigrants created unexpected demands, and the fledgling city was unable to provide even basic services, leading to slum-like conditions and unforeseen hazards. Also, food and housing costs were high; Brent rented a small room for an exorbitant rate of $16 per day. Adding to the city's problems, during 1850 and 1851 a beleaguered San Francisco suffered a half-dozen fires, including one hotel fire that partially destroyed Brent's law library. The rain, fog and bitter wind were an unwelcome mix to a Southerner accustomed to the warmly damp and soft air of the Deep South.[5] Brent would have surely agreed with Missourian Mark Twain, who once reportedly said that the coldest winter he ever spent was a summer in San Francisco. Encouraged by his physician-cousin, Thomas Brent, who preceded Brent west, he decided to move to the more temperate environs of Los Angeles where, he hoped, he might begin a successful law practice.[6]

Brent found rural Los Angeles much like the agrarian South, a pleasant contrast with the bustling intensity of San Francisco. Sprawling ranchos, undulating valleys and emerald fields dotted with cattle attracted Brent to Southern California as much as he was repelled by the urban nature of tenement dwelling in San Francisco. Brent soon fell in love with the romantic ambience of the pueblo, as had Abel Stearns, Alfred Robinson and William Heath Davis before him. He may have found the cottonwoods, adobe huts, beaches and meandering Indian trails enchanting; and he might also have found something of the spirit of New Orleans this society described by Helen Hunt Jackson in *Ramona* as "a picturesque life, with more sentiment and gayety than will ever be seen again on those sunny shores."[7] Brent's spirits soared, envigorated by the land and climate, he declared that "this (environ) in itself made me like the place."[8]

Southern California also fit into the young Brent's image of

the Far West, which he envisioned as a wilderness rather than
the boom town-style settlement of the northern mining camps
and centers. A wilderness offered adventure, and the adven-
turesome Brent was fascinated by men who not only could survive but also tame it. In his early days in Los Angeles, he would
spend hours at the local saloons listening to the trappers and
journeymen recount their pioneering exploits. Brent would sit
until dawn at the Bella Union Hotel, enthralled by the stories as
such legendary men as William Wolfskill described the Taos
trade, William Workman reminisced about the rancho era, or
Benjamin Wilson recalled facing a Mexican firing squad during
the recent war. Danger fascinated him, and he noted that these
trailblazers "spent most of their lives on the war path, fighting
the Indians, fighting the Mexicans, fighting each other." They
were a diverse lot. "Strong, original characters," he admiringly
observed, "Some of them rough, wild men, perhaps desperadoes and bandits." To Brent, these early residents were icons,
the sort of rugged individualists who had survived on the
Western frontier.[9]

Still, this idyllic setting of ranches and cattle had drawbacks
for a young man who expected to make his living practicing law
or even commerce. Los Angeles, remote from the economics of
the northern mines, was still struggling to attract settlers, having less than two thousand Anglo-American inhabitants by the
end of the 1850s.[10] Brent was surprised and disappointed that
"there seemed to be so little business or trade going on."[11] A
lack of hard currency retarded investment, and slow commercial growth also meant a small tax base for municipal improvements. The city itself conducted business out of rented homes.
Benjamin Hayes' home even served as a courtroom. Local officials enlisted a volunteer police forces, and the pueblo had no
permanent school, hospital or jail. "The dearth of capital," historian Robert Glass Cleland would later explain, "was unques-
tionably one of Southern California's greatest handicaps."[12]

The slow economy, tight money and few emigrants added

up to a difficult first year for the young Brent. He found work as a carpenter's apprentice, carrying bricks and mortar to build the first brick structures in the downtown section. With a meager savings gained from hard labor, he bravely opened his legal practice near the courthouse, across from the Stearns home on Main Street. But four lawyers had already begun practicing before Brent's arrival, which meant that too many attorneys and too few cases made the courtroom a highly competitive place. In a small town, a lawyer's personal reputation often determined whether his law firm would succeed or fail, so a relatively unknown newcomer was at a disadvantage.[13]

Brent had only a few dollars and even fewer clients to sustain his legal practice. Within three months he had exhausted his savings. Undaunted, either from overconfidence or naivete, he whimsically declared that his predicament was "a joke," and promptly borrowed $300 from Benjamin Wilson to continue his practice.[14] Over the next few years he steadily built a reputation and law practice. By 1853, Brent was licensed by the State Supreme Court and had developed expertise in land title cases, including a successful award of the city's claims to land.[15] He was an "able lawyer (and) one of California's most brilliant men," acknowledged historian W. W. Robinson.[16]

Brent made the best of a limited marketplace, and his success is indicative of both the man and the era. Legal references and law books were scarce, a major drawback in a profession based on written precedent. One commentator noted that a brief passage from Kent's *Commentaries*, "found somewhere in town," once decided a civil dispute.[17] "Probably more lawyers than law books," quipped one pundit.[18] Brent's library, although partially destroyed in the San Francisco fire, became an invaluable reference resource. He added Hugo Reid's Indian library to his collection, as repayment for his defense of Reid's claim to mission lands in San Gabriel.[19]

The small community of lawyers and judges shared resources and debated points of law. Brent quickly developed a network of professional and personal friends, many of whom were Southerners, including Dr. John Griffin, who'd come to Los Angeles at the same time as Brent, and Jonathan Scott, a prominent Missouri attorney who arrived in Los Angeles the year before Brent. Other early Los Angeles lawyers were Albert Clark and William C. Ferrill. Though competitors, the tiny group of barristers nevertheless shared legal advice and reference materials. In 1853, Brent served as a school commissioner with Lewis Granger, another attorney.[20]

Brent made many friends, an invaluable asset in a distant land where brotherhood ranked in value with gold. He admired hard workers and the Jacksonian ideals of the common man.[21] Brent was an egalitarian, and the American West seemed to highlight this virtue within the spirit of frontier life. To his clients, many of whom were laborers, men of "rough" manner, he embodied "a higher and gentler civilization." His network of associates and contacts among the community included traders, politicians, businessmen and soldiers. He almost forgot his Southern roots, so comfortably had they transplanted into the Californio's world of *fandango* and *rendezvous*. By 1854, Brent proudly considered himself a Westerner, and a Californian in particular. "(I am) estranged from all ties of family and former friendship," and he recalled that he was "entirely out of the world as I had known it."[22]

Brent developed close ties to the Hispanic elites. The rancheros still had an unmistakable influence in American California's everyday affairs, serving as overseers to an extended family of relatives, employees and compadres. The pueblo served as a weekend social spot for the dons, vaqueros and ranch hirelings. Rodeos were held in the town center, along with horse-races, cockfights and dances. The rancheros' large adobe homes in the Plaza center served as guest residences. Indeed, the rancho lifestyle still dominated Southern California, with land symbolizing wealth equivalent to the northern mining towns' gold. When statehood brought disputes over Mexican land titles and grants, Brent became a spokesman for the underdog, those rancheros and dons who argued for legitimacy before an indifferent courts. Dividing his time between San Francisco and Los Angeles, Brent represented claimants before the Land Commission. He defended the claims of the Lugo family and Manuel Nieto,

Joseph Lancaster Brent

and became a close friend of the Del Valle clan. Considered honest and forthright, Brent exercised considerable influence among the Californio elite.[23]

Although Brent benefited from his grateful ranchero clientele, he sincerely enjoyed the romance and charm of Hispanic culture. If for nothing else, being gregarious and high-spirited himself, Brent would have been drawn to Hispanic society from necessity. In 1850, the old pueblo offered little entertainment beyond the heavy drinking and male conversation found in the gaming rooms. Anglo women were few and, as a bachelor with a confident manner, Brent soon became acquainted with the senoritas of the upper echelon. He appreciated the charm of Antonio Coronel's dark-eyed daughters, who wore bright-colored *rebozos* knotted in their long flowing hair. He observed the submissive demeanor of Hispanic women in a male- dominated society. Hispanic women served meals, often did not converse at the same table and, according to Brent, "were not disinclined to marry the American men, who treated their wives with greater consideration.[24] He loved their delicacy, particularly at dances where they played festive games such as the *coscarones*, a breaking of eggshells filled with colored paper that produced a shower of gold and silver over the ballroom dancers. Brent led a carefree life in those pioneer days, with no responsibilities, and "nothing to arrest the flow of spirits, which had been generously bestowed by Nature and encouraged by health."[25]

For the Southern-bred Brent, Hispanic life held a familiar charm, in contrast to the aggressive bent of gold rush California. The Californios were a graceful people, profoundly religious and uncomplicated in their approach to the land. The rancheros valued integrity, a virtue that ran counter to the competitive sharp practice ethic of the gold rush era. Brent was comfortable with the rancheros' who conducted business with a handshake, as similar to the Southern code he'd grown up with as it was different from transactions with San Francisco bankers, whose interest on loans compounded monthly at inordinate rates. As miners feverishly toiled in the Northern diggings, gala processions decorated the Los Angeles plaza square in honor of feast days or Holy Week. The Californios knew little of the sophisticated technology behind steamers and railroads. But they were skillful masters of their land, driving wooden *carretas* to the marketplace, or handling a stallion with grace and ease. In fact, the horse was integral to the rancho world, just as the buffalo was central to Native Americans, or the Iron Road to Anglo expansion. So important was 'el canolo,' Brent recalled, that "a man never walked unless it was absolutely necessary."[26]

Many rancheros embraced Brent's courtroom talents with open arms: here was a man of their stripe who also could deal with incomprehensible Anglo laws and courts. The legal entanglements over land grants created tension among competing Anglo and Hispanic interests. American justice seemed unfair to the proud dons, many of whom felt they were not obliged to prove their claims. Honest legal representation within a system they strongly distrusted proved invaluable. Brent had a reputation for sound advice and shrewd logic. In 1851, he tried his first important case, successfully definding members of the Lugo family accused of murder. The grateful don reportedly paid Brent $20,000 for his services.[27] Professional success led to new friendships, and Joseph Lancaster Brent soon became a confidante of the Californio elite. He frequented Abel Stearns' home and socialized with members of influential families such as Alvarado, Pico and Bandini. The Del Valle clan adopted him as one of their own, and the eldest children affectionately called him *padrino*. Brent valued his friends and their hospitality, and would converse for hours with Ignacio Del Valle, polishing his Spanish while exchanging lively ideas on life, business, and politics. "Nothing disturbed his calm," wrote Brent of his compadre Don Ignacio. "When you got through his shell, he was warm hearted and had a good deal of humour."[28]

Brent became a prominent civic leader during the 1850s. Politics was a natural arena for him: as a successful attorney, popular, respected by the community elite, Brent had solid leadership qualities. He "stood high as a lawyer and Statesman," read one contemporary account.[29] Ever the diplomat, the affable Brent bolstered his political fortunes by consciously promoting good will with "everyone with whom I was brought in contact."[30] Most important, the great issues of the day electrified party politics and piqued Brent's sense of civic activism. He was sensitive to the race issues that threatened the slaveholding society of his birthplace. The legal-minded Brent understood the Constitutional questions regarding states' rights and popular sovereignty. As a Jacksonian Democrat, he could not ignore the sectional questions that threatened to divide his party.[31]

Brent became an influential force among Southern California Democrats. Like a puppeteer manipulating events from behind the scenes, he planned strategy, created alliances, counted enemies and elicited support for upcoming elections. "I have always preferred to put other men forward," he recalled, "and have them carry out my political ideas."[32] The men Brent supported were individualists themselves, capable leaders, and loyal Democrats. Throughout the 1850s, Brent supported the political ambitions of many friends: Jack Watson, I.S.K. Ogier, and Benjamin Wilson. William Gwin, a powerful party leader of the Chivalry wing, was one of Brent's close friends who urged him to retain a visible role in state and local politics.[33] Brent could rely on a strong Hispanic bloc and, in turn, he rallied political support behind Hispanic candidates such as Antonio Coronel and Agustín Olvera. Because of their regard for and trust in him, Brent virtually controlled the large ranchero families' votes, a potent political force. Of the Verdugo family, it was said that Brent could distribute ballots for instant tabulation. Harris Newmark recalled that Brent's "political influence with the old man was supreme."[34]

Control of the powerful Hispanic vote coupled with his Democratic allies among the Anglo populace allowed Brent to dominate county legislation and dictate local elections. By the mid-1850s he could boast that Los Angeles was "in his vest pocket."[35] Newmark believed that the invincible Brent could nominate candidates "at will."[36] As a delegate to the 1856 Democrat national convention at Cincinnati, Brent dutifully supported the convention nominee, James Buchanan. During the next two years Brent served in the California Legislature and sat on the Judiciary and Ways and Means committees.[37]

Brent's hold on local party machinery was damaged somewhat by the rise of bandidos like Juan Flores, and a corresponding increase of xenophobia within the pueblo. Brent's political opponents targeted Hispanics and other ethnic peoples as responsible for the rise in crime. Though Brent supported tough law enforcement as a member of the Los Angeles Rangers, he felt the rise in crime was a result of the gold rush gone bust, producing transients and displaced miners. "After the emigration into California became larger and the number of desperate men increased," Brent claimed, "the towns were visited by lawless characters."[38] His Hispanic loyalties weakened his credibility, and several rivals emerged within the pueblo: Sheriff Bill Getman, who defended the city against a mob attempt to lynch his deputy, William Jenkins, after the wrongful shooting of a Spanish-speaking citizen, Antonio Ruís; Columbus Sims, a fellow Southerner and proponent of vigilante justice and Jonathan Scott, Brent's friend and associate at odds with him on the use of vigliante justice. Scott acted as the hanging judge in the Flores trials and, in Brent's view, was an all too eager participant in a lynching party.[39]

Nevertheless, Brent won a few political battles in the years preceding the Civil War. He supported Benjamin Wilson's state Senate bid as a tactical move to thwart a Know-Nothing candidacy. Brent carried Los Angeles for James Buchanan in the 1856 Presidential election, and championed the Southern rights candidacy of John C. Breckinridge in the 1860 election. Yet his most satisfying victory may have been his last. In 1860, he vigorously campaigned for Tomás Sanchez in the election for sheriff. With law and order a persistent concern, the sheriff was considered a powerful city official and prejudices surfaced during the election. Explained Brent, "Many Americans bitterly opposed him, owing to their race and prejudices."[40] Sanchez narrowly won. Brent felt that the election was a personal vindication of past battles, and a rebuke to the xenophobia he had opposed in the mid-fifties.[41]

Nevertheless, Brent suffered his share of political setbacks, mainly because of party realignments on the state and national level. In 1859, Brent and rival John G. Downey led a divided Los Angeles Democrat delegation to the nominating convention for governor. When Brent supported the re-election of Governor John B. Weller, the convention rejected him and other Weller supporters, denying them a slate. Brent led a walk-out of delegates, while Downey remained at the convention in support of the party favorite, Milton Latham. The Democrats eventually nominated Downey for lieutenant governor, perhaps in a show of gratitude for his party loyalty. Brent believed that Downey's motives were self- serving, a blatant power move to gain control of the Los Angeles delegation, and pressed an unsuccessful challenge against the Latham-Downey ticket in the general election. The Brent-Downey feud divided Democrats statewide. "Before it was over," summarized historian David A. Williams, "new dimensions of political vituperation had been reached, the system of democratic politics seriously damaged, and the political issues buried in an avalanche of invective."[42]

The Democrats' failure suggested that political trends had passed Brent by, or at the very least were moving too quickly for him to control. Brent, increasingly an outsider within his own party, conceded that many Angelenos wanted to "break up the political influence which had governed the county for so many years."[43] The city population had doubled by the end of the decade, bringing settlers with new ideas and new ambitions. Los Angeles slowly evolved from a rancho community into a growing Anglo-American settlement; a larger city with broader issues made politics a more sophisticated venture than the uncomplicated era of barroom deals and stump rhetoric. A weary Joseph Lancaster Brent, disillusioned with his inability to control events, interpreted local opposition as a negative aspect of the westerning process. As the pueblo grew, Brent simply reasoned, those who took control were a "rougher element and men who looked upon politics as a money- making business."[44]

In October 1861, 11 years after he had landed at San Francisco, Joseph Lancaster Brent went east to fight for the Confederacy. He opposed abolition and felt the federal government had an obligation to protect the slaveowners' property in the territories, but he was not a secessionist at first, enlisting only after the war had started. Nor was he optimistic about the South's prospects for victory. He has the distinction of being the last Confederate general (eight total) commissioned from the state of California.

Brent's decision to leave Southern California and fight in a distant war was painful for him. He had accumulated properties throughout Southern California, including nearly 75,000 acres in Los Angeles and the Tejon mountains. In 1859, he purchased the Morengo ranch, a modest estate located two miles from Benjamin Wilson's residence at Lake Vineyard. Fearing that the Union would seize his holdings when he enlisted with the Confederacy, he knew that he would have to liquidate these properties, a slow process that would be left to his friends, with the risk that his properties would be sold at a loss.[45]

Brent also left behind cherished friends, including his neighbor Henry Rice Myles, "a Kentuckian and a very great friend"; Tennessee-born Benjamin Wilson, a confidante Brent admired for his devotion to family and children; James Watson, his political ally and a "Don Quixote" in Brent's words, someone Brent respected as a peacemaker who used force only when necessary; and Tomás Sanchez, a trusted ally with whom he had fought several political battles. To Sanchez, he said his good-byes with "tears streaming down his cheeks." He also respected some of the loyalists of the Northern cause, men like Winfield Hancock, commissioned in the Union Army, and Phineas Banning, a Republican adversary whom Brent admired for his frank and friendly demeanor. In his mid-thirties, this brief chapter in Brent's life was analogous to a shooting star across a dark sky, never to be repeated, "at the time of life when we form our warmest and most enduring friendships."[46]

Brent's return to the South would be risky. The Union Army had closed the borders and prepared to assert control over the state's southern counties. Federal authorities were deeply concerned about threats of subversion or rebellion in the Southern counties. They had good reason to be worried: the months that followed General Pierre Toutant Beauregard's attack on Fort Sumter, Southern Californians publicly defied the Union cause. Confederate rallies and demonstrations took place at El Monte and downtown Los Angeles, near the Bella Union Hotel. Holcomb Valley in the San Bernardino mountains reportedly was the scene of Confederate recruitment camps. "They deceive themselves," warned Benjamin Hayes, "who suppose that California could stand aloof from the contest."[47]

By the summer of 1861, rumors of widespread intrigue swept the state and led federal authorities to question Brent about his loyalties. He affirmed his sympathy with the Confederacy but denied any involvement in planning a local uprising. When Brent was approached by local residents interested in a coup, he vehemently rejected the idea, reasoning that Union gunboats would blockade the harbor, and eventually Federal forces would be sent south. Without control of the seas, or the possibility of reinforcements, it would be only a matter of time before the rebels would be overcome. Those Californios who supported the takeover "would be ruined."[48]

There was also a point of honor that went beyond practical matters, the question of secession itself. For Brent, the war was a revolutionary response in the best traditions of the American Revolution. Secession was a libertarian protest and the legal right of a state when confronted with an oppressive federal government, and was not without precedent. Had not the New England states very nearly seceded at the Hartford Convention, over sectional economic interests very similar to the South's? Brent, like most secessionists, believed their actions were justifiable in the spirit of the Founding Fathers. As Civil War historian James McPherson put it, "State sovereignty preceded national sovereignty. When they had ratified the Constitution, states delegated some of the functions of sovereignty to a federal government but did not yield its fundamental attributes."[49]

But what Brent's compatriots at Los Angeles were suggesting was rebellion in a state that had not seceded, an act both dishonorable and treasonable by law. Instead, he counseled sympathizers to go "South and join the Confederate army, where they would be of real service."[50] It was far easier for Brent to make that determination than it would have been for many of his *compadres*, who had wives and families deeply rooted in Southern California. Brent, by contrast, was a bachelor, law was a portable profession and the prospect of a prestigous commission awaited him in the Confederate army. Yet, despite personal and financial hardships on themselves and their families, many Southern Californians chose to return to fight for the Confederacy during the first year of the war.[51]

Brent never returned to Southern California. He fought in several campaigns in Louisiana and Mississippi. After the war, Brent returned to Maryland, and later operated a sugar plantation at New River, Louisiana, until his death in 1905. Always a man of energy and verve, he remained active in politics most of his life. He wrote political commentaries, delivered public addresses on foreign policy and domestic issues and participated in several Democratic conventions throughout the century. He always missed Los Angeles; when Brent's final properties at Morengo were sold in 1868, he wrote his longtime friend, Benjamin Wilson, that he felt the sadness of this passing chapter. The war years planted the seeds for a new beginning in an old homeland. "If I was able to reconcile a sense of duty, I would long since have returned."[52]

Although he never returned, Joseph Lancaster Brent left a distinctive imprint on the pueblo in law and politics, and perhaps saved the region from disaster by forestalling rebellion. He participated in a volatile period in local and national history when questions of violence and race were as hotly debated on the frontier as in Washington or Richmond. Perhaps the Far West shaped the man even more than his native South, which he chose in the end. For Brent, the great debate would be played out in other forums, on distant battlefields, and among different contemporaries in his life.

CHAPTER SIX

An Officer and the Outlaw:
James Barton
and
Juan Flores

O f the early Los Angeles lawmen, James Barton best represented the power and influence behind the badge. He
was colorful, rash and outspoken, with attitudes
shaped by the cultural prejudices of his era. Serving as sheriff
from 1851 until his death in January 1857, Barton wielded
police authority at a time when law enforcement was excep-
tionally important and therefore powerful in early Southern
California. Thieves, transients and bandidos threatened the
community, and the police represented safety to a fearful people who in turn were happy to accord excessive leeway to the
law enforcers.

Barton migrated to California during the early stages of
overland travel when Margaret Hereford, Benjamin Wilson and
other Southerners, particularly from the border states, were
attracted to the growing southwestern trade in hides and cattle.
A Missourian, Barton had traveled to Mexico early in 1841, and
two years later he wandered farther northwest to California. He

enlisted during the Mexican-American War and fought with Stephen Kearny's Army of the West.[1]

Barton and other early pioneers were pragmatic men, traders, trappers and frontiersmen all interested in the new opportunities for a better life offered by the West. During the 1840s, the Bidwell-Bartleson and Workman-Rowland parties utilized a workable network of trade routes throughout the Southwest, which included the Gila, Santa Fe and Old Spanish trails. Taos, Santa Fe and Yuma were trading centers where Angelenos could buy or trade goods, and also served to attract migrating people, encouraging them to settle in the area. Community building as well as the added protection against hostile Indians made locals especially eager to boost their populations in those days.[2]

Southern California benefited from Northern California's mining boom during the early 1850s. Main Street featured new store front construction, a Bella Union Hotel filled with newcomers, and a commercial center filled with corrals, *cantinas*, trading posts and adobes. In the words of writer Ed Ainsworth, "The Enchanted pueblo was losing its baby look and beginning at last to feel the pangs of growth."[3] Economic growth increased the demand for labor, and the resourceful Barton found plenty of work as a handyman during California's early days of statehood. He formed a partnership with '49er William Nordholt, and together they contracted as carpenters and construction laborers. Their firm built a section of Bell's Row located between Aliso and First Streets, near Francis Mellus' adobe home.

Nordholt and Barton created a public image for themselves through their involvement in civic and political organizations. Nordholt helped organize the first political rally in Los Angeles while Barton joined many societies and humanitarian organizations, developing a network of friends within the young city's upper elite. He joined the Masonic Order, the Los Angeles Lodge and had acquaintances in various fraternal groups like the Odd Fellows, City Guard and the *Los Angeles Rangers*. In

1851, he left the partnership with Nordholt and successfully ran for sheriff. His election placed him in a fish bowl, a focal point of community interest at a time when the old pueblo was afflicted by violent desperados.[4]

When Barton took office, the public had little confidence in the criminal justice system. Vigilantes, public hangings and quick justice were considered legitimate responses to crime. Benjamin Wilson, Abel Stearns and Joseph Lancaster Brent were just a few of the men of high caliber who participated as posse members as frequently as they enlisted as jurors, and Horace Bell's reputation as a vigilante mirrored the widespread public support for the *Los Angeles Rangers*. Bell's legendary reminiscences about outlaws and hangings made him a celebrity or at least a celebrated character. Crime threatened the general welfare to such an extent that most of the responsible citizenry approved of the blunt message that vigilante trials and lynchings sent throughout society. One account vividly recalled "the streets enlivened by the martial tread of the military companies required, from time to time, in our wild circumstances."[5]

Angelenos often saw Barton's self-confidence and rash behavior as a bold and welcome panacea for the crime plaguing their troubled community. He faced lawlessness with unrelenting fervor, often reacting with force and aplomb scorning caution. In one instance, Barton confronted an unruly patron at a local bar, the Figuera House, and then shot the unarmed man after a brief verbal altercation.[6] Unsavory, dangerous reputations of certain troublemakers did not deter Barton from making arrests. In 1852, the sheriff was shot at during the Fourth of July festivities by Joseph Caddick and Charles Norris, men who had connections with the notorious Jack Powers, a local ruffian and gambler. Norris had previously been accused of assault on another police officer. Nevertheless, Barton cooly apprehended the two thugs and not only held them for trial, but also testified against them in court.[7] Opinionated and outspoken, Barton would sometimes instigate trouble rather than restore peace. In one instance, an argument at the Bella Union Hotel between the sheriff and another patron led to a larger brawl between onlookers, which the sheriff was then forced to disperse with appropriate arrests.[8]

Bandidos constantly challenged the power of the pueblo's law enforcement officials. Legendary exploits of outlaws like Pio Linares, Joaquín Murrieta and Pancho Daniels had spread fear throughout the state, challenging local authorities and straining the patience of law abiding citizens to the point that they were willing to resort to lynch law tactics if necessary. Occasional reports of nearby fugitives prompted outlying residents to flee to the old pueblo for protection.[9] An underlying suspicion persisted that Hispanic residents, perhaps embittered by Anglo-American rule, sympathized with these self-styled Robin Hoods who covertly championed the bandidos' flight from justice.

Barton, a stalwart symbol of law and order, possessed the self-assuredness that galvanized support for swift action. He effectively organized posses by enlisting influential citizens to track desperados, no matter how thin the trail or suspect the rumor. In 1851, following one aborted attack on Benjamin Hayes, Barton quickly organized a four-man party and chased the suspects for 10 miles to a lone house, isolated from the reach of reinforcements. Outnumbered and exposed to attack, the posse was in a precarious position. The bandits recognized their advantage, and "charged upon them, fired several shots, and drove them from the ground."[10] The posse safely returned to the city, but the incident raised questions about the sheriff's judgment. Harris Newmark portrayed Barton as "brave but reckless," a backhanded but accurate compliment, foreshadowing the events that later led to Barton's demise.[11]

Recklessness on the lawman's part, however, inevitably came with the territory; many notorious villains of that era led police and vigilantes on fruitless chases throughout the state. The capture of famous bandidos would elevate the captors to a level of notoriety that Bat Masterson and Wyatt Earp would achieve in a later era. The notorious outlaw, Joaquín Murrieta, was a special prize whom Barton and other law enforcement officials were eager to pursue and capture. The case of "El Famoso" represented all that was wrong with Anglo settlement; a resourceful and talented Hispanic, soured by Anglo injustice, launched what many saw as a revenge-bent vendetta of ruthless crimes against the miners. "He robbed to live," wrote historian Frank Latta. "He (Murrieta) robbed only characters like the mob that abused him."[12] On several occasions throughout the early 1850s, the Murieta gang reportedly took refuge in Southern California to escape pursuing vigilantes.

In 1853, Barton received a tip that Murrieta was in hiding at a Hispanic settlement on the Arroyo Seco. The sheriff quickly formed a posse and led a raid on the settlement and, once again found he had landed his men in a precarious situation, outnumbered and surrounded by a hostile populace who gave posse members "black looks and scant courtesy."[13]

Barton was a confusing symbol, inextricably linked to controversy, reflecting the excesses of police power associated with frontier lawlessness, and yet the best hope of stability and order on the frontier, despite Hispanic resentment. Three events exemplify the agitation surrounding Barton's tenure.

In January 1855, the local courts found David Brown and Felipe Alvítre guilty of murdering a local resident. Both men received a temporary stay of execution. Yet Alvitre was hanged under Barton's supervision before the stay was delivered, while Brown's reprieve arrived before the hangman could do his duty. Hispanics and some Anglos were infuriated by this hasty, rush to justice. Judge Benjamin Hayes, for example, said that Alvítre seemed "poor and defenseless" when pitted against an indifferent legal system.[14]

Barton was at the center of this controversy: he personally had assumed responsibility for Alvítre's execution. After Hispanic outrage reached a crescendo of demands that David Brown be hung to balance the scales of justice, Barton was persuaded by friends to withdraw his jailhouse guard, in effect permitting an irate mob to rush the jail and hang Brown.[15]

Three months later, Barton was embroiled in a domestic feud that further tarnished his reputation among Hispanics. In April, the Los Angeles District Court sentenced Juan Flores and Juan Gonzalez to 5 years in state prison for horse theft. Both men claimed that Barton, seeking revenge over a prior incident, had fabricated the evidence. Gonzalez had intervened during a public quarrel between Barton and his common law Indian wife. According to Horace Bell, Gonzalez stopped Barton from "dragging her away." Only a few days later, Barton had the two men arrested on felony charges brought by claimant Garret Hardy, who was an occasional volunteer deputy and friend of Barton.[16] Barton took personal interest in the trial. He stood watch over the defendants and executed their transfer to San Quentin for their final incarceration.

Subsequent events placed Juan Flores at the center of rising tensions within Los Angeles. During the summer of 1856, Marshal Bill Getman, Barton and a large volunteer contingent defended the pueblo against an attack by Spanish-speaking residents, angered because Deputy Sheriff William Jenkins had shot an unarmed citizen, Antonio Ruís, after a verbal altercation over the repossession of a guitar. When the court released Jenkins pending a future court date, threats of retribution forced city officials to jail Jenkins for his own safety. A beseiged city waited three days while an angry crowd of nearly 300 Hispanic residents gathered outside the city limits to decide on a plan of action. On July 23, the mob stormed the pueblo, wounding Marshall Bill Getman in a brief gun battle that occurred at the center of town. Barton and other defenders repelled the attack, forcing the mob to retreat into the hillside, thus saving Jenkins from a vigilante execution. Barton later sat on the jury which convicted the two ringleaders of the uprising, while criminal charges against Jenkins were dismissed as an accidental shooting.[17]

Barton inadvertently slipped into a commanding position after the Jenkins-Ruis incident, emerging as the senior officer in Los Angeles when Getman was wounded. Barton's subsequent crackdown on crime translated into notably higher frequency of Hispanic prosecutions. In the six months prior to the July confrontation, there was a generally even distribution between Anglo and Hispanic cases but in the six months after the Jenkins-Ruis incident, more than two-thirds of all Los Angeles court cases involved Hispanic defendants.[18] These figures support historian David J. Weber's observation that "although some Californios participated in and approved of vigilante justice, more often the Spanish-speaking of Los Angeles were its victims."[19]

Hispanics remained skeptical of Anglo justice, which led to tension between police and commmunity. One Spanish-speaking resident resisted arrest and exchanged gunshots with a deputy sheriff, William Peterson.[20] Meanwhile, a more serious harbinger of trouble occurred when Juan Flores and Pancho Daniel escaped from San Quentin in the autumn of 1856. Daniel had a reputation as a hardened criminal, while the rueful Flores was a defiant symbol of Anglo injustice to the poor and displaced Spanish-speaking residents. By January of 1857, both desperados had attracted nearly a dozen bandido followers, including the escaped convict Juan Gonzalez, who had vowed to take his revenge on Barton for sending him to prison. The gang headed toward Southern California, then into the jurisdiction of Los Angeles officials. The renegades terrorized San Juan Capistrano, murdered a storekeeper and ambushed Barton's posse, ruthlessly killing the sheriff and two deputies.

For a brief time during the winter of 1857, the Juan Flores-Pancho Daniel gang transcended the world of ordinary crime and entered the realm of cult personality. The brazen murders of Barton and his deputies alarmed the region and made the outlaws instant legendary figures. But some citizens were convinced that lenient treatment of Hispanic dissidents during the

Jenkins-Ruis incident had emboldened criminals like Flores, encouraging them to wage the type of crime spree that resulted in the Barton ambush. "So much for the anti-vigilance of this county last summer," Henry Rice Myles sardonically noted. "Had the proper course been taken this would never have occurred."[21]

In general, Anglo Southern Californians interpreted the Flores rampage as a call to arms. Cave Johnson Couts, a prominent San Diego rancher, was warned that he might be an target assassination of the renegade band. "You (Couts) appear to be signaled out," wrote John Forster, "in case their (Flores gang) going below so that you must be on your guard."[22]

The desperados sojourn at San Juan Capistrano during most of January 1857 suggests tacit acceptance within the Hispanic community, even though three bandits were known to be ruthless, killing a storekeeper, George Pflugart, then ransacking his premises.[23] Perhaps it was widely understood in San Juan Capistrano that the murder of Pflugart was simply Flores' way of baiting the trap for the despised Barton, though there is no proof of this other than logic. In any case, when news of Flores and Daniels whereabouts reached Los Angeles, Barton quickly assembled a five-man citizens' posse and headed for San Juan Capistrano, brashly ignoring warnings of the outlaws superior numbers. Subsequently, Flores and his men ambushed Barton's posse, killing three law enforcement officials in a violent gun-battle.

Shock and dismay rocked Los Angeles when news arrived of the Barton ambush and Pflugart murder. Henry Rice Myles, a prominent resident and neighbor of Benjamin Wilson, was struck by the outpouring of grief over Barton's death. Myles felt as if the city had undergone a personal catharsis, realizing just how vulnerable they were to attack.[24] The killing spree prompted a call to arms. To the gringo, the Flores-Daniel gang could galvanize the existing disenchantment with American rule into a violent revolt in the worst traditions of the slave uprisings led by Nat Turner or Toussant L'Overture in a similarly repressive circumstance. "Lock the doors and bolt the windows," warned a panicked citizen, who apparently believed that "some of the outlaws were on their way to Los Angeles, to murder the white people."[25] One upstate observer speculated that the Flores-Daniel gang might be a puppet of a larger Mexican resistance to the Gadsden Purchase. "We fear," exclaimed the Sacramento *Daily Bee*, "a series of similar outrages in that portion of the country." The paper blamed Mexico for Hispanic-Anglo tensions and the widespread lawlessness that Flores and other bandidos represented. The paper hinted that the United States may need to engage in another conflict with Mexico. "If she (Mexico) cannot govern her own subjects, they must be governed for her."[26]

Wild rumors of an impending attack on the city panicked residents into immediate action. Henry Rice Myles reported that four men rode up to the Wilson home, then fled up the ravine when one of the servants sounded the alarm.[27] Local officials ushered all women and children to the town center, while citizen patrols, feeling beleaguered, guarded the city's perimeters.[28]

Los Angeles had never before witnessed such a united community effort and organized manhunt. Town leaders willingly turned authority over to a tough law-and-order group that included key Southerners and former Know-Nothing activists. Dr. John S. Griffin, W.W. Trist, Jonathan R. Scott and Jim Thompson assumed official roles, organized posses and administered swift justice to those captured. In all, at least four search parties and a military garrison from Fort Tejon were organized to pursue the bandidos.[29]

The criminal profiles of Flores and his men were neither glamorous nor unusual. Poverty was common among the bandidos, most of whom came from rural Sonoran communities or transient camps in outlying locales. Several outlaw members worked as everyday laborers or temporary hirelings at the ranchos. Some bandits had violent reputations, like Francisco

Ardilleo and Jóse Santos, known as "the worst of the bandidos."[30] Other desperados were considered good men turned bad. Harris Newmark believed Luciano Tapia, one of the last Flores gang members to be captured and hanged, was a tragic figure, a "respectable laborer" persuaded by Flores "to abandon honest work."[31]

Flores, Barton's nemesis, epitomized the complexity of the bandido profile. Although vindictive and ruthless in his crimes, Flores was seen in more sympathetic terms by his own people, many of whom regarded him as a symbol of hope amidst the poverty of his times. Surely Flores was keenly aware of the inequities between Hispanic and Anglo. An almost mythic symbol of defiance at only 21, Flores had the brash and impetuous nature that often accompanies youth. Horace Bell marvelled at Flores' self-confident demeanor, his "lithe and graceful" figure with a "tiger-like walk."[32] The Los Angeles *Star* also observed that Flores had a boyish charm and "pleasing countenance."[33]

Physical attributes aside, young Flores was not just another ordinary fugitive from San Quentin, a penitentiary known for harsh treatment of Hispanic inmates.[34] While at prison, Flores and Daniel developed a scheme to break out. In October 1856, they successfully scaled the prison walls and fled south, enlisting sympathizers and other fugitives on their behalf. By January of 1857, the gang made San Juan Capistrano their base of operations, moving freely among the local residents, buying from merchants, unchallenged by local authorities. Their intent, Horace Bell asserted, was "to go to Los Angeles, raise the standard of revolt and rid the country of the hated gringos."[35]

Flores lacked the revolutionary fervor needed to sustain a revolt, and had neither an ideology or a specific agenda of reform. As historian Richard Griswold del Castillo has analyzed this bandido, Juan Flores was an "anarchist rather than social reformer."[36] Even so, the hunt for the renegades highlighted Anglo-American fear and a deeply divided Mexican- American community. *El Clamor Publico* weighed the existing legal inequities against the undesirable alternatives of a violent uprising. "Although we see them as poor and without resources," the paper concluded, "we should aid the authorities to fulfill their duty."[37] The Californios who valued peace and order rallied behind the vigilante cause. Andrés Pico and Tomás Sanchez organized posses and demonstrated as much resolve as the gringos in hunting the fugitives. Juan Sepulveda offered his detailed knowledge of the rugged terrain of the Santiago Canyon, providing insight into potential hiding places of the band.[38]

The intense Hispanic-Anglo search and the swift capture of the gang reduced the possiblity of a serious rebellion, if such a possibility ever existed. Within days of the Barton ambush, law enforcement officials had sealed all escape routes leading from San Juan. San Diegan Cave Johnson Couts organized a group to block any flight to the border. Led by local tribal leaders Maucielito and Geronimo, nearly four dozen Indians scanned the southern mountain ranges and alerted Temecula.[39] Meanwhile, a large force from El Monte and forces under the command of Don Andrés Pico pressed toward San Juan Capistrano from San Gabriel.[40] El Cajon, San Fernando, and San Gorgonio passes were blocked to escape. Caught between the advancing posses from San Diego and Los Angeles, the gang could not hold its ground and expect to win against overwhelming odds.

Although Flores and his gang may have only been common bandits, they obviously represented a larger threat in the minds of Anglos, Californios and even the region's native Americans. The manhunt meant to rid the community of dissidents, to reassert the dominance of Anglo-American settlement but perhaps most of all to buttress the area's economic and political stability so that all could build, adjust and prosper.[41] Retreating into Santiago Canyon and the surrounding Santa Susanna Mountains, the bandidos never had a chance. The pursuers maintained an unrelenting pursuit in order to provide the fugitives with "no time for rest."[42] By mid-February, most of the gang had been captured, executed or fled the locale.

The Hispanic elites, rancheros and dons, attempted to assuage gringo fears by asserting their loyalty to American rule. *El Clamor Público* suggested that Spanish-speaking citizens stop calling themselves Californios. Tomás Sanchez, a popular figure among Anglos because of his participation in the Flores-Daniel hunt, was elected sheriff of Los Angeles County.[43] Juan Sepulveda organized a city militia comprised of ranchero and vaquero volunteers -a counterpart to the *Los Angeles Rangers*. Sepulveda's *California Lancers* acted as honor guards, assisted at Sunday Mass and marched in American holiday festivities. So it was not surprising that four Hispanic jurors rendered guilty verdicts when the last of the Flores-Daniel gang was brought to trial.[44]

Flores and his cohorts assumed their sinister profile as larger-than-life symbols of oppression and rebellion within the context of vigilante fervor, past incidents of ethnic friction, and breakdowns in frontier justice. The Flores bandidos' actual threat certainly did not warrant the widespread anxiety. Only three days after posses were formed, San Juan Capistrano resident John Forster said that "the Robbers are not by any means as strong as they have been represented."[45] Los Angeles returned to normal, after the capture and swift execution of the outlaws, by mid-February. "The excitement here is gradually dying out," observed attorney Cameron Thom.[46] Even the Hispanic community, sensing the overreaction, seemed relieved that the crisis had passed. *El Clamor Público* welcomed an end to vigilantism with the new election for sheriff, so "that justice will be administered legitimately."[47]

Yet, a somber pall blanketed the community for nearly a year, until law enforcement officials captured the last fugitives at large -Luciano Tapia and Pancho Daniel. Both men were executed in 1858, not by vigilantes, but through the due process of a district court trial. Whether justice was served in Tapia's case remains an open question. The jury was overwhelmingly Anglo, including prominent men such as retailer Isaias Hellman, civic activist Harris Newmark and former sheriff Alviron Beard. Some jurors, as ardent law and order advocates or even active participants in the Flores hunt, were hardly impartial or sympathetic toward a bandido defense. Several witnesses placed Tapia at the scene of the murders in San Juan Capistrano. The bandido maintained his innocence to the end, claiming to have worked as a laborer for a Rafael Martinez in San Luis Obispo during the time of the Pflugart and Barton murders. The court refused Tapia's request for a recess until Martinez could be summoned to testify at Los Angeles. On December 19, 1857, following two days of hearings, Tapia was sentenced to death by Judge Benjamin Hayes.[48] At the gallows, a rueful Luciano Tapia still insisted he was innocent and warned his compatriots "to leave this country, as it was no place for them."[49]

The execution of Tapia closed the last chapter in the Flores case, but not the storyline on the bandidos' significance to the era. Flores and Barton were adversaries during a truculent period of frontier settlement when the courts, police and civic institutions were in their infancy, often unable to quickly respond to Anglo or Hispanic concerns. Although Flores' men left an outlaw trail filled with greed and violence, the ambush of Barton stemmed from personal resentment against an unjust legal system. Flores generated alarm far beyond the norm, and the perceived threat coalesced vigilante efforts with the urgency of a wagon train under siege.

Public anxiety over lawlessness was predictable within the broader context of the era. The 1850s highlighted rapid population increases, cultural friction and boom/bust cycles against a pueblo backdrop in transition from Hispanic to Anglo rule. Tough law enforcement was a simple solution to complex social and economic dislocations in the California gold rush. For James Barton and Juan Flores, the outcome of such turmoil would be swift, but not forgotten in an unforgiving land of unrepentant participants.

CHAPTER SEVEN

Benjamin Hayes & Horace Bell Pioneer Perspectives on the Frontier

Benjamin Hayes and Horace Bell lived during California's transition between American and Mexican rule, a time of sweeping institutional change in the old pueblo. Between 1850 and 1870 Los Angeles' population tripled, crime increased and vigilantism periodically surfaced as both an imperfect yet legitimate response to the problem of violence. Meanwhile, a host of opportunists displaced the ranchero, symbol of Hispanic dignity and influence, from the landscape. Although the creation of new roads, government structures and schools provided Los Angeles with a tangible sense of permanence, these physical changes offered only limited stability within the scheme of Anglo-American settlement. By 1870, Los Angeles had replaced its sleepy pueblo ambience with a different hurried personality not unlike other towns in the Western landscape. As historian Remi Nadeau commented, Los Angeles was beginning to convey the fussy, overdone "furbellowed" styles of the Yankee immigrant.[1]

Bell and Hayes left a legacy of invaluable personal recollections and diaries that provide an intimate look into their era's politics, social customs and economic expansion. Hayes' diary and scrapbook (circa 1850s-1860s) reveal Angelenos confronting not only typical Western problems such as lawlessness and commercial growth but also increasingly divisive national issues, particularly slavery and secession. Bell's two colorful memoirs chronicle the evolving politics and culture in the old pueblo. Together, their works provide an unusually broad as well as deep insight into local politics and other civic affairs, while revealing sentiments representative of their community. In short, writer Kevin Starr succinctly put it, Bell and Hayes "stand like cactus plants in the desert of early expression in the Southland."[2]

Growing up in the Indiana wilderness, the young Horace Bell read the romantic adventures of Francis Marion, the Southern "Swamp Fox," along with the daring escapades of the conquistadores as reported in the accounts of Bernal Diaz. A daring, imaginative and romantic youth himself, Bell emigrated to Los Angeles during the early stages of Western settlement. He rubbed shoulders with the influential and the ordinary, willing to learn from both, and discussed the virtues of frontier life with such contemporaries as Benjamin Wilson and Joseph Lancaster Brent. His career encompassed a variety of occupations, indicative of his restless nature: attorney, soldier and land speculator in the 1850's and 1860's, then, in later years, author and editor. Never shrinking from conflict, verbal or physical, the volatile Bell championed both reputable and questionable causes with equal intensity. He engaged in a brief mercenary adventure in Latin America during the 1850's, followed by a stint as a Union soldier in the next decade, in between acting as a vigilante officer. For Bell, the good life often required a daring risk, so not surprisingly his vision of the frontier emphasized its danger and uncertainty.

Benjamin Hayes, cautious and meticulous, had a career and a vision that greatly contrasted with Bell's. Educated in law at St.

Mary's College in Baltimore, Hayes quickly established a professional reputation after arriving in Los Angeles in 1850. Even-tempered, precise, fond of history, Hayes quickly became a studious, highly civilized icon in his adopted pueblo's crude surroundings. Drawn to the political arena despite his fastidious temperament, Hayes was elected county attorney and, later, district judge, a position he held for 12 years. As one who recog-nized the importance of the written account,

Benjamin Hayes

he chronicled the life and times of a western settlement in search of stability. His diaries and notes record, in fine detail, the key events that shaped the early years of Southern California.

The writings of Hayes and Bell feature opposing views of how frontier justice in early Los Angeles settlement would be best conducted. Hayes believed that law enforcement was a matter of common sense, requiring judges and sheriffs to adopt reasonable procedures sufficiently flexible to fit the pueblo's uncertain and transitional situation. To Bell, however, early American Los Angeles was part of the frontier, therefore demanding an immediate codification of law, a rigid framework of statutes and written procedures into which one could stuff the odds and ends of an unstructured environment, thereby guaranteeing order, and, perhaps, justice.

Judge Hayes was sworn to interpret the law as well as to

uphold its due process. The informal atmosphere in frontier Los Angeles meant that fair and useful results were more important than protocol and rigid precedents, and Angelenos, both Hispanic and Anglo, valued ingenuity and hard work above lofty legal principles and rigid courtroom procedures. Hayes' beliefs about justice were rooted in common law principles that addressed local conditions. In 1863, for example, the Southern California tribes were being ravaged by a widespread smallpox epidemic at a time when Southern California had already undergone drought, famine and the loss of young men to the Civil War being fought back East. Fears that the smallpox epidemic would spread to the Anglo and Hispanic populace created widespread panic, worsening confusion in an era when so many were already devastated by painful alterations to life as it had been. Hayes recognized the need for a quick response in the outlying communities hardest hit by the disease, and took charge urging an expanded use of authority for local officials, empowering justices of the peace and judges of the plains with "an advisory, discretionary authority" in matters of quarantine and care in remote areas.[3]

When Hayes arrived at Los Angeles in 1850, California was in a delicate transition from Mexican to Anglo-American authority. The old pueblo underwent a dramatic change in the rule of law, requiring the formation of courts, jails, a police department and government buildings, along with a tax base to support these services. Civic institutions were badly needed for the improvement of roads, water supply and, in general, commercial growth. Hayes advocated the formation of a civic administration, city government and legal code. He oversaw a judicial system that handled minor offenses through a court of sessions and more serious offenses by a district court. To best meet the needs of a growing frontier community, as noted earlier, Hayes took a simplified, practical approach to legal problems. For example, he ordered judges in the pueblo's outlying rural areas to assume responsibilities for administering warrants

Los Angeles Courthouse (1859-1888),
where Judge Benjamin Hayes presided as District Judge.

and making criminal arrests. Judges, Hayes reasoned, "are a kind of police" in this remote backdrop, and their role as judge and jury should also be expanded to fulfilling the "functions of the police of a city."[4]

The Californio was still a visible and important part of Los Angeles society following the Mexican-American war. Familiar personages like Agustin Olvera, Juan Sepulveda and Antonio Coronel retained prominent positions in the courts, law enforcement and party politics. Even so, a delicate situation evolved when this proud, Spanish-speaking people was subjugated to the strange and alien rules of a minority of their pueblo's populace. For their part, many Anglos resented the language barriers and chafed at the relaxed style of Hispanic rule. Deals sealed with a handshake in particular irritated the Anglo settlers of the gold rush era; how could an economy develop on such an informal, seemingly amorphous basis?

Hayes recognized that the introduction of different customs and strange new legal procedures could lead to ambiguities, misunderstanding and eventually antagonism among the Hispanic majority. He therefore departed from the letter of the Yankee law and ardently defended indigenous customs even though they conflicted with the American legal system's technicalities. In one instance, Hayes adjourned court in deference to a Catholic feast day. On the other hand, he was willing to ignore specific laws when the circumstances warranted: during the health crisis of the early 1860s, for example, when local authorities outlawed open burial rites in an attempt to reduce further risks, Hayes countermanded the order. Anticipating violence from the devoutly Catholic Californios, he ruled that "it would be impossible to refuse" burial in such times of distress.[5]

Bell held a different view. Unlike Hayes, who sought to create harmony between Anglo law and Hispanic culture, Bell saw a hostile frontier filled with speculators and unscrupulous opportunists threatening the orderly progression of American settlement. For Bell, the sources of criminal activity may have seemed complex, ranging from excessive speculation, political graft and mob rule to the social grievances of the bandido, but he saw nothing complex about the remedy. Bell believed that swift enforcement would be a quick fix for this "old Mexican town" apparently "very loosely, very informally governed by its new masters."[6] At times, Bell reasoned, the old pueblo was in a "state of siege," and law enforcement had to prevail on the battleground that pitted civility and progress against savagery and deceit. Bringing his soldier's mind to the fray, Bell considered the law as the one constant capable of bringing order to a chaotic state.[7]

Bell approvingly cited one judge's solution to a dilemma, which arose when the jurist's sympathy for the accused came into conflict with his sworn duty to administer justice. The judge sentenced the defendant to the maximum penalty, explaining that "I am sworn to the execution of the law, and must discharge my duty, whatever my sympathies may be."[8] Bell also admired the notorious Judge Roy Bean, a frontier prototype of the man teetering on the line between respectability and wanton criminality. He reminded his contemporaries that the Texas judge, despite his outlaw reputation, had ruled by the "authority of the book" and often consulted the 1856 California statutes for legal countenance.[9]

Bell favored an impersonal legal system to bring structure to the nondescript place that Southern California had become: a dangerous and uncertain world filled with easy prey for an array of unsavory predators. Across frontier Los Angeles' proscenium paraded the villains and victims, charlatans and rogues who peopled Bell's recollections, supplying a lively courtroom drama of acrimony and woe. As Bell saw it, in Los Angeles (circa 1850s) naivete would be exploited, cunning rewarded. To him, the pueblo was a hardened place where individualism meant a stony approach to neighbor and stranger alike. Citizens did little to protect one another, and survival depended on one's instinct to survive: absent community institutions, which had yet to appear on the Los Angeles scene, residents took matters of law and order into their own hands as a way of protecting themselves against the most deviant opportunists in society. Conversely, Bell seemed to support this Social Darwinism, believing it proper behavior not to "spoil" a scam being run on an unknowing victim. "It wasn't supposed to be one man's business how another man bet his money," Bell declared.[10] The rancheros' fall seemed further proof of the triumph of cleverness over innocence. Bell reasoned that Anglos held an advantage over the *paisano* because the former knew the "judicial ropes," hired the best attorneys, and forced the Californios into protracted and ruinously expensive litigation.[11] Besides being masters of the sharp practices so dear to the hearts of Yankee businessmen, the Anglos were operating under a system of law quite different from the Spanish colonial codes and customs which the Californios understood. The "matrimonial shark" used still another nefarious tactic to siphon the wealth from the native populace. When men such as Abel Stearns and Benjamin Wilson married into Hispanic families, they may have done so at least partly out of affection for the demure yet exciting Hispanic women but also were certainly aware that wedding the daughters of the dons gave them access to land ownership and inherited fortunes. Bell saw this not as cross-cultural romance but as blatant exploitation, and he excoriated such marriages as "the worst infliction that fell upon the hapless Californians."[12]

Los Angeles' job market offered little pay and less opportunity to the settler: laborers toiled in the mines or rancho fields for day wages.[13] Bell, "quite dissatisfied" with the lack of opportunities in Southern California, had a love/hate relationship with the region that mirrored his own personal affairs as well as the overall boom/bust cycle of economic fortune. For example, Bell was first effusive about a real estate partnership with John Downey, then finding his investment halved three years later, by 1872 was so low in spirit that he was considering liquidation to fund for himself "a start in some new country."[14]

From their differing perspectives and out of their divergent temperaments Hayes and Bell wrote of the old pueblo in microscopic detail, recounting the charming atmosphere and rich traditions of this culturally diverse place as well as its problems. In recording the grand August festivals to commemorate the birthday of Emperor Napoleon III, Hayes also noted that the town's lone Jewish shop had closed, as its proprietor and his family observed their Sabbath.[15] Bell too emphasized the coming and going of individuals. He wrote glowingly, for example, about the deeds of English-born John Gilroy, and about the honorable Joseph Mascarel, elected mayor in 1866, whom he considered a "plain and honest Frenchman turned into a good American." A settler's regional identity provided instant acceptance in this rural land, descriptions that Bell used frequently like "Yankees"

*Horace Bell
during the heyday
of the Los Angeles Rangers.*

Stephen C. Foster and Don Abel Stearns.[16] Bell was part of an oncoming wave of Americans, boosters and enthusiasts who promoted the United States' style "Westerning" process. But although he was proud of his *gringo* identity, he also enjoyed being welcomed into the circle and confidence of the rancheros. He wrote of the Californio lifestyle admiringly, his work almost reading like a travelogue as he describes the rancheros and their pastoral lifestyle to an Anglo audience. He obviously enjoyed and appreciated the local enthusiasm for the national game of *monte*, the required dexterity for a rodeo *lazo* throw, and identified the elaborate, somewhat formal type of fiesta called *baile*, which celebrated the marriage of a rancher's daughter.[17]

Bell's memoirs were written long past the high tide of Mexican influence, so his recollections had to address the

Californios' demise, the sad tale of how power and wealth had been transferred in frontier Southern California. Bell's basic theory was that the noble traits of the Hispanic culture were considered a weaknesses among Anglos, who consequently did not hesitate to exploit those virtues.[18]

According to Bell's scenario, the Californio was a mixture of the era's dominant stereotypes, combining the elegance of Rousseau's "noble savage" (found in the same romantic literature that aggrandized Native Americans) with the docile profile that people often imposed over the reality of the antebellum slave. Bell's writings paralleled the popular view of the Southern plantation, in his numerous references painting an idyllic scene and a passive culture, in which people of naive assumptions lived innocently amidst an agrarian paradise. In essence, Bell's condescending treatment subtly condemned the Californio for the very qualities he admired. The Spanish-speaking community appeared a "gentle people," innocent of the ways of the gringo, and a contented lot "full of jovial good humor."[19] To Bell, California's isolation had created a unique sense of purity in the uncomplicated world of the rancho, and the serenity of the Southern California frontier complemented the Hispanic personality. This isolated paradise would end with the American takeover, for the frontier had created a bitter paradox: virtue to a fault.

Bell considered Anglos to be the intruders of an established society that was built upon Hispanic customs and traditions. As a landscape spoiled, the Californio was a casualty of an advancing conquest, just as, though he did not draw this comparison, the Hispanics had originally conquered the New World Indians. Bell wrote fulsomely of elaborate processions, parades and displays surrounding Holy Week in the old pueblo. He extolled the gala features of the Hispanic spirit rooted in the ceremonial traditions of the Roman Catholic faith. Then, in succinct contrast, he curtly stated that "after the gringo nation had nailed its flag to the mast in this angel land, the ceremonies attending the annual execution of Judas became less inspiring and satisfactory."[20] In sum, Horace Bell felt the Californio had been victimized. Of the emasculated ranchero, his empire lost, Bell sadly concluded that "he isn't half the man he was in the days of the revolutions and rawhides."[21] Bell's view of the Mexican-American as victim of his own passive culture's response to an aggressive pioneer migration, mirrored the widespread caricature of California's Native Americans as weak, dependent and thus unworthy of social or political equality. As scholars Ray Allen Billington and Albert Camarillo concluded of the Indian, that "by showing himself unable to conquer Nature, he had surrendered the right to exist."[22]

Judge Hayes, less verbose than his counterpart Bell, wrote more from the standpoint of participant rather than tour guide. Like Bell, he sympathized with the Californio, but on several levels. As a confidant in the legal affairs of his ranchero acquaintances, Hayes witnessed firsthand the gradual erosion of the rancho estates. Sharing a common faith, Hayes sat in pews of equal rank with the dons, attentively listening to Father Blas Rahó preach at the Sunday pulpit, sermons that stressed universal themes of brotherhood and community.

Hayes was further tied to Hispanic customs through his marriage to Dōna Adeleida Serrāno, which brought him into a Californio family after spending nearly a decade as a widower. Professionally tied to the Mexican world by his legal practice, bonded through marriage and baptism, Hayes' writings were both more balanced and more sympathetic than Bell's regarding Hispanic conditions. Hayes praised the Californio spirit and the "elegance of manners, natural hospitality, mirth, outgushing of gaiety and simple rural life." Yet he also recognized that the rancheros' "simple rural life" could not resist the Anglo settlers arriving in increasing numbers to "civilize" the West.[23] He himself embodied the brash frontier sentiment that blindly urged pioneers "to help in civilizing, educating, and elevating a class

who are now our fellow-citizens."[24] Hayes typified this xenophobic belief in America's destiny, a sentiment inherently hostile toward non-European traditions. Hayes, for example, disapproved of some Hispanic practices that offended his Yankee
upbringing. Within the traditional setting of the old pueblo, for
example, Hayes enjoyed the *rodeo*, but he disapproved of them
when they ran counter to his moral sensibilities, such as engaging in both *monte* and festivity on Sunday.[25]

Although Hayes embraced the triumphant spirit of Manifest
Destiny, he nevertheless sensed that the clash of cultures had
created injustices, particularly the rancheros' legal entanglements over land titles, law enforcement and the economic dislocations that followed rapid migration. He believed that fair-
ness was necessary to bring order to the frontier. Therefore, in
Hayes' view of law and society, Hispanics stood on level ground
with Anglos -a principle that cut both ways in the execution of
justice. Judge Benjamin Hayes was equally inclined to sentence
a Spanish-speaking criminal as any other guilty offender. The
Californio, Hayes evenly stated, "mixed good and bad, pretty
much like the rest of the people of the United States."[26]

Bell saw frontier justice at eye level. He wrote colorfully of
his own dangerous escapades involving brawls, posses and
saloons. Bell, an active member of the vigilante committee and
the pueblo's volunteer police force, understood the criminal
from an adversary's view. Criminal violence, he maintained,
required a community response of corresponding force.

Horace Bell interpreted the frontier in harsh terms. Personal
well-being was far more important than altruism in an era that
focused on quick riches, boom/bust cycles and widespread
commercial speculation. In Bell's equation, the gradual erosion
of Spanish-speaking influence proved a by-product of these
realities and the bandido merely presented the flip side of this
process -hospitality turned into hostility. Of the gracious
ranchero, Bell cautioned that "even if he choked one with his

Horace Bell during the era when he wrote his reminiscences on early Los Angeles.

lasso he would be polite about it."[27] An underlying tension seemed ever present. At a *fandango*, for example, Bell admitted to outfitting himself in an elaborate disguise of Mexican attire, "otherwise you would be taken for an American (Anglo) and be socially ignored."[28]

Racial friction in Southern California intensified in direct proportion to the advance of Anglo settlement. Population growth, inadequate government services and lawlessness heightened community tensions, but their immediate fears obscured the underlying problems of ethnic injustice. Temperance movements, men's organizations and citizens' police efforts emerged throughout the 1850s, but these moral crusades never fully addressed ethnic divisions. Communities remained segregated, barrios swelled, and Indian camps deteriorated all within the pueblo. The *Calle de los Negros* located near the Plaza symbolized the decadence of the era. The saloons, gaming halls, and rowdy clientele associated with Negro Alley threatened the quiet ambience of the Plaza lifestyle. "It was not like life in the simple 1830s and 1840s," observed historian W.W. Robinson, and some rancheros even contemplated returning to Mexico.[29] Lack of sanitation, inadequate law enforcement, and a dearth of public works accentuated the severity of disease, violence and severe flooding in many places like Chavez Ravine and outlying areas such as Agua Mansa. Even though Southern Californians understood that poverty and violence were barometers of injustice, they failed to enact meaningful political reform in order to address these problems. Instead, a vigilante mentality prevailed, and the lynching evolved as a immediate response to the inevitable frustrations to the residents and business people in this frontier setting beset by urban-style problems.[30]

Bell blamed prejudice and graft among Anglo leaders for the old pueblo's lawlessness and ethnic friction. Civic leaders, either indifferent or corrupt, had failed to inspire local confidence and as a result, Bell believed, panic and fear led to a town sometimes "ruled by a lawless mob."[31] As Hispanics often resorted to the same vigilante tactics as their Anglo counterparts, Bell dismissed the siege of the pueblo that followed the 1856 Antonio Ruís killing as just another lawless act in a lawless era. Bell's Californio thus experienced yet another sad transformation; soiled by injustice, reduced to the methods they once had disavowed, the Mexican-American community fell prey to the corrupting influence of lynch law tactics. He believed the Mexican-American were a spurned people, their demeanors soured by injustice and thus losing the innate gaiety of "olden times." Bitterness surfaced, as in the case of David Brown, who, as Bell explained it, was jailed in 1854 for murder, then kidnapped and hung "by an irate mob of Mexicans" who had adopted extralegal ways "in the most approved gringo fashion."[32]

Judge Hayes, unmoved by the fickle swings in public sentiment, saw struggling Southern California in its most rational
perspective -as engaged in a struggle to bring order from chaos.
"There are many bad Americans in this section," he concluded,
"and they will have to be looked after."[33] With a jurist's sense of
equity, Hayes proceeded with caution, always taking fact as
precedent over unsupported suspicion. In one instance, a disgruntled Hispanic laborer was charged with murdering his former Anglo employer, John Raines. The accused, Don Ramon
Carrillo, had been abruptly fired by Raines, and he was accused
of taking revenge in the ambush of a stage near the base of the
San Bernardino mountains. Suspicion of foul play heightened
when Raines' carriage and a blood-stained newspaper were discovered in the area traveled by the victim. Despite public pressure to arrest Carrillo, Hayes remained skeptical of the allegations in the absence of evidence. He acknowledged that "our
community is in very deep gloom" over the Raines murder, but
stubbornly maintained that "Ramon must be innocent without
proof of wrongdoing.[34] For Hayes, a man who personified logic
and deliberation, innuendo and the prejudice it spawned created a hopeless situation that was at best and at worst, as in the
case of the Raines murder, a miscarriage of justice and "reasoning from false premises, we must necessarily be led to the wrong
action."[35]

Hayes also viewed the slow and painful decline of the
Californio with less sentimentality than Horace Bell. As legal
counsel to many ranchero families who were at the mercy of an
indifferent judicial system, Hayes analytically noted the dons'
continual struggle to buy time, cheat fate and stave off economic ruin. He saw their plight less emotionally and in a larger context than did Bell. Although the injustices committed
against the rancheros were obvious and repugnant to Hayes, he
did not lament to one and all but instead catalogued the tedious
points of the struggle: adverse weather that eroded ranching
profits, extravagant spending, inordinate legal expenses and

endless litigation over boundary disputes. As confidant and counselor, Hayes participated in desperate efforts to reverse the fortunes that "brood over and close around them."[36] The case of the bedridden and dying Don Lorenzo Soto illustrated the overwhelming complexity of the rancheros' predicament. Hayes could only hope that medicine would keep the old paisano alive "a couple of weeks" so, he sadly concluded, "that we had better fix up all his temporal affairs."[37]

Obviously Bell and Hayes were very different men. Bell considered the misfortunes of the Hispanic community a necessary evil, the unpleasant result of two cultures at odds. In the spirit of American expansionism, he maintained that the fallen rancheros should "pine not over grandeur gone," but instead take "their stand in the ranks of American Progression resolved to curve their way onward and upward."[38] Hayes did not consider any such scenario; as a critic of mob rule, he lamented the "anti-social distrust" that led to extralegal methods: "Must each man provide his own safety? This cannot be."[39] Bell saw the posse as a cathartic experience and vigilante justice as a practical system; Hayes, the courtroom overseer of a procession of criminals, questioned the value of force as a deterrent to violence. Exasperated over the weekly reports of violent crimes, he wrote in 1857 that "to me it sometimes seems that capital punishment is useless."[40]

Bell's frontier represented a romantic quest akin to the vision of James Fenimore Cooper's *Pathfinder*, the pioneer's personal struggle to overcome the land and its hardships. Bell's Southern California was filled with pitfalls and will o' the wisps -a chance for unlimited success or certain failure. The ever-restless dreamer, Bell even looked to new frontiers during the early 1870s; perhaps of the uncertain economy and in search of new ventures, he whimsically mused of "going further west to the Fee Jee (Fiji) islands."[41]

Hayes' hope and vision of the frontier encompassed an

orderly progression of Western settlement emphasizing the law, church and rancho lifestyle as civilized efforts to soften a coarse pioneer existence. To Hayes, devoted to church and "higher" laws, the sins of a violent setting could be forgiven in the spirit of a prodigal son. Educated on the Roman Catholic precepts of reconciliation, a doctrinal emphasis separating the sin and sinner, the judge found that his violent world presented a dilemma. "I think it is a good thing," he once wrote, "even for great sinners to go to church, although some people must think differently."[42] Of Robert Carlisle, shot in a longstanding feud of his own making, Hayes fervently believed that "he must have had many redeeming qualities," despite the bad temper and abrasive personality that probably led to his demise.[43] The sudden death of Hayes' wife also reinforced his faith in a communal spirit, as the condolences offered by his Hispanic neighbors appeared an honest expression of "kindness so remarkable in those of the California population."[44] To Hayes, progress depended on harmony between Anglo and Hispanic, pioneer and ranchero and new and old customs, rather than an unfolding contest between peoples.

Finally, both Hayes and Bell represented American expansion in a broad context. As immigrants, they brought to the West an established set of mores from an emerging nation, a nation whose history included crisis and volatility. Hayes reflected the Eastern orthodoxy, with faith in community as solution and savior, but Bell, raised in the wilderness, steeped in the lore of honor and courage, saw the frontier as a heroic challenge to overcome the barbarism of his own times.

Thus do the writings of Hayes and Bell present a mixed portrait of the Southern California frontier, for both men reflected on the world around them through divergent, personal prisms. To Benjamin Hayes and Horace Bell, the quest for settlement, men in search of community and community in search of harmony, are themes that best explained the vitality of the frontier condition, and Southern California in particular.

CHAPTER EIGHT

Seceshers and Democrats:

Henry Hamilton and Edward John Cage Kewen

Southern Californians hardly noticed when Henry Hamilton and Edward John Cage Kewen settled in the old pueblo during the mid-1850s. Hamilton bought a local newspaper in 1856, while Kewen opened a modest law practice two years later. City leaders like Joseph Lancaster Brent, Abel Stearns, Benjamin Hayes and Charles Ducommun were preoccupied with growth and settlement. They built roads, forged political parties, established retail trade and impressed Anglo-American law on an agrarian society. Meanwhile, disheartened miners migrated south in hopes of new opportunity, Sonoran families passed through in search of work and a steady flow of Easterners eagerly sought a new land of milk and honey.

Hamilton and Kewen were only two of many early migrants coming west to start anew, traveling dusty trails and sailing clipper ships during the feverish climate of the gold rush, then drifting toward Southern California after inauspicious careers in the northern mines. Both men were Irish, both volatile and flamboyant, both transplanted Southerners full of the impassioned spirit of the pro-slavery firebrands with whom they felt

*Henry Hamilton (right) poses with a local representative
to the State Legislature during the Civil War.*

a kinship.

Hamilton and Kewen were bookends that closed an era of Southern California's relative isolation. The Civil War abruptly ended the provincial scope of the Far West. Hamilton and Kewen, like so many other Californians, were thrust center stage in that conflict, arguing the same partisan arguments that were being debated throughout the nation. While some rebel sympathizers such as Joseph Lancaster Brent returned to the South to enlist in the Confederate military, Hamilton and Kewen remained in Southern California to act as spokesmen for such Southern causes as states' rights, secession, tariffs and slavery.

Hamilton's voice was a professional one. He bought the Los Angeles *Star* in 1856, a Democratic newspaper that had barely survived under its three previous editors during the early 1850s. Tough-minded, opinionated and pragmatic, Hamilton was an experienced newspaperman. He arrived in the United States in 1848, and served as an apprentice for a New Orleans paper. He traveled west during the gold rush and found work as a reporter for a San Francisco newspaper. He began his own journal at Mokelumne Hill in the Mother Lode country and, at age 30, the seasoned journalist brought his partisan Southern passion to the Los Angeles *Star*, adroitly making a profit in a depressed economy while competing with no less than three rival Southern California papers.[1]

Los Angeles was a perfect fit for Henry Hamilton, with its Southern feelings and independent frontier spirit. As an avowed Democrat, the fiery editor championed vigilante justice, state division, and the xenophobic vision of a pure Anglo society similar to those of many Southern Californians. Among Hamilton's friends were the most visible Democrats in the Southern counties, including Benjamin Hayes, John S. Griffin, John A. Watson and Cave Johnson Couts. These civic leaders often wrote articles for the Los Angeles *Star*, actively supporting Democratic candidates endorsed by Hamilton's paper. To

Hamilton, politics was a battlefield of worthy ideas: his news-paper would supply the partisan weaponry for Southern Democrats.

Hamilton's flamboyant editorials against Republican lead-ers, abolitionists and the Union military had helped polarize his readership. "Republicanism has been swept out of existence," he prematurely boasted after the Frémont ticket was defeated in the 1856 presidential election; a boast that, ironically, was in the best Frémont style.[2] In the volatile late 1850s, Hamilton doggedly supported Southern rights. He defended Buchanan's policy on the Kansas question, opposed Stephen Douglas' ambiguous position on popular sovereignty, and considered the aborted John Brown affair an example of Northern fanaticism.[3] Hamilton believed that the national issues increasingly dividing North and South were far more important than the mundane happenings of this "far western outpost."[4] By the end of the 1850s, believing that war was inevitable, he proclaimed that his paper served "in the struggle which is approaching...that our trumpet shall give no uncertain sound."[5] In that respect, if no other, his wish was granted.

Edward John Cage Kewen arrived in California during the same period as Hamilton. His life personified the Jacksonian ideal -that of a common man overcoming life's adversities through hard work and honest living. Born in Mississippi, orphaned as an adolescent, young Edward curtailed his formal education to raise his two younger brothers. Because of an early interest in law, government and politics, the ambitious youth read law books by candlelight then developed his own legal practice, rather like the young Abraham Lincoln except that Kewen became involved in Whig politics during the 1840s. Personal tragedy struck Kewen in the early 1850s. It was a unit-ed and idealistic America in those days and the Kewen family, like so many of their countrymen, believed in Manifest Destiny and the rightness of spreading the American Dream to Latin America. Kewen's brothers, Thomas and Achilles, enlisted as mercenaries in an aborted filibuster scheme. Kewen lost both his brothers to distant lands for vague goals: Thomas at Panama in 1854, and Achilles a year later at the Battle of Rivas in Nicaragua. The grief over Achilles' death was a final blow, leading Edward to take up his brothers' cause in an effort to bring meaning to their deaths, just as he'd worked so singlemindedly to enable them to get the education that he had once hoped would bring meaning to their lives.

The young Edward Kewen enlisted in William Walker's ill-fated military foray into Nicaragua. The daring Walker, a one-hundred-pound Tennesseean, envisioned an expanding slaveocracy into Latin America. In 1855, he declared himself the elected leader of Nicaragua, legalizing slavery and planning to ask for admission into the United States. Nicaraguans thwarted Walker's coup with the help of the British Navy. Kewen had recruited nearly 800 enlistees in Louisiana to the doomed cause, and never questioned the goals of the Walker expedition despite its disastrous outcome.[6] He proudly assumed the title of "Colonel," returned to the States and began looking for a new start in Southern California.

Kewen's passion was the political arena, and when he came west he brought with him his Southern beliefs in states' rights. Considering the Republican party responsible for anti-slavery agitation, he chastised the Douglas Democrats for their betrayal of the Lecompton Constitution and the Buchanan presidency. He blasted William Seward for proclaiming allegiance to a "higher law," ridiculed Joshua Giddings for welcoming slave insurrections and scolded preacher Theodore Parker for standing at the pulpit in defense of abolition with "bared brows in the face of heaven."[7] Acerbic, truculent and highly opinionated, the young firebrand Kewen was nonetheless grudgingly admired by his opponents. Kewen's "oratorical abilities," Oscar T. Shuck observed, "so eminently peculiar, have often been condemned by those most fascinated by their display."[8]

Kewen briefly held state office and occasionally gave public addresses in defense of slavery. He often spoke of California's future, warning of the state's need to invest in education and avoid the parsimonious short-sighted aims of the gold rush mania. In an 1854 address to the Society of California Pioneers, Kewen said he feared that greed was the unhappy legacy of the state. "The only lesson our people have studied with earnestness and practiced with assiduity," he exclaimed, was to "put money in thy purse."[9]

By 1858, Colonel Kewen had married Fanny White and opened a Los Angeles law practice on Main Street near the drug store of father-in-law, Dr.Thomas White. A year later, White gave the young couple a plantation-style tract once owned by the mission padres, *El Molino Viejo*, situated next to Benjamin Wilson's Lake Vineyard estate in present-day Pasadena. Whereas the pragmatic Hamilton worried as much about newspaper circulation as principle, the impetuous Kewen displayed a more reckless spirit. The Colonel fancied himself a meteor among fixed stars, a romantic within the context of the sentimental ideals of mid-19th century America.[10]

By the close of the 1850s, Kewen and Hamilton had acquired a long list of civic accomplishments, both rising to prominence in public affairs. Kewen shared advertisements with entrepreneurs like dentist H.P. Swain, participated in hunting contests with such local notables as Benjamin Wilson and Sheriff James Thompson and enlisted as a director for the Los Angeles Library Association. Kewen spoke at the national 40th anniversary celebration of the Odd Fellows and at political mass meetings in El Monte and San Bernardino. Never hesitant to criticize opponents, the volatile Kewen blasted J.J. Warner, editor of the *Southern Vineyard*, on a host of issues ranging from Stephen Douglas' popular sovereignty, the Kansas question and the Lecompton Constitution. "Pardon is for men, and not for reptiles; We have none for Warner."[11] Hamilton too led an active public life. He joined various groups for weekend excursions around Southern California, supported the Freemasons and was an honorary member of the Mechanics' Institute, a literary group that promoted readings and recitations on popular subjects of the day.[12]

Both Hamilton and Kewen thought that abolitionists were the root cause of sectional divisions, and they blamed the Republican party for the threat of disunion. As early as 1856, Kewen warned that a Republican presidential victory would destroy the South.[13] Henry Hamilton bluntly charged the Republican party with instigating the national crisis, and he identified the real culprit as the "irrepressible doctrine" of slavery, and the "chief movers in this aggression were Seward, Giddings, Chase, and Trumbull."[14] San Bernardino assemblyman Charles W. Piercy offered a resolution that faulted national disruption on "the sectional doctrines advocated by the Republican Party."[15]

Hamilton, Kewen and other Democrats defended Southern states' rights, blamed abolitionists for the national crisis, claimed that secession was a last-ditch alternative and deftly made these charges in the spirit of maintaining national peace without compromising the South's honor. Hamilton's pointed editorials shaped the debate. He asserted that the slaveholding states were victims of Northern aggression, and peaceful secession remained the only possibility left for Southern survival. The Los Angeles *Star* argued that a "right of self-preservation had compelled the South to take the stand she has."[16] Kewen's brother-in-law, Assemblyman Murray Morrison, thought the rebellious states had the right to leave the Union peacefully. Hamilton believed that efforts to keep the South within the Union would prove a hollow victory for the Northern states, and the South "would be merely held as conquered provinces."[17]

In Southern eyes, this prediction was fulfilled. By early 1861, the Republican victory moved the nation still closer to war. South Carolina and a half-dozen other Southern states, angered by ruinous tariffs and aggressive abolitionist attacks,

Colonel
Edward John Cage Kewen

left the Union within three months after Lincoln's election. Southern Californians debated the legality of secession as the movement toward a Confederacy gathered momentum in the Southern states. Southern Californians rallied to the Confederate cause after General Pierre Toutant Beauregard ordered the bombardment of Fort Sumter in Charleston's harbor in April of 1861. El Monte residents paraded downtown in support of the Confederacy. At the Bella Union Hotel in Los Angeles, rebel sympathizers publicly applauded Beauregard and other Southerners who had led the siege of the Charleston fort, and in the following months, hung portraits of their heroes in the Montgomery Hotel lobby. Reports circulated that Confederate enlistment camps were being organized at the mining community of Holcomb Valley in the San Bernardino Mountains. Recruits were to be trained locally and then sent into the armies of Confederate states by way of Arizona and Texas.[18] "Temescal appears to be one of the most central points for secessionists," reported one correspondent; "scarcely a day passes but what companies pass here going East sometimes in small squads from 15 to 20."[19] Judge Benjamin Hayes cautioned Union sympathizers against the notion that Westerners were indifferent toward disunion: "They deceive themselves who suppose that California could stand aloof from the contest."[20]

By the fall of 1861, Union military strategists had become alarmed that the seemingly-splintering Union would encourage the many Confederate partisans in Southern California to revolt. The surprise rebel victory at Bull Run, or Manassas Junction as its called by Southerners, had given the Confederates new hope, along with new recruits. Although Federal officials were worried about a mass exodus of California soldiers to the Confederacy, they were even more concerned by the possibility of insurrection in the southern counties. As the Union officer Winfield Hancock noted the Hispanic Californios, with only a few exceptions, supported the Confederacy along with their Southern partisan Anglo friends and family. The army feared that covert activity and sabotage would be only a prelude to future Confederate liberation. "Dissatisfaction in the southern part of the state is increasing," declared General E.V. Sumner; "the rebels are organizing, collecting supplies and evidently preparing to receive a force from Texas."[21] One onlooker reported that "since the Seceshers' left here, we have all sort of rumors that they were going to return here again."[22]

The discovery of gold at Holcomb Valley in 1860 provided another incentive for the Confederate military to make a stab at the Southwest. In comparison with the industrial North, the agrarian South was poor, particularly in the materials and manufacturing facilities needed to wage a war. Also, as one Union soldier recalled, to "furnish the Confederacy with the gold of western mines and prestige (would be) to win recognition from European countries."[23] Union troops confiscated several letters from former residents living in Texas encouraging others to flee the state. Joseph Lancaster Brent recalled that the schemers "proposed to organize an expedition to cross the desert and come into Southern California, and accomplish what (they) could for the Confederate cause."[24] General Sumner personally interviewed Brent and John Griffin, recipients of these letters, and felt assured the men had no involvement in any plot.[25]

Along with the standoff at Bull Run and the public display of Confederate support in Southern California, the Union military became further alarmed when a Confederate regiment advanced into northern Arizona during the summer of 1861. Approximately 100 Texas rebels intercepted the overland trails, halted stagelines and destroyed supplies at Union storage centers. The Confederate foray in the Southwest seemed a menacing threat despite its limited strategy of harassment and observation. Northern California newspapers duly reported enemy advances: as, for example, when the Confederate detail moved closer to the Colorado River, the Sacramento *Daily Union* warned of potential rebellion along California's southern border with Arizona. By September 1861, after the South's small initial victories at Fort Sumter and Bull Run, Confederate enthusiasm had carried the Texas recruits past the Pima villages to within 50 miles of Fort Yuma.[26]

Covert resistance in the southern counties, an exodus of Confederate sympathizers and the potential threat of a Southern advance into the Far West led to an immediate Federal military build-up in Southern California. Guard barracks and army camps were quickly organized at Baldwin Hills, San Pedro, and Los Angeles. Union strategists also increased reserves at the border forts in the Yuma and Mohave deserts, while sentinels were instructed to detain any suspicious caravans leaving or entering the state. The operation worked. In 1861, approximately 200 residents had left California to join the Confederacy and by the following year the migration had nearly stopped since most of the disaffected had already left, or the threat of internment proved a sufficient deterrent to remain in the state.[27]

In reality, the Confederacy posed little danger to Southern

California. Although the South might possibly have mounted a southwestern offensive early in the war, the rebels fared so badly later that there was little likelihood of any serious Confederate invasion of Southern California. By 1862, the Confederates were on the defensive in the Midwest, and their strategy centered on regaining control of the Mississippi River and overcoming the Union blockade in the Gulf of Mexico. The Southwest, therefore, far removed from the crucial points of conflict, held only a tactical advantage in that Southern partisans could survey Union troop activity. The Arizona forces were "a cord of observation," noted Hamilton, "to watch and report any movements made from California upon New Mexico and Texas."[28]

By late summer of 1862, the Union military changed its attitude regarding the potential for a Confederate advance into the Far West. Union forces seemed more concerned with Navajo Indian uprisings than with any potential Confederate western offensive. The tables were beginning to turn in favor of the North, and any new encounters with Southern forces provided an opportunity for the Union army to harass their combatants. "If a force of rebels comes," ordered General James H. Carleton, "you know how to annoy it; how to stir up their camps and stock by night; how to lay waste to prairies by fire; how to make the country very warm for them and the road a difficult one."[29]

Meanwhile, Hamilton and Kewen called the stationing of Union troops in Southern California an unwarranted and blatant effort to stifle dissent. If anything, the presence of Union forces galvanized the opposition and reinforced Democrat party loyalty. "We hold, there can be no disunion among Democrats," intoned the Los Angeles *Star*.[30] "It is of the highest importance," Kewen noted, "that the State should be fully represented (voter turn out) in order to give encouragement to our party organization."[31] Legal challenges of election returns provided a courtroom forum for Southern partisans to influence public sentiment, and Kewen expressed disappointment with one of his party's candidates who "did not contest" his election defeat, Kewen also considered the next legislative session to be "an opportunity however of ventilating that and other matters," while party members "will have to stand from under."[32]

Hamilton and Kewen were part of a struggle for control of local government. After the Union and Confederate call to arms, partisan Democratic rhetoric shifted from secession to libertarian protests over Republican war policies. Hamilton and Kewen complained about the adverse effects of the Union war effort on the locale. Both men protested federal government control, taxation and military occupation. This subtle shift from a pro-Confederate to anti-Union polemic also changed the focus from disloyalty to dissent, a posture that temporarily shielded Democrats from direct allegations of sedition.

Kewen, Hamilton and other Southern Californians opposed federal authority and supported the loosely organized Confederacy, similar grounds to those on which the American colonies, less than 100 years earlier, had staked their bid for independence and subsequently organized themselves into a highly decentralized nation. In addition, the largely pastoral Southern California rarely enjoyed the prosperity that Northern California's mining and commerce was experiencing in the early 1850s, almost mirroring the contrast between the agrarian, non-industrial South and the North which, in completing its transition from mercantilism to industrialism, had become quite wealthy. Certainly these parallels were not lost on the Southern Californians, and the bold act of secession made the division of California seem not only viable but also rational on economic as well as libertarian grounds. Hamilton agitated for state division. "The people of these southern counties," the Los Angeles *Star* pronounced, "have (been) noted time and again to be disconnected from the State Government."[33]

Hamilton, Kewen and other Democrats also attacked Lincoln for playing politics with the war by supressing legitimate partisan dissent. The Knights of the Golden Circle maintained that Lincoln had violated "the most sacred palladium of American liberty by the suspension of the writ of habeas corpus."[34] Hamilton further asserted that loyalty oaths were illegal and an invasion of individual privacy. The Los Angeles *Star* claimed that the country had never experienced "such a total surrender of the right of private judgement."[35] Southern Californians also resented mandatory conscription, and even the presence of Union soldiers seemed to them an excessive display of force by an occupying army. One military official conceded that army personnel were "not very welcome" among the citizenry.[36]

Democrats characterized Southern Californians as the victim of repressive Union policies, and held Republicans responsible for conducting "an abolition war," a damning accusation in an era when most white Northerners, including Abraham Lincoln, did not regard blacks as their equals in any regard and did not want to mingle the races on an equal footing, whether social or political.[37] The abolition war argument handily reelected most Democrats in 1861 in Southern California. Kewen's brother-in-law, Murray Morrison, and a close friend, Colonel John "Little Jack" A. Watson, both won state legislative seats while otherwise popular Republican candidates such as Abel Stearns and Juan Sepulveda were soundly defeated.[38] Stearns finished a distant second to J.R. Vineyard in the state senate contest, while Sepulveda ran fourth in a five-man field for the assembly[39] The gubernatorial campaign also highlighted the unpopularity of Republicans in Southern California: though Republican Leland Stanford won the election, in Los Angeles County he captured only Anaheim and San Pedro among the 10 county precincts.[40]

Democratic strength in Southern California ran counter to larger statewide trends. Fears of rebellion or, worse still, a Confederate invasion of the state, had worried the electorate more than the harsh Union wartime measures annoyed them. Republicans gained a majority of assembly seats in Northern

California, particularly in San Francisco. Stanford's gubernatorial victory was a pivotal election, because control of state political machinery translated into pork barrel and patronage advantages at the local level.[41] "But the times are changed, and we have to change with them," admitted a chagrined Henry Hamilton.[42] Southern California Democrats gloomily predicted more military repression under the guise of patriotism, and the even-handed Judge Benjamin Hayes worried that any criticism of Union policy would be interpreted as subversive behavior.[43]Local resident Augustus Ensworth characterized the era as "tough times," because "it appears dangerous for one to try and defend himself in his right according to the civil law of the land."[44] Hamilton pleaded for an end to "sensational humbug about secession and treason" after the conclusion of the 1861 campaign. "It has had the effect intended -to influence the election."[45]

Hamilton and Kewen directly benefited from anti-Union sentiment, winning elections to the State Legislature in 1862 and 1863. Victory, however, did not come easy: their Republican opponents contested the election results, prompting Kewen and Hamilton to counter with equally damning allegations of voter fraud. Both political parties were probably guilty of voting irregularities. Union authorities attempted to control local government by manipulating of the political process; i.e., polling booths often resembled armed camps, and some said that the military took a more active role than mere overseer. There may have been some truth to that allegation. In one instance, a Union officer stationed in San Bernardino requested 150 additional rifles for an upcoming election.[46] Kimball H. Dimmick, a government agent and Los Angeles' former district attorney, believed that Republican candidates had an excellent chance of defeating their opponents, confidently writing that "we shall make a strong effort to overthrow them at the election."[47] Kewen asserted that 250 soldiers from Camp Latham illegally voted during his 1862 election bid and that board of election inspectors at the La Ballona precinct were "constituted and appointed not by the qualified voters but by the soldiers of Camp Latham."[48] Hamilton's opponent, Francisco P. Ramirez, the Republican editor of *El Clamor Público*, claimed that voter fraud throughout Los Angeles County had cost him 250 votes.[49] Kewen and Hamilton were eventually awarded their legislative seats in the State Assembly, but only after withstanding humiliating courtroom accusations of political chicanery and disloyalty.

Southern California Democrats had reached the pinnacle of influence and power by the end of 1862. Kewen had taken his seat in the state legislature, and Henry Hamilton would soon follow. After Hamilton's Los Angeles *Star*, the city's leading newspaper, was banned from the mail by Union officials, locals distributed it through private means, an indication of the region's widespread support for Hamilton's views. Also by this time, the second year of the war the fortunes of war were buoying Southern hopes. The Confederacy had been victorious on the Virginia Peninsula and at Manassas Junction and fought to a standoff at Antietam. Finally, the South and her supporters were encouraged by the possiblity that Great Britain would recognize their independence. Every month the war continued, the rebel cause was gaining international support as a legitimate nation fighting for independence.

In 1863, however, events took a turn for the worse for the Confederacy. The Emancipation Proclamation lent moral authority to the Union cause, prevented England and France from supporting the South, and reinforced many Northerners belief that it was a just war. Union victories at Vicksburg and Gettysburg improved the military outlook, dividing the Confederacy and challenging the mystique surrounding Robert E. Lee's military invincibility. Thus, partisan Democratic characterizations of the 1862 Union campaigns as "paralyzed" had lost credibility through Union victories in the following year.[50]

Hamilton, Kewen and other Southern partisans continued

their attacks, despite finding themselves on the unpopular side of events. They often sounded mean-spirited against a backdrop of growing patriotic fervor. They labeled the Emancipation Proclamation as a blatant theft of "private property." Some Democrats ignored obvious military trends or misinterpreted battlefield news that suggested Confederate defeats because of unreliable information and delays in communication, or a refusal to admit the worst. Aware of this, John G. Downey desperately wanted more information than Hamilton's newspaper or other "little Democratic papers" could supply.[51] John Forster, an ally and confidant of Henry Hamilton, admitted that he was perplexed by the surrender at Vicksburg and Lee's advance into Pennsylvania. He suspected – at least hoped – that "they know what they are about. Quien sabe."[52]

California's Republicans took the offensive by the close of 1863, demanding that the state present a unifed war effort, and labeling their opponents as disloyal. The charges raised in the bitter campaigns involving Hamilton and Kewen led to their brief incarceration on charges of subversion. So ubiquitous and implacable was the censorship that John Forster cautioned a fellow resident to not criticize the taxation policy because "too free use of words" could lead to arrest.[53] "Damned black souls (or republicans) however they may be called," José Estudillo wrote of the harassing Unionists, exasperated over his arrest for failing to register for the draft with local authorities.[54] "Disloyalty to the Union cause," recalled one observer, "had become about as perilous as had been the expression of abolition sentiment but a few years before."[55]

By the end of 1863, Democrat complaints of oppressive Union policies had lost their credibility in the face of continuing battlefield defeats. Hamilton, however, still counseled vigilance regarding potential military intervention into the mining camps. "Our mines will wake up some fine morning," he warned through his Los Angeles *Star*, "and find a military guard prospecting their claims for and on account of Uncle Abe."[56] But this prophecy of Hamilton's never materialized, weakening his paper's credibility. The mines thrived as a haven for refugees, pacifists and opportunists seeking fortune rather than conflict. One traveler to Warner's Ranch in late 1863 conceded that "everyone gives a good account of the mines."[57]

The election of Hamilton and Kewen were mixed blessings because their legislative responsibilites kept them in Sacramento, robbing their region of its most ardent organizers for and supporters of the Southern Cause. If anything, political momentum was lost. During 1863-1864, coinciding with a decline in voter participation, the Los Angeles *Star* lost money. Hamilton decried public apathy, denouncing "men pretending to be Democrats who absented themselves from the polls."[58] Kewen acted as a booster from afar, encouraging his fellow Democrats to maintain a viable organization, but this did not have the same impact on Democrat voter turnout as his presence might have generated.[59]

Democratic party loyalty in California began to diminish as the Union victory seemed more likely. In 1863, a Republican won the Los Angeles race for city marshal, an influential position coveted by many in the frontier era. The Republican gubernatorial candidate, Frederick F. Low, won the election statewide, even finishing a close runner-up in the lower counties to hometown favorite John G. Downey (Downey, ironically, had forecast an end to Democratic control over local patronage in the aftermath of Lincoln's 1860 presidential victory).[60] Some Democrats downplayed the war in their campaigns, in an effort to counter these adverse trends. Benjamin Hayes, for one, stressed his own independence, impartiality and integrity. "The office of Judge should be maintained free forever from any influence of mere party politics," he declared.[61] But a large Republican turnout in Santa Barbara tipped the scales in a close election, ending Hayes' tenure as district judge.

Democrats faced an even tougher uphill battle in the 1864 campaign, faced with continued Union military victories. Hamilton, Kewen and other Copperheads pragmatically shifted their emphasis from anti-Union rhetoric to demands for immediate peace. "One experiment is left," declared Kewen, "it is Peace -peace to a distracted country -peace to a nation drunk with horrors."[62] Hamilton, caught in one of the war's ironies, found himself with no one to support but a former Union general, George McClellan, whom he had vehemently criticized only a few years before when McClellan led the Union forces. Now, there naturally being no prospect of a Southern Democrat presidential nominee except McClellan, a disgruntled Henry Hamilton could only support a "peace platform" as the only feasible alternative to Lincoln's reelection.[63]

Several factors hampered Democratic efforts to win votes in 1864: internal problems with party organization, declining voter registration over the past two years, and the Los Angeles *Star's* declining subscriptions during that time, a harbinger of the steady erosion in party rank and file. By October, Hamilton's financial difficulties forced his newspaper into bankruptcy, leaving Democrats without a major political organ in Southern California during the closing weeks of the campaign.[64] San Juan Capistrano Democrats worried that the power of incumbency had galvanized Republicans: "Every effort will be made to carry the election in this County against us," fretted Democrat regular John S. Griffin.[65] John Forster called the election "very warm" and "Don Abel (Abel Stearns) is running about stumping everywhere that they can get an audience to understand English."[66]

As Republican momentum peaked at the election, Hamilton, Kewen and other Democrats tried a last-ditch effort to blunt their opponents' energy with a rally at the Montgomery Hotel. Kewen spoke for an hour, and Hamilton characterized the event in glowing terms in one of the last issues of the Los Angeles *Star*. All these efforts were to no avail, for Republicans countered with their own galas during the closing days of the campaign. Phineas Banning hosted a grand barbecue for Republican candidates at Wilmington. One bitter partisan warned that if Republicans flaunted this rally as the "beginning of the feast in anticipation of the Election the majority will hide snakes in their boots."[67] Such remarks, of course, expressed honest frustration instead of political reality: Lincoln carried the state by 30,000 votes. In Southern California, Republicans captured Wilmington and Anaheim to offset Democratic strength in El Monte, San Gabriel and Azusa. Historian John Robinson notes that "the initial return indicated a stunning upset. There was jubilation among Union men in Los Angeles, and artillery boomed at Drum Barracks."[68]

The bitterness associated with wartime politics subsided once the Confederacy surrendered in the spring of 1865. The reduction of military forces in California eased tensions, returning the southern communities to civilian control and beginning an era of reconciliation. Soon commercial expansion reemerged as the civic priority. Benjamin Wilson encouraged one Confederate expatriate to come home, declaring that any postwar restrictions would be repealed, and "we are in hopes of brighter times."[69] Old themes again came to the forefront: railroad construction, law and order, education, and social progress. The future offered renewed vitality in commerce, with increased speculation in petroleum and mining. "There are riches in store for Los Angeles," promised the Los Angeles *Semi-Weekly News*.[70]

Hamilton and Kewen mirrored the temper of those postwar times, returning to quiet, private lives. Hamilton managed a San Gabriel citrus ranch, acquired real estate during the boom of the late 1860s and briefly owned a printing press during his later years. Kewen reopened his law practice and attended to his properties at *El Molino Viejo*. Financial difficulties forced him to sell his properties less than profitably in later years, leaving him to spend his latter years in relative obscurity.

Both men continued to speak on political issues throughout the postwar years, but only as shadows of their former influence and power. The Democratic party rejected Kewen's bid for an 1872 Congressional nomination, while Hamilton served an inauspicious term as justice of the peace for Mission San Gabriel. Politics had passed them by. Southern California had put the Civil War's ideological divisions behind, if not totally reconciled. Edward John Cage Kewen and Henry Hamilton and their beliefs were soon eclipsed by the practical concerns of the continuing settlement of the West.

But oh, what those bygone days represented, with the country's fate in the balance! Future Americans could only speculate what life had been like in the Civil War era, and maybe even envy the great issues that moved men like Hamilton and Kewen to sacrifice themselves for a Lost Cause. But the cold realities of war are, always have been, sobering. Kewen's poetry, written years before the Civil War on his arrival in Southern California, perhaps best captured the musings of those later generations of Americans:

> The golden visions of our youth!
> They come and mock us with their spell,
> They seem all loveliness and truth,
> But oh, how soon the sad farewell[71]

CHAPTER NINE

Charles Louis Ducommun:
From Pioneer to Entrepreneur

The life of Charles Louis Ducommun was a metaphor for his age, in that he represented the oncoming tide of journeymen, speculators and opportunists who made the gold rush an epic adventure. His reasons for coming west paralleled those of his contemporaries, men like Joseph Lancaster Brent, Edward John Cage Kewen and Horace Bell: pioneers who had journeyed west in search of opportunity and riches. It was the mid-19th century, an era in which it was fashionable to travel an uncharted course, take risks in faraway lands, explore and seek new challenges in uncharted waters. Sir Richard Burton traversed the Nile River, searching for its source, John Charles Frémont became known as the Pathfinder while cataloguing the geologic and topographical details of the wilderness of the West; and, Stanley and Livingston wandered the uncharted African interior. These adventurers' published accounts of their explorations, captured the popular imagination and exemplified the frontier spirit in Europe as well as America. And the California gold rush merely heightened this global curiosity concerning trade and travel with its get-rich-quick potential. Ducommun, a Swiss-French watchmaker from a family of modest means, was one of those youths burning with the ambition to find his personal fortune in the American West.

The Ducommun family included Catholics and Huguenots, embodying the opposing religious divisions that had been at war for two centuries, characterizing European politics since the Reformation. In 1820, the family decided to migrate to Switzerland. The alpine country offered a new start in the post-Napoleonic era, free of political strife at a time when it appeared that France had exhausted herself after decades of war and conquest.[1]

Ducommun was one of 13 children, born en route to Calvinist Switzerland near Besancon, France. Because this family's survival had always depended less on good fortune than on common sense and ingenuity, Charles' father had diverse skills. A watchmaker, he also dabbled in jewelry making and dry goods sales to supplement his income -much as European Jews of an earlier era, forbidden to own land, had survived by diverse and portable skills. The large Ducommun family was often threatened by economic hardship, forcing them to separate for several months at a time, during which the children were placed with relatives and friends until better times allowed the parents to reunite their offspring.

Young Ducommun learned his father's watchmaking craft, apprenticing with another family in Locle, Switzerland. Meanwhile, a fire destroyed his father's business, forcing the breakup of the family. Theirs is a story common among the ordinary mid-19th century Europeans, scarred by centuries of conflict, feudal repression and economic hardship. Once again, the Ducommun offspring were placed with relatives or in foster homes. Charles Louis' mother eventually migrated to Italy, where she died without ever seeing her son again. The Ducommun brothers scattered throughout France, Italy and Switzerland.

Alone in the world, Ducommun began his nomadic life adventures in the two great pilasters of Europe: Paris and London. He polished his professional craftsmanship and honed his entrepreneurial acumen in a post-Napoleonic Europe that was still recovering from decades of continental conflict. Working as a jeweler and watchmaker in Paris, Charles familiarized himself with nautical instruments and chronometers along the English docks, all the while living in near poverty., often hungry, but nevertheless surviving on cunning and resourcefulness.

Throughout his travails Ducommun endured, and probably listened to romantic tales of the vast New World to the west, perhaps reading of the young United States' applications of the democratic principles of equality and liberty that Alexis De Tocqueville's writings had articulated for a curious audience back home. In any case, America must have beckoned to the young, rootless Swiss, for in 1841 he sailed for New York. There, he hoped, he would start a new life in an egalitarian world caring little for aristocratic circumstance to which he had no claim at all.

Ducommun's early years in America were filled with misfortune. At New York, during a winter epidemic he contracted smallpox, which damaged his eyesight and led to the loss of his right eye. During his protracted recovery at Bellevue Hospital, Ducommun had time to reflect on his options as well as misfortunes. Handicapped, weakened by illness and a foreigner with limited language skills, Ducommun nonetheless knew that he had willingly accepted the risk of an unknown environ, impetuously leaving Europe thinking only of new riches. Now, it seemed, illness and disfigurement might dampen his expectations but also eventually, led him to the Far West, for his maladies, like those of Thomas Hereford, required a milder climate.

As soon as he was able to travel, Ducommun went south during the mid-1840s, traveling between Augusta and Mobile much as he junketed between Paris and London. The ambience of farms and plantation life may have reminded him of the society and landscape of the English countryside, perhaps even of the stately gardens and woods of Versailles. The lush, rural

South was probably quite similar to the fanciful setting he may have imagined while working as an apprentice to his father.

In the South, Ducommun soon had built a modest trade in watchmaking; nonetheless he was still restless, still hoping for greater opportunities. The discovery of California gold was the impetus Ducommun needed to fire up and pursue those ambitions dampened by his

Charles Louis Ducommun

encounter with smallpox. Now everything must have seemed possible again, for he moved quickly to join the rush to the Feather River. By late 1848, Ducommun was in Fort Smith, Arkansas, where he enlisted with a mule train destined for Southern California.

The mule train Ducommun joined at Fort Smith traveled west along the Gila Trail, a route through the New Mexico and Arizona deserts leading to California's southern border. The Gila Trail was shorter in distance than the more popular Santa Fe or California trails, an appealing characteristic to impatient argonauts bewitched by gold fever. Yet though the trail was shorter it was also riskier to the novice and unsuspecting traveler. Severe weather, harsh terrain and hostile Apache and Comanche tribes were the dangerous, often fatal side of the deceptively simple face of the Gila. Writer Ralph Moody noted that "to the west of the Colorado, it was even worse, for there were ninety miles of waterless, grassless desert to be crossed before reaching the California mountains."[2]

Ducommun, like many novice travelers, was so besotted by the prospect of quick riches in the gold mines that he ignored the warnings and risked the dangerous journey to reach California as quickly as possible. His party traveled to New Mexico via the Cimarron cut-off, through the western tip of the Oklahoma plains, and arched southward below the rugged Sangre de Cristo Mountains. At Santa Fe, the travelers recouped for two months and plotted the next leg of the journey, which traversed barren deserts and hostile Indian territory from Santa Fe to Yuma, Arizona. In the spring of 1849, the group proceeded south through Zuni and Apache country, parallel with the Rio Grande and near the Black Range. The party then turned west along the Gila river, over fault blocks formed in prehistoric ages and dry lakes bleached white with salt and gravel, a torpid surface covered in bunch grass, junipers, oak and pinions. This austere, difficult road snaked along the Basin and Range country of the Empty Quarter, a name given to the dirt trails throughout mid-America that connected the far-flung civilized extremities of American society.[3]

Ducommun, like so many, had underestimated the risks associated with an overland journey through hostile Indian country, across austere terrain and treacherous weather. Prudent reason meant little to anyone smitten with the illusions of wealth that had captured the imagination of the Brents, the Herefords and others of this era. Ducommun may have possibly brushed shoulders with Thomas or Margaret Hereford somewhere along the way, sharing mutual dreams and hopes for the future. They may have broken bread at Santa Fe, crossed paths along a dry creek near the Salt River, or squinted in the bright Arizona sun that covered the desert ground like dull chalk. Even if the Herefords and Ducommun never met, they shared a common spirit, like a broad wind swirling to its own rhythm: pioneers in search of opportunity within the larger context of the Westward settlement.

Ducommun's party suffered from the risks they had perhaps rashly undertaken in their zeal to reach the gold fields: Apache attacks, rugged deserts, and no stopovers to replenish supplies. Near starvation and exhausted, the mule train limped across southern Arizona and staggered into Yuma during the late spring of 1849. From Yuma, the route proceeded northward into Southern California, passing San Diego toward Los Angeles. The Spanish had forged part of the trail under Juan Bautista de Anza and Father Eusebio Kino, and in contemporary times trailblazers like the Patties, Ewing Young and Stephen Kearny with his Army of the West had covered the area.[4] The Gila Trail's craggy hills, wide sand dunes and oppressive summer heat made timing critical to any desert crossing. Ducommun's party braved the trail in the early summer: time was a serious concern, requiring a quick crossing of the western deserts. They rested at Yuma and then proceeded, arriving at Warner's Ranch by late August, 1849. Like the Herefords and so many wanderers of that era, Ducommun's party had survived with ambition their chief sustenance. Historian John Walton Caughey characterized the stragglers along the Gila Trail as "used up, walking 'with the kind of dead march step, ragged, dirty, starved, worn down, and exhausted."[5]

When Ducommun arrived in California he stopped at Los Angeles, then continued toward the Mariposa mining country. There, Ducommun like Joseph Lancaster Brent, Thomas Hereford and Edward John Cage Kewen, quickly learned that mining itself, in the overcrowded camps, afforded few opportunities. Fortunes passed from miner to merchant as retailers demanded exorbitant prices and bankers offered currency at compounded interest.

During his travels between San Francisco and the mining camps near Sacramento, Ducommun met John G. Downey. The two men developed a lasting friendship and later became business partners. They shared mutual interests, recognizing as they did that the gold rush had created unique demands for the basic, everyday necessities. They visited Mariposa County, built a network of friends among the miners, and occasionally worked the diggings near the Feather and American Rivers. Ducommun and Downey were part of a new merchant class, men who saw that the real fortunes to be made in the goldfields rested on scarcity of supplies in the mining camps. "For the shrewd, the tactful, the risk takers, and those with access to credit, the world lay before them," noted Western scholar William G. Robbins.[6]

Ducommun and Downey targeted Southern California for their business, part of the steady flow of migrants who passed through Los Angeles in the years following the gold rush. They had little money when they landed at San Pedro in 1850. Their *carreta* had broken down on the path to Los Angeles, so the two men walked from the docks with belongings in tow, a small feat in determination that Ducommun later recalled with great pride.[7] Dogged, youthful and opportunistic, Ducommun and Downey represented a different brand of settler from the earlier wave of emigrant characterized by Abel Stearns or Hugo Reid. By the time Ducommun and Downey arrived, land titles, ranching, fiestas and the missions were part of a distant past. As historian Robert Hine has commented, "the speculative Yankee came from another world, another age, with far less acceptance of class responsibility and position."[8]

The resourceful Ducommun relied on his old familiar skills to make his way in Los Angeles, opening a small shop repairing watches and peddling jewelry and cutlery.[9] He also sold a variety of other merchandise from a wholesale trade he worked out in San Francisco, ferrying down goods through San Pedro and then moving them by stagecoach to Los Angeles. Ducommun made several trips to San Francisco, managing his own shipments of stock, purchasing toys, trinkets, stationery and books to meet consumer needs.[10] In 1853, he returned to the mining counties, establishing business contacts, surveying the commercial activity in the region and identifying new speculative

Main St. toward the Plaza,
which includes the Temple Block (at left). The white circular object
which was a clock stood in front of the Ducommun Building.

adventures. Some of his earliest stock purchases were made possible through minor commercial coups in the goldfields.[11]

Ducommun steadily expanded his operation throughout the 1850s, purchasing additional land along the commercial center of the growing town. In 1853, he acquired an 848-square-foot parcel of land from Benjamin Wilson, situated at the northeast side of Commercial Street, which became the basis for his future expansion, purchasing of additional properties along the block. Two years later, Ducommun acquired an adjacent lot for $2,500 from Joseph Bernstein, nearly doubling the square footage under his ownership and giving him a substantial portion of the entire block. Ducommun continued making land purchases along Commercial and Main streets, and also at Vineyard and Los Angeles streets near the Francisco Alvarado properties.[12]

By 1860, Ducommun had become a leading businessman in Los Angeles, with his wholesale operation favorably located in the heart of the city's economic community, across Main Street from John Temple's store (later absorbed into the Downey Block); across Commercial Street to the south was located Benjamin Wilson's general store, Maximo Alaniz's townhouse and John Goller's wagon shop; a few doors away in the opposite direction stood the Bella Union Hotel, the city's first major hospice; and Mateo Keller's store of merchandise and wine as well as McFarland and Downey's apothecary shop were east on Commercial and Los Angeles streets.[13]

Several of Ducommun's commercial enterprises failed in the early 1850s, vulnerable to the gold rush era's boom/bust economic climate, but Ducommun was able to adapt to the changing demands by expanding his inventory. One contemporary, Boyle Workman, marveled at Ducommun's diverse trade and his ability to satisfy consumer needs. The Swiss merchant had avoided the pitfall of others by going them one better in his hardware store. "You could buy anything from a watch to a washtub, and from a necklace to a scrub brush."[14] His inventory also had items not readily found in the Far West, including oil paints, art objects, porcelain, domino sets, violins, *Bibles* and cigars. His stock lists enumerated a variety of metalworks, including brass, bronze and silver rolls and rods. No customer whose wallet was full was too insignificant, and Ducommun advertised in the Los Angeles *Star*, selling his goods to both Spanish-speaking and Anglo customers.

In short, Ducommun was simply applying valuable lessons learned during his early days in Europe and America. Survival in a cyclical business environment required a basic understanding of markets, the dynamics of supply and demand and the fluctuating and diverse needs of a frontier in transition. Personal tragedy had also taught him the basic tenets of survival, through his own family's separations and forced migrations to distant lands in search of health and opportunity. Besides capitalizing on the material demands of western settlement and the new gold rush markets, he lent hard currency at commercial interest rates, assayed gold ore, operated as a pawnbroker and deposited customers' gold in the store safe. He was all things to all people, but for a price. Rival retailer Harris Newmark described Ducommun's store as the most complete operation in the old pueblo. According to Newmark, his competitor had "a sort of curiosity-shop containing many articles not obtainable elsewhere; and he was clever enough, when asked for any rarity, to charge all that the traffic would bear."[15] When businessman and real estate developer John Temple decorated the front of his store with shade trees, providing a new and appealing look to his establishment, Ducommun immediately followed suit, gracing his storefront property with pepper trees and shrubs. He would also be one of the first to construct asphalt sidewalks, which the Los Angeles *Star* praised as a progressive step in "mending our (city's) dusty ways."[16]

Ducommun also became a visible civic leader, joining fraternal organizations such as the Masons, acting as a juror and volunteering when needed for the citizens police force, *Los Guardines de la Ciudad*.[17] He was a defender of the city and part of the era's patriotic vigilante fervor. Ducommun often slept with a loaded gun beneath his bed and was always ready to join the official and unofficial posses to combat bandido threats to the community. He was a juror in the trial of the ringleader of the 1856 Los Angeles riot, and participated in the trial of Luciano Tapia, a bandido hanged in 1858 for his participation in the Juan Flores crimes.[18] He financed part of the aggressive manhunt for the Juan Flores gang, which extended from Los Angeles to San Diego. The city paid him $40 from a vigilante budget entitled *The Fund for Suppression of Armed Banditti in the Counties of Los Angeles and San Bernardino*. Throughout the decade, Ducommun's financial assistance in the arrest of outlaws was always reimbursed.[19]

By the end of the Civil War, Ducommun had assumed an influential role in Los Angeles. His was not a meteoric rise; rather, this disfigured, nomadic Swiss migrant had gradually assimilated into western society, eventually achieving respectability among his peers. He became a naturalized citizen in 1855, joined the ranks of the Democrat party, and watched his good friend, John G. Downey, gain prominence in the state.

Ducommun began thinking of marriage and family as his business prospered and middle-age was fast approaching. In 1857, 37 year old Ducommun married San Francisco resident Bertha Rontex. The couple had two daughters by the end of the decade, when Ducommun's young wife died following the birth of their second daughter. A widower for the next seven years, Ducommun returned to his boyhood home, Neufchatel, Switzerland for a visit and found romance in the person of a language teacher, Zelie Leonide Petitpierre, whom he married in 1867. The couple returned to Los Angeles to begin a new life together, rearing six more children during the next three decades. The Ducommuns lived at the LaFayette Hotel for three years, eventually moving into a home near the Ducommun store in 1871.[20]

By the close of the 1860s, Los Angeles had transformed itself from frontier outpost to a bustling western settlement. The demand for internal improvements accelerated. A new school and a paid police force became a reality by 1870, and the city council contracted for five thousand feet of irrigation pipe and built a dam and reservoir. The city outlined plans for a new bridge across Macy Street, and new towns emerged throughout the region: Santa Ana, Tustin, Newport, Florence and Riverside, subdivided for future development.[21] The expectation of railway transit from the city to the coast raised hopes among local business leaders. Benjamin Wilson, a Ducommun friend and once a pessimist about the future, confidently wrote in 1868 that future rail transit "is all the talk," and "our country is fast improving. People are moving in constantly and many of a very good class."[22]

Ducommun, like many Southern Californians, invested in new commercial ventures, believing in the aggressive capitalization of new enterprises, whether railroad, oil, transportation, natural gas, engineering, or finance. He financed many speculative schemes in new oil and mining ventures, supporting his friends' investments while solidifying his entree to a tight-knit

*Ducommun Building at the corner
of Main St. and Commercial St. circa 1875*

work of business colleagues. By 1870, he was one of the city's top two dozen wealthiest men, and his increasing stature paralleled with the rise of prominent friends. John G. Downey accumulated properties along Main Street, subdivided ranchos, and became an important political figure within the state. Other local icons such as John Temple, Phineas Banning and Benjamin Wilson were also among Ducommun's intimates.

Ducommun was daring, and he supported some questionable enterprises that were popular ventures in frontier California. The Comstock Lode in Nevada and the demand for hard currency to support the Civil War effort created renewed interest in gold and silver mining. In 1863, Ducommun purchased stock in Chimawabo Consolidated Copper and Silver Mining Company, a San Bernardino operation working along the Colorado River.[23] Two years later, oil was discovered in the San Fernando region, sparking an immmediate frenzy of quick claims and drilling projects in the surrounding Santa Susanna,

San Francisquito and San Gabriel mountains. Many elite personalities, including Andres Pico, Dr. Vincent Geleich, and Benjamin D. Wilson became associated with the formation of new oil companies. John Rowland and Burdette Chandler began oil drilling operations in La Puente and the Wilshire District, and Sunset Oil Company put down wells on the La Brea Rancho. Ducommun was part of this feverish speculation, purchasing shares in the Los Angeles Pioneer Oil Company. Pioneer Oil Company was headed by Phineas Banning, with a membership including several of Ducommun's old friends: Benjamin Wilson, John G. Downey and John S. Griffin. The petroleum company secured title to the San Pasqual Rancho.[24]

Though Pioneer Oil was a minor success, producing a limited amount of asphaltum and oil, the overall oil industry at this stage was a premature phenomenon, nearly 15 years before the Santa Paula strike that would propel Lyman Stewart and the Union Oil Company into regional prominence. Pioneer Oil was one among many unfortunate casualties of their owners ambitious vision. "Because of the extravagant claims made for the industry during the period of feverish activity," according to historian Robert Glass Cleland, "the general opinion prevailed that the whole petroleum business was a complete fiasco."[25]

Despite the outcome, however, the early oil experience forged lasting bonds of friendship among its participants. Ducommun frequently entertained his associates over a good meal, Havana cigars, dice and a full deck of cards. Comfortable with and confident in one another, they discussed business trends, assessing competitiors and arranging new ventures in commerce and industry. At the center of this consanguine group was Isaias W. Hellman, a financier and visionary whose many segments of Los Angeles society, including large landowners, politicians, and entrepreneurs which made him a driving force behind Los Angeles commerce and industry. Hellman "was fortunate in securing their confidence and patronage," recalled Harris Newmark, and "he laid the foundation for his subsequent career as a banker, in which he has attained such success."[26]

California eased its restrictive banking laws during the Civil War years, which encouraged the growth of small banks throughout the state. Hellman, Ducommun and other businessmen recognized and quickly took

Ducommun Hardware Store at 204 Main St.

advantage of these favorable trends in local economic policy. In 1868, Hellman, John Temple and John Downey formed a small lending institution to meet the demand for capital. Three years later, Hellman and Downey reorganized a larger financial operation, the Farmers and Merchants Bank, securing pledges totaling $500,000 in capitalization from several local businessmen and speculators.[27] Ducommun had a subtle but important role in these developments as the largest investor aside from the two principals, and pledged $25,000 in financial backing. As a charter board member, he shaped bank policy by casting key votes on several financial decisions throughout the turbulent

1870s. But the economic depression that swept the country in the mid-1870s destroyed regional banks, muted credit and led to bankruptcy and foreclosure on farmers and businessmen, much as earlier depressions, drought and land disputes had ruined the rancheros many of these farmers and businessmen had replaced. Ducommun painfully watched his longtime associate, John Downey, withdraw from the Bank's leadership as a result of questionable lending practices during the 1875 depression.[28]

Despite hard times, board members of the Farmers and Merchants Bank recognized the region's economic potential and positioned themselves as key players in any economic recovery. Ducommun and Hellman were particularly undaunted by the economic dislocations of the mid-1870s. They invested their personal fortunes in the region, jointly purchasing the Alanis Vineyard Tract in 1871, then subdividing and selling the lots.[29] In 1876, the bank supported a railroad connection between San Francisco and Los Angeles, which further tied the Southern California economy with other portions of the state.

Throughout volatile business cycles, Ducommun became a symbol of stability and integrity to many residents. In 1874, a grateful city council honored him by harking back to his skills as a watchmaker and Swiss heritage, declaring the city to be on "Ducommun time." He continued to preside as a director of the Merchant and Farmers Bank for two decades, maintaining a seat on the board until his death in 1896.[30]

Charles Louis Ducommun was indeed a one-eyed king of an expanding kingdom that once was blinded by the singular dependence on the gold rush era, which finally emerged as a diverse economy that mirrored the late-19th century Industrial Age. As a tinker, a dabbler and a creative dilettante, his rich imagination personified the innovative spirit of the time. His wholesale operation supplied materials for an array of improvements that reflected the city's growth and development, the ultimate goal of the Manifest Destiny that finally spawned the country sea to sea and north to south, with the West successfully wrested from Mexico and the South an agrarian colony open to the Northern textile industry and railroads. Ducommun metals were used to develop a telephone system, electrical lighting and a public elevator in the 1880s. The orange-picker he patented in 1888 was significant in the growth of the citrus business in Southern California. Ducommun built Los Angeles' second three-story brick building in the commercial district, and his "grandfather clock" was considered the most accurate in the city. His achievements were indicative of Andrew Carnegie's spirit of social activism, a time when the "Gospel of Wealth" required upper class responsibility to the larger society. Ducommun became associated with several philanthropic endeavors, including the development of a city library. He was active in the Masons Lodge and nurtured, on his estate, a lavish garden of various species of flowers, including a Marshal Neil rose bush containing 3,000 blossoms.[31]

Los Angeles' population had risen to over 50,000 residents by the mid-1890s. The last semblance of the old pueblo and frontier town had dropped away, and the city was now as an urban milieu displaying the bustling growth found in such midwestern townships as Omaha, Kansas City and Chicago. Henry Huntington and Isaias Hellman formed a transit system that would dominate the region for a half-century; Edward L. Doheny and Charles A. Canfield discovered oil near Second Street and Glendale Boulevard; the fight over a free harbor was resolved with a Congressional appropriation of $3,900,000 for construction at San Pedro. And Ducommun, who had come west overland when hostile Indians were still a threat to the California-bound pioneers, had lived to see Los Angeles become a significant urban center poised to enter the next century. In 1896, 75-year-old Charles Louis Ducommun died while at work, surprising no one familiar with the forthright lifestyle that had led him to find family and fortune in the changing West.

CHAPTER TEN

Antonio Coronel and Southern California's Romantic Lore, Ramona

Antonio Coronel lived through six decades of Southern California history, spanning the rancho period, American conquest, Civil War years and the late-19th-century economic volatility in commerce and industry. His position in the small elite strata of almost feudally-organized Mexican society shaped his perceptions concerning problems of acculturation during that period, an influential perspective that shaped the romantic view of those bygone days of padres, rancherias, adobes and cattle -subjects immortalized in Helen Hunt Jackson's popular literary classic, *Ramona*. Coronel's images took on a life of their own largely because of his relationship with Jackson, one of the most celebrated friendships in 19th-century Southern California history. Don Antonio acted as tour guide, mentor and confidant to Mrs. Jackson, provided research sources and contributed the underlying idealistic picture of local history so integral to her novel's tone and character, forever popularizing Southern California's history as he saw it through Mrs. Jackson's romantic writings.

The 1880s were a watershed in Southern California's transition from frontier to bustling center of western settlement. Los Angeles had grown to a town of more than 11,000 residents, five times the pueblo's population at the time of statehood. Gilded Age Los Angeles was a boom town, a commercial marketplace firmly connected to the Midwest by the Southern Pacific Railroad, no longer geographically remote. The gold rush era was gone forever and so was the wide-open town: there was a corresponding decrease in vigilantism as California developed permanent settlements, community institutions and a stable, family-based populace. Southern California's new college (University of Southern California) and newspaper (Los Angeles *Times*) added a new dimension of cultural prestige to the area.

Fresh leadership had emerged in Southern California within a few decades after statehood: Charles Ducommun represented a new breed of patricians that replaced the likes of Abel Stearns, Henry Hamilton and Benjamin Hayes as well as Joseph Lancaster Brent and other Confederate loyalists who had left California during the war years. Lawlessness subsided, and bandits like Juan Flores had been captured, hanged or chased away. Sheriff James Barton and his lone posse were replaced with a professional police force and improved regional coordination of law enforcement. Fortunes were won and lost in the boom times of the late 1860s. Even Horace Bell, a holdover from the old days, caught the speculative fever and squandered his meager savings in land schemes and failed business ventures. In sum, Southern California's growth and expansion brought fresh meaning to the word "civilized" on the Western frontier.

During this new epoch in Southern California settlement some noticed that old lifestyles were quickly disappearing without a trace and felt the need to provide a historical record of the fading mission period and Hispanic ambience that had so long dominated the locale. Jackson's *Ramona*, though written for the

Helen Hunt Jackson

purpose of conveying the author's social message regarding the plight of the American Indian, was also, thanks to the influence of Don Antonio Coronel, the first literary attempt to capture the pastoral era within the context of the Anglo-American conquest. The love story between Ramona, an orphaned Indian girl raised on a rancho, and Alessandro, a proud Indian *vaquero*, found a late 19th-century audience who identified with this enchanting tale of two lovers against a world of bigotry and injustice.

Ramona is a classic romantic tragedy of love and misfortune, filled with melodrama, sentimentality and idealized settings. Ramona and Alessandro are Native American outcasts in a land dominated by Anglo speculators and opportunists (It is perhaps Don Antonio's perspective or Mrs. Jackson's desire to simplify the message that the unpleasantness of the Spanish and Mexican encounters with the California Indians is glossed over, with the exception of Señora Moreno's distate for Hispanic/Indio *mestizos*). The young lovers elope and encounter the cruel indifference of Yankee settlement. This forced them to retreat further into the wilderness to find peace and harmony, but the hardships of health and poverty cause them to lose a child in the process. Prejudice and misunderstanding eventually lead to the senseless killing of Alessandro. Ramona, widowed and left with a young child, is eventually vindicated and recaptures her rightful inheritance. Alessandro's death is a bittersweet ending to a life of travail, lost loves and stolen liberties. The reader is compelled to address the central issue of the novel, which concerns the protection of Native American rights.

Ramona's publication in 1884 brought instant success and focused national attention on Native Americans. "The nation must now take up in good faith and with an unwearying patience the task of raising the Indians to the comfort and dignity of self-support," observed S. A. Galpin, a former Interior Department official.[1] Activists seized upon the novel's success to influence public opinion and press Congressional leaders into creating a reservation system similar to that in California designed by Edward Beale in the 1850s. In 1887, the Ramona Indian Memorial School was established at Albuquerque, New Mexico for Apache tribes. Post offices, hotels and cities in Southern California were named to commemorate the heroine of the novel. Boosters felt the Hemet-San Jacinto locale would profit from the notoriety of the region. By 1912, a Ramona carnival had been organized, and the San Jacinto *Register* urged the construction of a permanent outdoor amphitheatre to dramatize "California's greatest outdoor play."[2]

Ramona found a wider audience with the advent of motion pictures. Hollywood director David Wark Griffith retold the romance in one of his earliest movies, placing light-skinned Mary Pickford in the lead role against the natural backdrop of cottonwoods and chapparal found in the San Gabriel foothills. Writer Kevin Starr noted that Griffith's movie version of *Ramona* highlighted "panoramic views of Southern California's coastal mountain range, as well as following up the use of visual detail with highly articulated close-up scenes of sheepshearing."[3]

The story of Ramona and Alessandro connects with major themes in classic literature. The sad circumstances of the two lovers cut against a hostile world filled with bigotry, similar in theme to Shakespeare's *Romeo and Juliet*, a tale of lovers caught between the family divisions of a city-state hierarchy, or Harriet Beecher Stowe's *Uncle Tom's Cabin*, which highlights an African American family threatened by the cruelty of slavery. *Ramona* indeed makes a larger point about the temper of the times by admonishing western settlers and government officials for disavowing of land grants, discriminating against non-Anglos and the systematic removal of Native Americans from the Southern California landscape.

Ramona, as a historical novel, captured the mystery of a romantic past and crystalized the contemporary problems of Native American rights. Many characters metaphorically underscore problems of race and inequality in western settlement. Because Coronel acted as tutor and mentor to Jackson, her work cannot be considered without understanding Coronel's position as well as the circumstances that existed in frontier Southern California.

Coronel's life spanned 60 years of Southern California history, transcending both the Mexican and Anglo-American periods. His family was influential in Southern California, arriving there in 1834 when Coronel was only 17, during the zenith of Mexican rule. The Coronels became closely associated with the rancheros and pueblo politics of that era, when the missions were left in disarray and the Indian labor force became vulnerable to unrestricted economic forces, a point lamented in the early chapters of *Ramona*. Antonio's father, Ignacio F. Coronel, was a Mexican officer under General Yturbide and had emigrated to Southern California during the celebrated Padres "Colonia." On arriving at Los Angeles, Ignacio Coronel established a school and educated his sons in Lancastrian traditions of language, literature and music. He was an active spokesman for progressive reform in the old pueblo, and established a network of influential acqaintances, including Abel Stearns and Benjamin Wilson.[4]

Antonio Coronel stayed involved in civic affairs after California became a state in 1850. In the next two decades, he supported Hispanic land titles and his own claim to properties at Rancho Sierra de los Verdugos. In 1857, he traveled to Mexico and secured documents and political support for several Hispanic claims around the San Francisco area. Coronel also championed partisan views in a heavily Democratic area, challenging Lincoln's wartime policies as unfair and oppressive.[5] He supported community beautification projects, the horticultural and historical societies, a county museum, restoration of the San Carlos Mission, and became a charter member of the Historical Society of Southern California.[6]

Resident authority, local patron and political leader to the vanquished Indians of Anglo American conquest, Coronel had survived war and foreign settlement, even the bitter partisan divisions of the foreigner's Civil War. He emerged as a respected sage in a region with one foot still firmly planted in the Old World aristocracy and the other angling for a toehold in the rough-and-tumble new period of Yankee capitalism and urban expansion.

Conversely, Jackson was a relative newcomer to Native American issues, and consequently had not had as much impact as she would have liked with her academic writings on the plight of the Indians. Inspired by Harriet Beecher Stowe's fictional Uncle Tom's Cabin, she decided that fiction might be more compelling than fact. She was a New England resident who became interested in the Indian question when she traveled west in 1879. She researched several southwestern tribes and explored the failed government policy toward Native Americans, likening the native tribes' condition to African American slavery. According to writer Susan Coultrap-McQuin

"Until her fight for Indian rights she was not a rebel in the sense of wanting to change society"[7]

These two unlikely characters found commonality in spirit and goals. Jackson was the creative talent but lacked knowledge of the California Indians and was unfamiliar with the Southern California locale. Coronel was the expert she needed to bring credibility to her writing.

In 1881, Jackson had published *A Century of Dishonor*, a factual study highlighting government mistreatment of seven Indian tribes; their homeless state and poor living standards: the Delaware, Cheyenne, Nez Perce, Sioux, Ponca, Winnebagoe and Cherokee. Jackson hoped her work could influence legislation pending before Congress, and encourage the appointment of dedicated United States attorneys willing to protect Indian rights.[8]

A Century of Dishonor received favorable reviews although, as Rosemary Whitaker critically noted, it was "stylistically flawed, by hasty writing."[9] Still, a Presidential commission on Indian affairs issued a report that supported many of her claims, and *Century Magazine* commissioned her to write a series of articles on the Southern California Indians. Within months, Jackson was appointed Indian Agent of the Southern California region.

Jackson returned to Los Angeles and began research for a new government study dealing with the Native Americans. She visited several tribes and developed a working relationship with Coronel, Benjamin Wilson and the del Valle family. Coronel offered insights into the mission era, detailed the decline of the Church during the period of secularization, and recounted the eventual loss of Hispanic land grants after the conquest. He also supplied her with information regarding Junipero Serra and the Mission days, characterizing Serra as a "great man (to whom) it is owing that Spain should not lose this country."[10]

Jackson was impressed with Coronel's recall of Hispanic tradition and ceremony. As one observer noted, she became "as a little child in the society of the childlike, Catholic christian

Antonio Coronel

Coronel."[11] Jackson spent days at the Coronel home in western Los Angeles, listening to an animated Antonio Coronel detail sentimental tales about the rancho era, while his wife acted as hostess and interpreter.[12] He frequently played the guitar, sang ballads, and embellished yarns of Hispanic yesteryear, just as Alessandro charms Ramona with his violin and clear voice in a scene Jackson may have visualized from her encounters with the Coronels.[13]

Jackson was not the only vistor to the Coronel home who found the hospitality and setting intoxicating. At El Recreo, located at the northwest corner of Seventh and Alameda streets, one could stroll in the pleasant confines of vineyards and orange groves. Artist Henry Y. Sandham, commissioned by *Century Magazine* to sketch various California subjects, visited the Coronel residence and was inspired to draw a series of local scenes. "I often think of the happy time I had while your guest," effusively wrote the artist; "we are indebted to you for some of our best subjects."[14] Trips through the southern counties, visits with the local Indian tribes and wanderings about the countryside caught Jackson's imagination, providing the construct for the story of Alessandro and Ramona.

These two *compadres* traveled the Riverside-Hemet region, discussed the plight of the Indian, shared strategies about national Indian policy, and visited the missions and rancherias to capture the tone and setting necessary to Jackson's story. She fell in love with Coronel's descriptions of place and time, while he was equally enthralled with Jackson's passionate defense of Native Americans. "Don Antonio loved this brilliant woman," recalled one contemporary.[15]

Coronel directed Jackson to people and places during her stay in Southern California. Jackson visited with Andres Pico, traveled to the missions at San Fernando and Santa Barbara, and spent time at the Camulos ranch of the del Valles, a model for the Moreno home in Jackson's novel.[16] Along with fellow Indian agent Abbott Kinney, she traveled through the Santa Ysabel and Mesa Grande Indian reservations.[17] Coronel also arranged interviews with the San Luis Rey Indians near Temecula. Antonio acted as guide, tutor and mentor, providing leads and contacts to assist in her research.[18]

Mutual political interests cemented the relationship of these two reformers and helped the author develop an empathy for the historical period. After all, *Ramona* is about human passion, injustice and Native American rights. The dynamics between Jackson and Coronel created an underlying energy for the novel, which brought exigency to the Indians' plight.

They were fervent about their politics, fiercely loyal to their allies, and interested in finding practical reforms for national problems. They were activists, reformers, and partisans interested in promoting a political agenda. With that in mind,

Jackson and Coronel stepped up their efforts as the rapidly disappearing frontier threatened the extinction of Native Americans. In the years since the Civil War, Northern generals who had honed their tactics against the Confederacy easily translated them to removing the Native Americans. William Tecumseh Sherman continued to scorch the earth, and George Armstrong Custer, flamboyant to the end, tackled the proud Sioux nation to make the country safe for Anglo settlers, railroads and commerce. Thus, *Ramona* is a political document written with a sense of time running out, with an urgency and passion that reflects the ideological beliefs of both author and confidant. In 1883, Jackson finished her report and returned to her western residence in Colorado Springs. With the encouragement of her editor at *Century Magazine*, she made ambitious plans to write a novel based on her research and experiences. By fall, Jackson was back in New York and prepared to devote herself to a long winter of relatively uninterrupted writing. Working at a feverish pace, she completed *Ramona* in the spring of 1884.

Ramona was written when Americans sensed an end of a historic era: the passing of the Native American, when Custer's fate at Little Big Horn and the Sioux massacre at Wounded Knee acted as bookends to the period. Within a decade, historian Frederick Jackson Turner identified the closing of the frontier, signaling a time in American history when Western settlement had finally reached the natural limits of America's physical borders.

Coronel and Jackson agreed that public support was essential to protect Native American lands and rights. Coronel actively corresponded with various supporters of Native American rights, suggesting legislative strategy and tactics to influence national sentiment. "I hope we will succeed," wrote Indian Agent Charles C. Painter concerning Congressional lobbying efforts.[19] "As you know," Coronel asserted, "I am and have been for thirty years intimately and minutely acquainted with their condition, rights, troubles, and needs."[20]

Coronel and Jackson were ardent supporters of a legislative plan to establish a reservation system, recognizing Indian rights to autonomy and equal protection of land and personal liberties. Coronel felt that public support was essential in shaping national policy, a strategy Jackson embraced in her writings. Concerning a strategy for passing the Dawes Act, a Congressional bill to establish a reservation system, Coronel wrote that "it would be wise to have all of the particulars of our Indians laid before the house Committee and make a clean sweep of all the difficulties connected with the Mission Indian problem."[21]

Coronel's career provides insight into his passionate faith in public service, a belief anchored in his youthful ambitions. The teenage Coronel learned the importance of civic duty from his father, and in the next decade he held elected positions as judge, mission inspector and commissioner. After the Mexican-American war, Coronel continued an active public life, serving as mayor, county assessor and member of the city council. He acted as a singular voice for the Hispanic electorate, urging them to vote and participate in community affairs rather than withdraw into the isolated life of the barrio. He wholly supported the publication of all state laws into both Spanish and English. Coronel believed in the uses of power and participatory government, and his strong sense of moral conviction found expression in his view of public sevice. Politics, he once noted, was "a simple endeavor in good and evil, not unlike the simple precepts of the Catholic faith. Democracy was based on morality and religion."[22]

His early years in Southern California shaped Coronel's desire to redress the social injustices that had occurred during the American conquest. He had migrated to the area when Mexico wrested California from Spain, a period of time that saw the secularization of the missions. Ideally, the mission Indian

Some scholars believe that Helen Hunt Jackson based her fictious character on an Indian woman, Ramona Lubo, shown here at her home in Cahuilla.

labor force was supposed to receive the divided-up mission lands but in fact corrupt Mexican administrators gave themselves and their friends large grants of mission land, leaving the mission Indians destitute and dependent upon the new owners of the lands, who used them at best as serfs and at worse as virtual slaves, without the former mission padres to protect them. Later, when another turn of the conquest wheel saw California taken from Mexico by the United States, Coronel defended Hispanic rights during the 1850s and 1860s on two major fronts: in land title disputes and law-and-order anxieties which accelerated into vigilantism and violence against the Hispanic populace. Jackson, tutored by Coronel, was also critical of American rule (though largely silent on Hispanic exploitation of the Indians) as a destructive force affecting both Indians and Californians. She alludes to this cultural resentment in *Ramona*, suggesting that "taking possession of California was not only a conquering of Mexico, but a conquering of California as well; that the real bitterness of the surrender was not so much to the empire which gave up the country, as to the country itself which was given up."[23]

Coronel, a founder of the Historical Society of Southern California, appreciated the importance of history and the need to preserve and interpret the events of his era, individual occurrences that taken together would constitute the narrative of Southern California's past. He vividly recounted the first subdivision of the city, how certain locations were reserved for the plaza church (Lady of Angels), a central *plaza real* with the east side reserved for public buildings and chapel (popularly known today as Olvera Street and the Plaza in Los Angeles). He valued the symbolism of pomp and ceremony as historical metaphors, and so carefully recounted are the trappings of public events such as landmark dedications, parades highlighting past battles and church ceremonies mixing feast days with community events. "The cornerstone of the church in the plaza was laid with all solemnity," Coronel reverently recorded, "then a solemn mass was said by the minister of San Gabriel [and] for the solemnities of the day temporary shelter was erected."[24]

Given his firm belief that events represented larger themes, Coronel saw feast days and community gatherings as important factors that held the community together and infused the Hispanic flavor during the pueblo's years of transition. Coronel's accounts were "not faithful in the matter of dates," conceded one contemporary, but "they would be very worthy when they spoke of the ceremonies attending the founding of the pueblo."[25]

Coronel supported Mexico during the American conquest of California, bravely defending Southern California and participating in the battles at La Mesa and Paso de Bartolo, fighting on in the surrounding hillsides as the Americans occupied the land below. When the United States surrendered the flag at San Pedro in 1846, Coronel eagerly took responsibility for sending the trophy to Mexico. He did not surrender until 1848, when he finally was convinced that peace had been negotiated between the United States and Mexico (This may seem strange to modern readers used to the instantaneous transmission of information worldwide, but was not uncommon in the 19th-century. For example, the last Confederate general to surrender -the Cherokee leader Stand Watie- was not convinced of that war's conclusion for several months after Lee surrendered to Grant at Appomattox).[26]

The American conquest not only brought a political power change, but it also presented a new set of ideological challenges. Coronel's ambivalence about the merits of Yankee capitalism can be seen clearly in Jackson's characterization of Angus Phail, the Scottish merchant who gave the infant Ramona to his lover, Senōra Ortega. Phail's character embodies the disparate traits of various early Anglo pioneers such as Abel Stearns (frugal, prudent and measured capitalist) and, in contrast, the flamboyant, hard-drinking and animated Hugo Reid. Whether Coronel had these specific men in mind during his discussions with Jackson is unknown, but the image of Angus Phail certainly embodies both the noble and parsimonious qualities of the Yankee traders and settlers.[27]

Caught between two peoples, Coronel deftly shaped his role within the pueblo as an interpreter, in the broader cultural sense, for two very different peoples who did not fully understand or appreciate one another. This role rendered Coronel into a complex figure as he adapted to Anglo politics while retaining the Spanish language and Hispanic customs. Coronel supported Native American rights, yet remained loyal to a Democratic party that defended the enslavement of African Americans. He embraced Anglo friends and confidants, but attacked the capitalist ethic that had displaced the Hispanic ranchero. In Coronel's eyes, friendship was earned and not inherited. As one of his admirers recalled, Coronel "judges people by their personal qualities rather than by their nationality or by their political or religious creed."[28]

These paradoxical attitudes can best be explained by the

one constant in Coronel's life: a close identification with his Hispanic ancestry. He consciously tried to preserve the romance and lore of the pastoral era through his work with the Historical Society of Southern California. He acquired one of the most extensive collections of Native American and Hispanic art and his unique role as an authority and primary source for Jackson allowed him to present myth as reality, for Jackson was less a researcher than a willing vessel into which the charming Don Antonio could pour the romantic ambrosia of his vision of the rancho days. What emerged in Jackson's novel, therefore, was the image of the rancho period as an Eden spoiled by the wily advance of cunning Yankee opportunists.

Yet there is a powerful kernel of truth at the heart of the novel. Surely, Ramona's desperate circumstances parallel the plight of the California Indians (If not other Native Americans for whom the earliest European contacts were quite different and had different outcomes). The orphaned Ramona is told by Señora Moreno of her rootless origins and vague background, just as the Indian though originally taken into the missions by the Spanish padres, was abandoned when Mexico took California, evicted from the mission lands by the Mexican government's policy of secularization and left to be victimized first by the predatory rancheros and their cattle empire and later by Anglo settlement. The analogy is not lost in Ramona's flight from the Moreno household, and later, in the character of Alessandro through his experiences with Anglos. "They say the Americans drive the Indians away as if they were dogs. Do you think that can be so, Father, when we have always lived on them (the land)?" remarks Alessandro ruefully to an empathetic padre.[29]

Alessandro's comparison of aborigines to the lowest social class is important. Coronel's Angelenos, Hisanic and Anglo alike, associated Native Americans with crime, springing from the same impulse that led many a New World family to stress their "pure" Spanish blood and deny any Afro or Indio taint. As judge and mayor, Coronel was keenly aware of the community's concern over law and order. Most Angelenos felt that the depravity of the Native American led to public disorder, drunkenness and idleness. "Theft" and "Indian" were synonymous, an unfounded assumption ignoring the fact that the most notorious outlaws were Hispanic and Anglo, but which neverthless affects Ramona. The heroine is first subjected to the prejudice attached to her lowly status when she is confronted with the unhappy prospect of being labeled a common thief simply for taking her own horse when she elopes with Alessandro.

Coronel also witnessed the mistreatment of Native Americans under lynch law tactics. During the early 1850s, the Los Angeles *Star* proposed that a military garrison be established to insure the protection of the county against Indian raids. The paper further hinted that in "the absence of an efficient police, our citizens must take measures to protect their property."[30] Advocates of such measures, of course, never fully spelled out what should be done when and to whom, but several Native Americans became the victims of unsolved murders. In February 1852, two Indians were found dead at a construction site. The Los Angeles *Star* noted that "all inquiries were unsuccessful in ascertaining the perpetrators of the murder."[31] At Mission Viejo in August of 1852, an Indian child was kidnapped while the parents attended a local festival and later was found drowned in a pond with "its throat cut."[31] Two months later the Tulare Indians presented a complaint to the Indian agent, stating that their white neighbors had encroached upon their grounds and had stolen "several of their children."[33] Under such conditions, it is not stretching fact too much to suggest that Alessandro would be shot on sight, a common occurrence for that period even though the novel shocked the more naive among its readership.

The subordinate characters in *Ramona* seem created to represent larger class and ethnic tensions. Ramona is raised by a reluctant foster parent, Señora Moreno. The matronly overseer of a large estate, she has a complex demeanor: aristocratic, devout, recalcitrant, but loyal to her familial obligations. She is a women of dramatic virtues and faults. The señora dutifully agrees to raise Ramona out of loyalty to her dying sister, Señora Ortega. The heroine is raised in a sequestered atmosphere, an idyllic but isolated lifestyle, situated on a sprawling Southern California rancho under the tutelage of her adopted Hispanic family. As an Indian, however, she is never completely accepted by the señora as a full member of the Moreno family.

The division between the Native Americans and Hispanics is also underscored in subordinate characters in the novel. Felipe, a foster brother, embodied the civilized manners of a privileged society. He is forthright, dedicated and hard-working, yet all his education and breeding pale in comparison to the raw courage possessed by Alessandro. The innate virtues of the "noble savage" stand in sharp contrast to the refinement of European colonization, in the Rousseauean context still fashionable in that time. Just as Rhett Butler remarked "that a reputation is something someone with courage can live without," Alessandro has strong convictions, virtue without social status: "Alessandro would not lie; Felipe might."[34]

Jackson also uses religious symbolism to enhance her story and dramatize the church's influence in Mexican Southern California. Father Salvierderra, a compassionate Franciscan padre, captures the mythic grace and dignity of the mission period. From the Hispanic point of view, the Church was a benevolent defender of and parent to the California Indians, just as the old padre assumes the role of confidant and mentor to Señora Moreno, Felipe, Alessandro and Ramona. He patiently listens to Alessandro discuss the loss of his land, instructs Felipe on the saintly heroes of the past and becomes the humble confessor for the señora in her most vulnerable moments. He represents the conscience of the novel, a catalyst enabling others to search their souls, reflect and estimate the gravity of their sins against those who have sinned against them. Father

Antonio and Mariana Coronel

Salvierderra symbolizes the underlying religious tenets of the era: penance and prayer. The Franciscan padre has the benevolence associated with the persona of Junipero Serra and Juan Crespi of an earlier era. The old padre "was a Franciscan, one of the few now left in the country; so revered and beloved by all who had come under his influence."[35]

The guiding spirit of Father Salvierderra is probably also

intended to incorporate, along with the Church, Coronel himself. Those among the Gabrieleños who came and stayed, loved Don Antonio as a protector and mentor. He was the natives' "padre," and his wife, Doña Mariana, was "little less than a saint" in their eyes.[36] So too, the good priest was the soul of Ramona, the man for whom she mourned even while her son was being baptized, and the omnipotent figure of wisdom and counsel in the waning years of the rancho era.

Ramona also subtly addressed gender, focusing on Native American women as victims of circumstance. Ramona's birth was the product of a Yankee-Native American relationship, briefly outlined in the novel. The heroine vainly searches for an identity while controlled by an overbearing foster mother. She is socially displaced by racial prejudice and further isolated by a persecuted, half-crazed husband.

Ramona typified the plight of many Native American women, her story a familiar scenario to Coronel and other reformers, and the perpetrators of outrages against the Native American women were as likely to be Hispanic or Indian as Anglo: gender, in that era, transcended race. "There is no portion of the poverty-stricken women of our large cities so degraded as Indian women," asserted one activist.[37] During the early 1850s, Indian women were exposed to cruelty and domestic violence, often without adequate due process in court. One Native American, Josefa, refused a proposition and was then attacked and beaten with a club. The court found the defendant guilty and fined him one dollar.[38] Another Indian woman, Rosa, was nearly drowned by her attacker. One witness provided startling testimony, stating that "I heard the woman, Rosa, crying out and when looking up I saw Fernando Vacquites have Rosa in the water." The witness claimed that Vacquites had "his hand in her hair and was hitting her in the ribs and cursing her. Afterwards I saw him knock her down with his fist and then punch her with a stick about 18 inches long and 2 inches thick." The defendant Fernando Vacquites, admitted that "it is all true that the witnesses have said with the exception of striking with the stick." The court dismissed the case and had Vacquites pay the court costs.[39]

Jackson's sentimental view of history, largely dominated by Don Antonio's views, is tied to the environment, as a land spoiled by Western settlement. Many scenes from *Ramona* create interesting contrasts in mood and tone. There are the austere settings at Temecula, the sprawling Moreno Rancho, and the imposing San Jacinto Mountains; all picturesque scenes of a land seemingly undisturbed by the advance of civilization. Each locale, however, is compromised by the fateful events that befall Ramona and Alessandro. A somber pall envelops the Moreno home after Ramona's departure and until the senōra's death; Temecula becomes a threatening land with the eviction of Alessandro's people and the majestic, expansive San Jacinto Mountains, instead of a sanctuary, turn the young couple into fugitives on a frantic race against the white man's advance.

Images of a hostile landscape are directly linked to the declining fortunes of Ramona and Alessandro and, in turn, a disappearing wilderness coincided with the vanishing of the Native Americans. Western settlement, with its railroads, wagon wheels, mining camps and commercial centers, had displaced the serenity of cottonwoods, chaparral and grapevines. Exploitation of people led to the exploitation of land, an underlying argument behind the environmental decline, and a defining point of the vanishing frontier. As historian Will Jacobs remarked, "this assault on the land was closely tied to dispossession of Indian people."[40] And so, Alessandro cries out as he discovers Ramona looking towards San Pasqual as they flee toward what little wilderness is left, "Do not look back! It is gone!"[41]

On her travels through Southern California, Jackson probably picked up individual incidents to weave into the story of *Ramona*. Alessandro's murder, for example, may be based on the circumstances of an Indian named Juan Diego. In 1883, Diego was shot by an Anglo resident, Sam Temple, followed by a trial reportedly held at San Jacinto. Judge S.V. Tripp found Temple innocent, ruling that the killing was justifiable homicide. Tripp also ruled that no crime was committed because no one had appeared in court to present a prosecution.[42]

A few contemporaries claimed credit for the story and have even been considered as the basis for characters used in the novel. Early Ramona Pageant promotional literature claimed that Mr. & Mrs. J.C. Jordan, hosts of Jackson during her visit to San Jacinto Valley, first told the novelist of the Juan Diego case. "Mrs. Jackson wrote *Ramona* on the information she got from me," asserted Mrs. Jordan.[43] "These two became the Jeff Hyer and Aunt Ri of the book," claimed one account.[44] Mrs. Cinciona Norte, a longtime Indian resident had a version of the Juan Diego account, as did Dr. H.G. Hewitt, a member of a pioneer San Jacinto family. Still, others say that Ysabel del Valle, whose hacienda extended its hospitality to Mrs. Jackson, inspired the character of Señora Moreno.[45]

The extent of Coronel's role in providing Jackson with the Temple-Diego story is difficult to determine. It is also problematic as to whether *Ramona* herself was real or imagined. What is significant is that the author's objective was not to retell history but to provide insight and inspire interest for the Indian's plight among her generation. Jackson crystalized the deplorable condition of Native Americans in general, rather than focusing on the wrongful murder of only one Indian. Coronel's guidance affected the research behind Jackson's work by supplying his picture of Southern Californina against which backdrop the author could tell a story of larger context, the Native American issues.

Just as Coronel molded Jackson's research, the most influential figure in *Ramona* has no lines or scenes: the spectre of Señor Moreno melds the novel's relationships. The fatherly don is the silent overseer evident at the beginning and end of the story, his rancho the idyllic environ that nurtures Ramona to adulthood, while his roots in Mexico City become the sanctuary where Ramona can finally begin a new life with Felipe.

Helen Hunt Jackson may have patterned the Moreno figure after Don Antonio's father, Ignacio, the Coronel family's guiding spirit and the influential force behind his son's years of civic participation. Duty, honor and military service were worn as badges of familial loyalty in Mexican California. The characters in *Ramona* represent the romance of an era gone by, and the virtues of an agrarian people that are inevitably lost amidst the advance of Yankee settlement. Though Ramona eventually finds a safe haven in Mexico, she never escapes her identity, and those "undying memories stood like sentinels in her breast."[46]

So too, Southern California has never lost the Native American and Hispanic legacies. In architecture, namesakes and in the diverse ethnic composition of our communities, a tapastry woven of many cultures overlays the landscape, reminding Southern Californians of their richly variegated heritage. The spirit of *Ramona* is alive and well in the sprawling pueblo we call home today.

Conclusion

This compendium of pioneers who came west in their youth illustrates the fervor with which they embraced Southern California and invested their skills and talents to build a settlement. Some of these migrants filled a variety of leadership positions -boosters, civic leaders, law enforcement officials- while other settlers took on those ordinary but essential roles such as raising families, working as day laborers, operating small businesses and otherwise providing the basic building blocks of true community. The less fortunate came west as slaves, were dismissed as savages, or lost their land through an unfamiliar legal system. For them, Anglo American settlement meant the passing of Native American tribes first disrupted by the Spanish missions, then impoverished by the ranchero elites who took the mission lands for their own at the time of secularization and in turn were dispossessed in the alien business and legal practices of the Yankee. Their lives on various points of the conquest cycle mirrored frontier tensions over problems of acculturation, law and order, commercial growth and sectionalism.

Each of these migrants personally identified in some way with the Southern California frontier, which led them on an uncharted course into a new land where their dreams materialized through the creation of new communities and settlements. They were, simply stated, colorful individuals who lived in a unique and exciting time in Southern California's past.

Abel Stearns became one of the wealthiest men in Southern

California, acquiring vast tracts of land from the San Gabriel foothills to the Pacific coastline. "Old Horseface" was a Republican, antislavery proponent, loyal Unionist, and defender of the ranchero against unscrupulous bankers and financiers. His sprawling estate, *Rancho Los Alamitos*, vulnerable to poor economic times, forced him, like so many other Anglo and Hispanic landowners, to liquidate his vast holdings after the Civil War. The subdivision of these huge ranches led to future urban development through the creation of housing tracts, commercial districts and new roads to support an expanding populace. When Stearns died in 1871, Los Angeles had tripled in size, and the Southern Pacific Railroad was about to connect Southern California with the Midwest, opening the Far West to new markets, more immigrants and the multiplicity of industries that sprang up during the late 19th-century's Industrial Revolution.

Although Hugo Reid died before a reservation system could be organized, his writings focused on the Native Americans' needs and inspired Benjamin Wilson (the first Indian Agent in Southern California), Helen Hunt Jackson and others to press for continued reforms in United States Indian policy. One contemporary summed up the nature of Reid, recalling that he "was a native of Scotland, of great intelligence, and always held in high esteem."[1]

Margaret (Hereford) Wilson survived her second husband, Benjamin, and lived to see two daughters marry into prominent Southern California families: the de Shorb and Patton clans. She also witnessed the radical transformation of the frontier she'd known as a young wife, an economic depression, two land booms, the introduction of electricity, growth of the citrus industry and the creation of a major college (University of Southern California). Margaret Wilson died in 1898. Wilson family biographer Midge Sherwood observed that Los Angeles "was in a hurry not only to replace the old, crumbling adobes with modern buildings and blocks, but to establish itself on a

parallel, if not non-pareil, with American cities in the East."[2]
The present-day Huntington Art Gallery at San Marino stands
on a portion of the Wilson estate.

Joseph Lancaster Brent commanded a steamboat expedition
along the Mississippi River, captured a Union ironclad and participated in the negotiations over the Confederate surrender of
New Orleans. Family considerations kept him from returning
to Southern California. He practiced law at Baltimore with his
brother, Robert; married a Southerner, Rossella Kenner; and
operated a sugar plantation on his father-in-law's estate in
Louisiana. Brent later returned to Baltimore and became general counsel to the Baltimore & Ohio Railroad and was active in
various state societies until his death in 1905. His Southern
California friends missed his wit, charm and energy, and they
often tried to cajole him into returning to the West. Margaret
Wilson wrote that "the first question we ask when Mr. Wilson
receives a letter from you (Brent), is when is Mr. Brent coming
to California? We still cling to the hope that you will return and
keep awaiting you all the time."[3]

There are no narrative records on the lives of Judah and
John Evertson following the 1850 court case, which leaves their
fates open to speculation. Evertson may have migrated to the
slave states at the opening of the Civil War, or remained in
Southern California and militated for the Confederate cause.
African Americans like Judah would continue the struggle for
legal equality. In mid-19th century America, however, the
Judah may well have found new freedom, some dignity, and a
fresh start in the Far West.

Horace Bell lived to be 88 years of age, dying in 1918. He
was opinionated, controversial and a staunch reformer during
his advanced years. He criticized local officials for ignoring
inadequate services in law enforcement and fire protection, and
he wanted all gaming halls closed, corrupt politicians ousted
and civic virtue restored to a changing urban landscape. Bell
fought with his daughters, discouraged them from marrying,

and even chased away suitors when they called at the Bell residence. His biographer, James Harrison, recalled that Bell had "witnessed the coming of the Iron Horse, the piping of melted snows from the High Sierras to water a thirsty land, and the migration of a half-million homeseekers to his loved town."[4]

Benjamin Hayes, like many Civil War Democrats, lost his judgeship in 1864, marking the end of his 12-year career in public service. In 1866, Hayes married into a Californio family, and he and the former Doña Adeleida Serrano had one daughter. They briefly lived in San Diego, then returned to Hayes' beloved residence at the Lafayette Hotel in Los Angeles. At 62, he co-authored with J.J. Warner and J.P. Widney a brief history of Southern California and died shortly after the completion of the book in 1877.

The Los Angeles *Star* never regained the prominence it held before the Civil War. Henry Hamilton repurchased the failing press after the war, revived the paper's circulation, then resold the operation within a year. Perhaps the war's conclusion sapped his interest in politics and controversies. In any case, Hamilton remained active in local affairs, serving as Justice of the Peace for the Mission San Gabriel and as a director for the San Gabriel Water Company. He bought a lemon and orange grove near the San Gabriel Mission, becoming a respected citrus grower in the valley. His estate, as one contemporary observed, was a "place of beauty which Shenstone may have envied."[5] Hamilton died of asthma at the Alhambra Hotel in 1891.

Edward John Cage Kewen, unabashed by the Confederacy's military defeat, remained an ambitious and loyal Democrat. Returning to the political arena, he unsuccessfully ran for a Congressional seat from the southern district, then returned to private law practice in the 1870s. Kewen suffered financial difficulties during the nationwide depression of the 1870s. Hoping to stave off ruin, he liquidated his property at *El Molino Viejo*, later restored by the City of San Marino in the 1970s. Kewen died in 1879 following a sudden illness. His funeral took place on Thanksgiving Day at St. Athanasius Church. The ceremony was attended by many of Kewen's political allies and legal associates. One account recalled that it was a solemn occasion for "one who had for so long a time filled a prominent place in the social and political circles of this state."[6]

When the Los Angeles *Times* obituary was written for Charles Louis Ducommun, the paper also reported on an upcoming mass meeting of suffragists at the downtown music hall, a county convention for the temperance movement at the Baptist Church, and the Free Harbor Fight that pitted Stephen Mallory White against the power and influence of the Southern Pacific Railroad. Ducommun saw Los Angeles evolve from a pueblo to a Western town then into a progressive city, propelling Southern California into the 20th-century and ushering in a new era of civic reform. Ducommun, active in his business until a few days before his death, died in 1896 at 75 years of age. He passed away at the end of Holy Week, and next to his Los Angeles *Times* obituary appeared an Easter Sunday poem written by Julia Ward Howe. Speaking as much in spirit to the determined character and forthright nature of a religious man who worked until the day he died, one stanza appropriately read:

> And Thou, consigned to lonely tomb,
> Come forth in Easter's radiant bloom!
> In robes of glory walk the earth,
> Lead Nature to a nobler birth![7]

Helen Hunt Jackson continued to correspond with Antonio Coronel after leaving Southern California in 1883. Coronel edited drafts of *Ramona*, offering suggestions on local detail and proofreading for historical accuracy. The elderly don had provided Jackson with the "proper coloring" for her novel, but she wanted more. Jackson had decided to write a sequel to *Ramona*, hoping Coronel would recount "some romantic story or legend of the older time here."[8] She queried him about the customs of the Temecula tribes, the history of Mexican California, topography and other details about the locale. Sadly, there would be no sequel to *Ramona*. Writing, traveling, and lobbying for Native American rights had physically drained Jackson, leaving her exhausted by the end of 1884. Stubbornly ignoring her need to rest, she persevered with her projects, lamenting "the irreparable loss of time" caused by illness. Her health further deteriorated while she was visiting San Francisco during the spring of 1885, leaving her bedridden. She could sit up for only 30 minutes at a time, tersely conceding in a letter to Antonio Coronel that she "can do nothing" regarding her sequel to *Ramona*.[9] Jackson died later that year at the zenith of her popularity. As one epitaph read, "How she loved us! It was for that she was so dear! These are the only words' that I shall mile to hear."[10]

Antonio Coronel lived for a decade after the publication of *Ramona*, tirelessly promoting civic improvements that highlighted the Spanish-speaking traditions of the rancho period and frontier era. He donated his personal art collection and manuscripts to the Los Angeles Chamber of Commerce, promoted community efforts to build a library, highlighted historic landmarks in the region, and organized festivities memorializing the Mexican traditions of bygone days. Coronel was an elder statesman in the locale and a 60-year resident of California when he died in 1894. Gracious to the end, his altruism and generosity were matched only by his keen memory of historical events. One contemporary believed that Coronel's importance would stand the test of time, just as the rancho traditions of yesteryear had endured, and he (Coronel) would "become more and more a striking figure in the annals of the times in which he lived."[11]

Meanwhile, it can be said that Ramona and Allesandro are alive and well, together in spirit, dwelling in the hearts of Southern Californians, and living happily somewhere in the foothills surrounding Temecula.

Notes

ABBREVIATIONS

BL– Bancroft Library, University of California, Berkeley

HEH – Henry E. Huntington Library, San Mariono, CA

SCWH– Seaver Center for Western History, Los Angeles County Museum

INTRODUCTION

[1] Jackson K. Putnam, "The Turner Thesis And The Westward Movement: A Reappraisal," *Western Historical Quarterly* 7 (October 1976): 398, 402.

[2] Ivan Doig review of Wallace Stegner, *Where the Blue Bird Sings to the Lemonade Springs*, Los Angeles *Times*, Book Review Section (12 April 1992): 2.

CHAPTER ONE

[1] Cursory updates on the theme of wealth and success in Stearns' life are noted in Kevin Starr, *Inventing the Dream, California Through the Progressive Era* (Oxford University Press, 1985), 17-19; and W.W. Robinson, *Los Angeles from the Days of the Pueblo, A Brief History and Guide to the Plaza Area*, revised with an introduction by Doyce B. Nunis, Jr. (Los Angeles: California Historical Society, 1959, 1981), 83-85.

The best biographical works on Stearns' life are Doris Marion Wright, *A Yankee in Mexican California, Abel Stearns 1798-1848* (Santa Barbara: Wallace Hebbard, 1977), Pearl Pauline Stamps, "Abel Stearns: California Pioneer," *Grizzly Bear* 39 (May 1926): 1-2, 4, 12; (June 1926): 54, 59; (July 1926): 4, 52-53, 61-62; (August 1926): 8, 57, and John Cushing Hough, "Abel Stearns, 1848-1871," Ph.D. dissertation, University of California at Los Angeles, 1961. Also see Woolsey, "A Capitalist in a Foreign Land: Abel Stearns in Southern California Before the Conquest," *Southern California Quarterly* 75 (Summer 1993): 101-118.

[2] Alpheus Basil Thompson to Abel Stearns, 22 September 1831, California Historical Documents Collection, Box 1, Huntington E. Huntington Library, San Marino, CA.

[3] Robert Glass Cleland, *Cattle on a Thousand Hills* (San Marino: Huntington Library, 1941), 44.

⁴Alexander Forbes to Abel Stearns, 18 April 1831, Stearns Collection, SG Box 27, HEH.

⁵Stearns to Jefe politico de la Alta California 31 August 1831 in Papelas viejos, Jefes politicos, 1831-1833, Bancroft Library, University of California, Berkeley; also, see Wright, *A Yankee in Mexican California*, 23. Actually, Stearns' antagonisms with the Mexican government represented a larger suspicion between officials and foreigners. Jedediah Smith encountered similar resistance during his travels to Southern California, and Smith's lack of forthright intentions may have set the stage for the problems Stearns and other emigrants encountered. On Smith, see David J. Weber, *The Californios versus Jedediah Smith 1826-1827, A New Cache of Documents* (Spokane, Washington: Arthur H. Clark Co., 1990).

⁶Oliver Vickery, *Harbor Heritage, Tales of the Harbor Area of Los Angeles, California* (Mountain View, CA: Morgan Press, 1979), 7-10. For an overview of the harbor's early history, see J.M. Guinn, "Historic Seaports of Los Angeles," *San Pedro Historical Society Shoreline* 8 (February 1981): 7-10.

⁷Stearns, "Road Improvements at San Pedro," SG Box 61, HEH. As early as December of 1832, Stearns had become involved in transactions of hides at San Pedro. See, Stearns Collection, Box 81. On development of the San Pedro warehouse, see Jose Antonio Ezequiel Carillo and Abel Stearns, "Permit to construct warehouse," 8 March 1834 Stearns to Jose Figueroa, 8 April 1834 (petition of water rights), and Tomas Estenaga and Jose Perez, Deed transfer of Mission warehouse to Stearns, 23 August 1834, Box 81, HEH.

⁸Stearns' relationship with other Yankee merchants predates his move to Southern California. Numbered among his acquaintances were Thomas Larkin, William Dana, and Nathan Spear. See the Stearns Collection, Box 61, and California Historical Collections, Box 1, HEH for various correspondences. On trade along the coast, see Paul W. Gates, "The Land Business of Thomas O. Larkin," *California Historical Society Quarterly* 54 (Winter 1975): 323-344, Sherwood D. Burgess, "Lumbering in Hispanic California," *California Historical Society Quarterly* 41 (September 1962):237-248, and David Lavender, *California: Land of New Beginning* (New York: Harper & Row, 1972), 65-94. A fine biographical look at several of Stearns' contemporaries is Charles B. Churchill, *Adventurers and Prophets, American Autobiographers in Mexican California 1828-1847* (Spokane, WA: Arthur H. Clark Co., 1995), and a recent bibliographical update in Richard B. Rice, William A. Bullough, and Richard J. Orsi, *The Elusive Eden: A New History of California* (New York: Alfred A. Knopf, 1988), 152-153.

⁹Stearns, "Road Improvements at San Pedro," SG Box 61, HEH.

[10]William Heath Davis, *Seventy-Five Years in California, A History of Events and Life in California: Personal, Political and Military* (San Francisco: John Howell, 1889, 1967), 168.

[11] Stearns to Frederick G. Becher, 25 December 1837, SG Box 61, HEH.

[12] The familiar problem of poor weather contributed to the decline of the local economy in the early 1840s. Stearns to Pierce & Brewer, 5 July 1841, SG Box 62, HEH. Also see Wright, *A Yankee in Mexican California*, 98. Comparative figures compiled from Stearns' accounts. Day Books 1840, 1843-1844, SG Boxes 72 & 73, HEH.

[13] Comparative figures compiled from Stearns' accounts. Day Books 1840, 1843-1844, SG Boxes 72 & 73, HEH.

[14] Abel Stearns to Levi Stearns, 23 February 1837, SG Box 61, HEH.

[15] David Waldo to John Rowland, 10 August 1840, Box 1, HEH.

[16] William Keith to Stearns, 27 February 1844, Box 1, HEH.

[17] Thomas O. Larkin, "List of Foreigners Compiled for 1840," (San Francisco, 1856), longhand, HM47356, HEH. Admittedly, the records for this period are incomplete. Larkin counts 23 settlers at Los Angeles. J.J. Warner substantiates these numbers in principle. He estimated that 21 Americans resided at the pueblo based on the Padrones of 1836. Col. J.J. Warner, Judge Benjamin Hayes, Dr. J.P. Widney, *An Historical Sketch of Los Angeles County California* (Los Angeles: O.W. Smith, 1876, 1936), 35-36.

[18] Although incomplete, the Day Books provide insight into the economic trends of Stearns' business. The retail sale receipts between January-June, 1840 totaled $8,601, averaging nearly $1,500 per month. Those figures are reasonably constant compared to the wide variations in hides traded. Day Book (1840), SG Box 72, HEH.

[19] Howard J. Nelson, "The Two Pueblos of Los Angeles: Agricultural Village and Embryo Town," *Southern California Quarterly* 59 (Spring 1977): 9. By 1840, American settlers had become equally involved in commercial interests as compared to agricultural ventures. Accordingly, professions among the Anglo populace totaled 6 merchants, 3 shippers, 2 carpenters, 4 ranchers, and 4 vineyard growers. See Larkin, "List of Foreigners," HEH.

[20] Stearns embodied capitalist instincts that underscored the early Yankee migrants. For a discussion of the larger context of the far western migration see, Arrell Morgan Gibson, *Yankees in Paradise: The Pacific Basin* (Albuquerque: University of New Mexico Press, 1993), William G. Robbins, "Western History: A Dialectic on the Modern Condition," *Western Historical Quarterly* 20 (Nov. 1989):430-432. On related aspects of materialism and the work ethic as central to pioneer life, see W.H. Hutchinson, "Westward: The Vision and the Purpose," *The Pacific Historian* 27 (Summer 1983): 22-30.

[21] Stearns to Larkin, 5 September 1840, SG Box 61, HEH.

[22] Stearns to Becher, 25 December 1837, SG Box 61, HEH.

23 Stearns to Ferdinand Deppe, 27 September 1833, SG Box 61, HEH.

24 Stearns to John Forster, 12 August 1844, SG Box 61, HEH.

25 Forster to Stearns, 12 August 1844, SG Box 29, HEH.

26 Ray Allen Billington, *The Frontier and American Culture* (San Marino: California Library Association, 1965), 8.

27 Stearns to Larkin, 13 May 1845, SG Box 61, HEH.

28 Stearns often acted as intermediary between Latin rancheros and Anglos. For example, see Joseph Walker to Stearns, 7 April 1841, SG Box 61, Paul Anderson to Stearns, 5 March 1834, Anderson to William Wolfskill c/o Abel Stearns, 5 March 1834, and James Johnson to Stearns, 11 October 1833, Box 1, HEH. Stearns was representative of many Yankee merchants who acted as middlemen. See David J. Langum, *Law and Community on the Mexican California Frontier, Anglo-American Expatriates and the Clash of Legal Traditions, 1821-1846*(Norman: University of Oklahoma Press, 1987), 18.

29 Davis, *Seventy-Five Years in California*, 37.

30 Alfred Robinson, *Life in California, and Friar Geronimo Boscana, Chinigchinich*, with an introduction by Andrew Rolle (Santa Barbara: Peregrine Publishers, Inc., 1970), 186-187.

31 Intermarriage was common to the period and throughout the Mexican Southwest. For a general comment, see David Montejano, *Anglos and Mexicans in the Making of Texas, 1836-1986* (Austin: University of Texas Press, 1987), 34-37, and Harlan Hague and David J. Langum, *Thomas O. Larkin, A life of Patriotism and Profit in Old California* (Norman: University of Oklahoma Press, 1990), 7.

32 Davis, *Seventy-Five Years in California*, 25, 322.

33 Wright, *A Yankee in Mexican California,* 92-97.

34 Certainly, the Bandini marriage was instrumental in Stearns' ventures into ranching. Nevertheless, Don Abel had begun inquiries into rancho Los Alamitos prior to his marriage, suggesting an interest along those lines before his inclusion into the Californio elite. Stearns to Jose Antonio Aguirre, 9 April 1840, SG Box 61, HEH. Stearns was also part of a larger statewide trend in the acceleration of land grants by the Mexican government during the 1840s. See Gloria Ricci Lothrop, "Rancheras and the Land: Women and Property Rights in Hispanic California," *Southern California Quarterly* 76 (Spring 1994): 61-62.

35 Wright, *A Yankee in Mexican California*, 98-110.

36 Horace Bell, *On the Old West Coast: Being Further Reminiscences of a Ranger*, ed. by Lanier Bartlett (New York: Grosset & Dunlap, (1930),255. Conversely, one argument maintains the upper class Californio was willing to intermarry in order "to disassociate itself from the poorer and darker complexioned groups in the territory." See Gloria E. Miranda, "Racial and Cultural Dimensions of Gente de Razon Status in Spanish and Mexican California," *Southern California*

Quarterly 60 (Fall 1988): 273.

[37] Stearns, "Application for Church Dispensation," 29 April 1839, SG Box 61, HEH.

[38] Stearns to Marcelin Giraudeau, 24 August 1839, SG Box 30, HEH.

[39] Stearns to John Wilson, 22 July 1836, SG Box 61, HEH.

[40] Forster to Stearns, 19 November 1837, SG Box 29, HEH.

[41] Marsh to Stearns, 27 March 1837, Box 1, HEH; Wright, A *Yankee in Mexican California,* 49-64.

[42] Robinson, *Life in California,* 69. Recent works on the destructive nature of secularization include Nicholas Beck, "The Vanishing Californians: The Education of Indians in the Nineteenth Century," *Southern California Quarterly* 69 (Spring 1987): 33-50, Robert F. Heizer and Alan F. Almquist, *The Other Californians: Prejudice and Discrimination Under Spain, Mexico, and the United States to 1920* (Los Angeles: University of California Press, 1971), Clement W. Meighan, "Indians and California Missions," *Southern California Quarterly* 69 (Fall, 1987): 187-202, and W.W. Robinson, "The Indians of Los Angeles and What Became of Them," *Historical Society of Southern California Quarterly* 17 (December 1938): 156-172.

[43] John R. Brumgardt and William David Putney, "San Salvador: New Mexican Settlement in Alta California," *Southern California Quarterly* 59 (Winter 1977): 353.

[44] Los Angeles, Criminal Cases, "Versus Antonio for wounding Francisco Sepulveda, administrator of San Juan Capistrano Mission," (1837), versus Torquato, Julian, and Raymond for disorder at San Juan Capistrano Mission," (1839), and versus Torquato for theft at the Los Angeles Church," (1842), Archives, 7 vols., 1836-1845 Seaver Center for Western History Research, Los Angeles 1: 378, 711, 1009; 6: 604.

[45] Robinson, *Life in California,* 69.

[46] Statistics can be drawn from the criminal cases at the Seaver Center and the California Historical Documents at the Huntington Library. Court records at both repositories indicate an increase in criminal activity in the 1840s, although the rate of increase does not reflect alarming proportions in terms of the total number of cases. The number of criminal cases for the 1836-1845 period are as follows: (4) 1836; (9) 1837; (3) 1838; (15) 1839; (12) 1840; (22) 1841; (24) 1842; (17) 1843; (16) 1844; (20) 1845. Total cases: 142; Indian related cases total 38. Thus, the trend of aberrant occurrences is steadily upward. See Criminal Cases, 7 vols., (1836-1845), and California Courts, Court of the First Instance, "Index to Criminal Cases," (1830-1846), in Stearns to Benjamin Davis Wilson, 5 July 1850, Box 1 (Spanish), HEH.

[47] Nelson, "Two Pueblos," 7-8.

[48] Versus William Day, testimony (1835), SG Box 61, HEH. Day was upset with the purchase of sour wine from Stearns'store, a common

problem of that era. In fact, Stearns had remarked on the poor quality of Southern California wines to Larkin, 25 March 1834, SG Box 61, HEH. However, he felt Day had every opportunity to refuse purchase at the time of sale. Day demanded a refund. Sadly, their disagreement degenerated into a clash of personalities that led to violence. For details, see Wright, *A Yankee in Mexican California*, 68-70.

[49] On Mexico's fading military presence in the Southwest, see David J. Weber, *The Mexican Frontier 1821-1846, The American Southwest Under Mexico* (Albuquerque: University of New Mexico Press, 1982), 107-121.

[50] Case summaries can be found in Criminal Cases, 1: 274-302, 810-837; 2: 832-866; 3: 767-790; 4: 149-224; 5:827-949; 6: 397-423, 672- 695. Also, see "Index to Criminal Cases (1830-1846), Nos. 7, 18, 33, 52, 64, 90, 112, SCWH.

[51] It is important to note that government intervention may not have occurred because criminal activity was not perceived as excessive. The increases, nevertheless, occurred within the context of Mexico permitting considerable regional autonomy which facilitated political volatility. See Weber, *The Mexican Frontier*, 20-29. In addition, these political revolts represented power struggles among the elite, common to 19th-century Mexican politics. See George Tays, "Revolutionary California: The Political History of California During the Mexican Period 1822-1846," Ph.D. dissertation, University of California, Berkeley, 1955.

[52] James Johnson, Rafael Guirado, Jose Antonio Carrillo, Vicente Antonio Maria Osio, Jose Perez, and Francisco Pantoja to Abel Stearns, 27 June 1833, Stearns Collection, HEH; On Stearns' prominence in local matters, see Wright, *A Yankee in Mexican California,* 65-75.

[53] In 1836, a vigilante committee hanged a couple for the murder of the woman's husband. Stearns, then a member of the Ayuntamiento, objected to the execution. Ibid., 65-75.

[54] Robert Elwell to Abel Stearns, 1 June 1837, Box 1, HEH.

[55] David Waldo to John Rowland, 1 May 1841, HEH.

[56] Anglo expatriates did not adapt to the Mexican California legal system. Their frustrations reflected conflicts in values between a homogeneous California society and the pluralistic views of Anglo emigrants. See Langum, *Law and Community*, 268-277.

[57] Stearns to Juan Bautista Rogers Cooper, 26 January 1830, SG Box 61, HEH.

[58] Stearns to Levi Stearns 23 February 1837, SG Box 61, HEH. Many of Stearns' acquaintances were exasperated with the political instability and encouraged independence or annexation. See Robert Elwell to Stearns, 1 June 1837, John Marsh to Stearns, 27 March 1837, and David Waldo to John Rowland, 1 May 1841, Box 1, HEH. Thomas Larkin also expressed similar feelings after the brief American occupation during the Thomas C. Jones affair in 1842. See Thomas O.

Larkin, *The Affair at Monterey, October 20 & 21, 1842,* with an introduction by Doyce B. Nunis, Jr. (Los Angeles: The Zamorano Club,
1964), 6,9.

[59] Stearns to Larkin, 14 May 1846, SG Box 62, HEH.

[60] Hague and Langum, *Larkin,* 146-148.

[61] Larkin would also express ambivalent feeling about the conquest.
Although he eventually accepted the invasion as inevitable, Larkin still
felt the conquest would bring dire economic consequences to the
region. See Hangue and Langum, *Larkin,* 159, and Langum, *Law and
Community,* 277. The Larkin correspondence with Stearns during the
March to July 1846 period can be found in John A. Hawgood ed., *First
and Last Consul, Thomas Oliver Larkin and the Americanization of
California* (San Marino, CA: Huntington Library, 1962), 53, 58-62, 67-
69, 72-73, 76-77.

[62] Benjamin Davis Wilson, "Reflections," 1853 notes, Benjamin Davis
Wilson Collection, Box 3, HEH.

[63] Stearns to Larkin, 12 June 1846, SG Box 62, HEH; George P.
Hammond ed., *The Larkin Papers* (Berkeley: University of California
Press, 1955), 5: 18-21.

[64] Ibid., Stearns to Larkin, 12 June 1846. On Larkin and Stockton's attitude toward a Southern California invasion, see Hague and Langum,
Larkin, 146.

[65] Stearns to Fremont, 23 May 1847, SG Box 62, HEH; Hawgood, ed.,
First Consul, 91.

[66] Wright, *A Yankee in Mexican California,* 139. Stearns, like other Yankee
expatriates who had married into the Californio elite, found they were
at a crossroads, caught between allegiance to family and state. William
Heath Davis, like Stearns, was in this dilemma, finding that he supported the American conquest, but who sympathized with the plight
of Mexicans and admired their valiant fight against superior forces. On
Davis, see Charles B. Churchill, "Hawaiian, American, Californio: The
Acculturation of William Heath Davis," *Southern California Quarterly*
76 (Winter 1994): 347, 370-371.

CHAPTER TWO

[1] Hugo Reid to Abel Stearns 5 April 1841, Abel Stearns Collection, SG
Box 52, Henry E. Huntington Library, San Marino, CA.

[2] Harris Newmark, *Sixty Years in Southern California,* 89.

[3] Reid to Stearns 29 July 1841, SG Box 52 HEH.

[4] Reid to Stearns Dec. 1839, SG Box 52, HEH.

[5] Reid to Stearns 26 April 1841, SG Box 52, HEH.

[6] Reid to Stearns 25 October 1841, SG Box 52, HEH.

[7] Reid to Stearns 26 April 1841, SG Box 52, HEH.

[8] Susanna Bryant Dakin, *A Scotch Paisano* (Berkeley: University of California Press, 1939), 153-156. Reid's daughter passed away during an 1849 smallpox epidemic while he was away seeking fortune during the gold rush sensation that pervaded the locale. According to Dakin, Doña Victoria felt her spouse had deserted her and the family. Resentment turned to outright blame for the daughter's death. Doña Victoria later believed that Reid's efforts to educate his daughter had kept her from the active life necessary to overcome illness.

Susanna Dakin's study is the most comprehensive biography of Hugo Reid, although further analysis of this early pioneer would be beneficial in order to understand Reid within the larger context of Southern California history. In the words of W.W. Robinson, Dakin's study "is essentially a novelized biography, successfully handled and presented. As time goes on, I believe it will continue to be thought of as one of California's most important literary products." See, W.W. Robinson, *Woman of California: Susanna Bryant Dakin* (Friends of the Bancroft Library, The California Arboretum Foundation Inc. 1967), 4-5. This discussion of Reid is based on a previous monograph. See Woolsey, "Hugo Reid and the Southern California Indians Revisited," *The Branding Iron* 186 (Winter 1991-92): 10-14.

[9] Reid to Stearns 26 April 1841, SG Box 52, HEH.

[10] The Los Angeles *Star* published the Reid articles in 1852 and again, in 1868. The *Star* scrapbook collection is located at the Bancroft Library. An incomplete version of the articles was later published in 1885. Arthur M. Ellis privately published a more comphrehensive 1926 edition, while Robert F. Heizer edited a complete version in 1968. The Heizer and Ellis versions are referenced in this text.

[11] Hugo Reid to Messrs. Lewis and Rand 15 February 1852, Folder 18, Hugo Reid Collection. Seaver Center for Western History, Los Angeles County Museum.

[12] Hugo Reid, *The Indians of Southern California*, with a forward by Arthur M. Ellis (Los Angeles: Privately Printed, 1926), and Robert F. Heizer ed., *The Indians of Los Angeles County, Hugo Reid's Letters of 1852* (Highland Park, Los Angeles: Southwest Museum, 1968), v. 21 Letter No. I.

[13] Ibid., Letter No. XIV.

[14] Ibid., Letters No. I & III.

[15] Ibid., Letter No. X.

[16] Alfred Robinson, *Life in California, and Friar Geronimo Boscana, Chinigchinich*, with an introduction by Andrew Rolle (Santa Barbara: Peregrine Publishers, Inc., 1970), 111.

[17] William Heath Davis, *Seventy-Five Years in California, A History of Events and Life in California: Personal Political and Military* (San Francisco: John Howell, 1889, 1967), 15.

[18] Robinson, *Life in California*, 128.

[19] Helen Hunt Jackson, *Ramona*, with an introduction by Michael Dorris (New York: New American Library, 1988, 1884), 22.

[20] Reid to Stearns 20 July 1838, SG Box 52, HEH.

[21] Reid to Stearns 15 June 1840, SG Box 52, HEH.

[22] Reid to William [David Merry] Howard c.1840, SG Box 52, HEH.

[23] Reid, Letter No. I.

[24] George Harwood Phillips, *Chiefs and Challengers, Indian Resistance and Cooperation in Southern California* (Berkeley: University of California Press, 1975), 17. Reid corroborated these findings in his newspaper articles. See Letter No. I

[25] Ibid., Letter No. VIII.

[26] Ibid., Letters No. III & IX.

[27] C. Alan Hutchinson, *Frontier Settlement in Mexican California, The Hijar-Padres Colony, and Its Origins 1769-1835* (New Haven, CT: Yale University Press, 1969), 397. The question of Indian treatment at the missions is hotly debated among intellectuals, and current scholarship and documentation have not resolved the issue. Sympathetic views of church policy include Maynard Geiger, O.F.M., *Franciscan Missionaries in Hispanic California, 1769-1848* (San Marino: Huntington Library, 1969), Francis F. Guest, O.F.M., "An Inquiry Into the Role of the Discipline in California Mission Life," *Southern California Quarterly* 71 (Spring 1989): 1-68.

Alternative views of mission treatment are presented in Michael C. Neri, "Jose Gonzalez Rubio: A Biographical Sketch" *Southern California Historical Quarterly* 73 (Summer 1991): 107-124, Edward D. Castillo ed., "The Assassination of Padre Andres Auintana by the Indians of Mission Santa Cruz in 1812: The Narration of Lorenzo Asisara," *California History* 68 (Fall 1989): 117-213, and Albert L. Hurtado, "California Indian Demography, Sherburne F. Cook, and the revision of American History," *Pacific Historical Review* 58 (August 1989): 323-344. Hurtado also believed that Indians found ways to temporarily survive through assimilation, adaptation, and preservation of their indigenous culture during the era of mission influence in the Western frontier interior. See Albert L. Hurtado, *Indian Survival On The California Frontier* (New Haven, CT: Yale University Press, 1988). A concise look at the polemic between scholars can be found in the exchange between Doyce B. Nunis Jr. and Edward D. Castillo "California Mission Indians: Two Perspectives," *California History* 70 (Summer 1991): 206-215.

On the general theme of the frontier and conquest, which places the Native American in a larger context, see Patricia Nelson Limerick, *The Legacy of Conquest: The Unbroken Past of the American West* (New York: Norton Publishers, 1987), and Donald Worster, Susan Armitage, Michael P. Malone, David J. Weber, and Patricia Nelson Limerick, "*The Legacy of Conquest*, by Patricia Nelson Limerick: A Panel of Appraisal,"

Western Historical Quarterly 20 (August 1989): 303-322.

[28] Reid, Letters No. IV, XVIII & XIX.

[29] Reid to Stearns 26 April 1841, S.G. Box 52, HEH.

[30] Ibid., Reid to Stearns 30 March 1848, S.G. Box 53.

[31] Reid, Letters No. I & XXI.

[32] Los Angeles *Star* 8 November 1851. On the motivation behind Indian attacks on settlements, particularly in the regions adjacent to the southern county, see George Harwood Philips, *Indians and Intruders* (Norman: University of Oklahoma Press, 1993).

[33] Ibid., 21 February 1852.

[34] Ibid., 9 August 1851. On Indian raids in Southern California during this period, see Phillips, *Chiefs and Challengers*, 71-111.

[35] Reid to Stearns 30 March 1848, S.G. Box 53, HEH.

[36] Reid to "Dear Star" n.d., Reid Collection, Folder #20, SCWH.

[37] Ibid., Folder #20, SCWH..

[38] Los Angeles *Star* 14 August 1852.

[39] Heizer ed., *Hugo Reid's Letters*, 3.

CHAPTER THREE

[1] Midge Sherwood, *San Marino: From Ranch to City* (San Marino: San Marino Historical Society, 1977): 5.

[2] Margaret S. Hereford to Thomas Hereford 2-5 June 1842 Tuscumbia, Alabama; Margaret S. Hereford to Thomas Hereford 21 June 1840 Pontotoc, Mississippi, Benjamin Davis Wilson Collection Huntington Library, San Marino, California, Box 1, Henry E. Huntington Library, San Marino, CA.

[3] Margaret S. Hereford to Thomas A. Hereford 13 May 1840 Pontotoc, Mississippi, Wilson Collection, Box 1, HEH.

[4] Ibid.

[5] Margaret S. Hereford, "A Glimpse at Female Biography" est. 1841, Box 1, HEH. An interesting look at female moral leadership in the mid-19th century Western frontier is Peggy Pascoe, *Relations of Rescue: The Search for Female Moral Authority in the American West* (New York: Oxford University Press, 1990); and on 19th century feminism, see Catherine Clinton, *The Other Civil War: American Women in the Nineteenth Century* (New York: Hill and Wang, 1984). On the need to focus on the multi-dimensional aspects to the Western female identity, see Joan M. Jensen and Darlis A. Miller, "The Gentle Tamers Revisited: New Approaches to the History of Women in the American West," *Pacific Historical Review* 49 (May 1980): 173-213; also, see a general study by Ellen Carol Dubois and Vicki L. Ruiz ed., *Unequal Sisters: A Multi-cultural Reader in U.S. Women's History* (New York: Routledge, 1990).

[6] Ibid.

[7] Excellent primary readings on slave revolts and slavery as a positive good are in Eric McKitrick ed., *Slavery Defended: The Views of the Old South* (Englewood Cliffs, NJ: Prentice-Hall, 1963), and a specialized study by Eric Foner, comp., *Nat Turner* (Englewood Cliffs, NJ: Prentice-Hall, 1971). On Southern female perspectives on plantation slavery, see Catherine Clinton, *The Plantation Mistress: Woman's World in the Old South* (New York: Pantheon Books, 1982). The economic nexus between slavery and the South is aptly considered in Eugene Genovese, *Political Economy of Slavery: Studies in the Economy & Society of the Slave South* (Middletown, CT: Wesleyan University Press, 1967, 1989); and Kenneth M. Stampp, *The Peculiar Institution: Slavery in the Ante- Bellum South* (New York: Knopf, 1956).

[8] Margaret S. Hereford to Thomas A. Hereford 2-5 June 1842 Tuscumbia, Alabama, Box 1, HEH.

[9] Mary [Catherine Hereford] Cooper to Margaret S. Hereford 17 January 1847 St. Louis, Missouri; Margaret S. Hereford to Thomas A. Hereford 13 May 1840 Pontotoc, Mississippi, Box 1, HEH.

[10] Ibid., Jim B. W... to Margaret S. Hereford 20 June 1836 Florence, Alabama; Jim B. W....n to Margaret S. Hereford 16 July 1836 Vicksburg, Mississippi, Box 1, HEH.

[11] Ibid., Margaret S. Hereford to Thomas A. Hereford 3 August 1846 St. Louis Missouri, Wilson Collection, Box 1, HEH.

[12] Ibid., Margaret S. Hereford to Thomas A. Hereford 6 April 1847 St. Louis, Missouri, Wilson Collection, Box 1, HEH.

[13] On pioneer motivations to emigrate West, see Ray Allen Billington, *The Far Western Frontier 1830-1860* (New York: Harper & Brothers, 1956),and William H. Goetzmann, *Exploration and Empire; The Explorer and the Scientist in the Winning of the American West* (New York: Knopf, 1966), and Goetzmann, *The West of the Imagination* (New York: Norton, 1986). For alternative perspectives to the Manifest Destiny theme as a central motivation behind migration, see Mario Barrera, *Race and Class in the Southwest: A Theory of Racial Inequality* (University of Notre Dame Press, 1979); and Howard Lamar, *The Far Southwest 1846-1912, A Territorial History* (New York: Norton, 1966).

[14] Francis Parkman, *The Oregon Trail*, with notations by William R. Taylor (New York: The Library of America, 1847, 1991).

[15] On the economic importance of the Southwest trade, see David J. Weber, *The Taos Trappers, The Fur Trade in the Far Southwest, 1540-1846* (Norman: University of Oklahoma Press, 1971), and Seymour V. Connor and Jimmy M. Skaggs, *Broadcloth and Britches: The Santa Fe Trade* (College Station: Texas A&M University Press, 1977).

[16] Thomas A. Hereford to Margaret S. Hereford 8 June 1847 Cimarron, Kansas; 10 June Upper Cimarron Springs, Kansas, Wilson Collection, Box 1. The classic description of the significance of the military to the Great Plains frontier is David Lavender, *Bent's Fort* (Garden City, NY:

Doubleday and Co., 1954), and a broader study by William H. Goetzmann, *Army Exploration in the American West, 1803-1863* (Austin: Texas A&M University Press, 1959, 1991). For a description of the Gila, Southwest, Santa Fe, and other overland routes, see the familiar descriptions by Ralph Moody, *The Old Trails West* (New York: Thomas Y. Crowell Co., 1963); and George R. Stewart, *The California Trail, An Epic With Many Heroes* (New York: McGraw-Hill Book Co., 1962).

[17] Thomas A. Hereford to Margaret S. Hereford 4 July 1847 Santa Fe, New Mexico, Box 1, HEH.

[18] David J. Weber, *The Mexican Frontier, 1821-1846, The American Southwest Under Mexico* (Albuquerque: University of New Mexico Press, 1982).

[19] Thomas A. Hereford to Margaret S. Hereford 4, 26 July 1847 Santa Fe, New Mexico, Box 1, HEH. Hereford's disgust may also represent a negative response to his first contact with Hispanic life, a common reaction among Anglo travelers in the Southwest. See Gloria E. Miranda, "Racial and Cultural Dimensions of Gente de Razon Status in Spanish and Mexican California," *Southern California Quarterly* 70 (Fall 1988): 265-278; and primary accounts from W.H. Davis, *El Gringo; or, New Mexico and Her People* (New York: Harper & Brothers, 1857); and Stella M. Drumm ed., *Down the Santa Fe Trail and Into Mexico: The Diary of Susan Shelby Magoffin, 1846-1847* (New Haven, CT: Yale University Press, 1926); for a comparative view, see Sarah Deutsch, *No Separate Refuge: Culture, Class, and Gender on an Anglo-Hispanic Frontier in the American Southwest, 1880-1940* (Oxford University Press, 1987).

[20] Ibid.

[21] Margaret S. Hereford to Thomas A. Hereford 19 April 1847, Box 1, HEH. On women pioneers along the Midwestern frontier, see Glenda Riley, *The Female Frontier: A Comparative View of Women on the Prairie and the Plains* (Lawrence, Kansas: University Press of Kansas, 1988); Martha Mitten Allen, *Traveling West: 19th Century Women on the Overland Routes* (El Paso, Texas: Texas Western Press, 1987); and Melissa Day Kiefer, "Female Heroes on the Overland Trails" (Thesis B.A. Scripps College, Claremont, CA, 1989); and Lillian Schlissel, *Women Diaries of the Westward Journey* (New York: Schocken Books, 1982).

[22] Sublette and Hereford (firm), "Articles of Co-partnership and Business Papers, 1848-1849," Box 1, HEH.

[23] Thomas A. Hereford to Esther Sale Hereford 12 December 1848 Santa Fe, NM, Box 1, HEH.

[24] Margaret S. Hereford to Esther S. Hereford August 1848 Santa Fe, Box 1, HEH. For a comparative look at female attitudes and experiences along the Northern borderlands, see Cheryl J. Foote, *Women of the New Mexico Frontier, 1846-1912* (Niwot, CO: University Press of Colorado, 1990), and Joan M. Jensen and Darlis A. Miller eds., *New Mexico*

Women: Intercultural Perspectives (Albuquerque: University of New Mexico Press, 1986).

25 The link between the increasing Anglo-American presence and the rise in Indian raids was a familiar complaint. See Antonio Jose Martinez, "Exposicion" in David J. Weber ed., *Northern Mexico On The Eve of the United States Invasion, Rare Imprints Concerning California, Arizona, New Mexico, and Texas, 1821-1846* (New York: Arno Press, 1976), Imprint No. 5; and Weber, *The Mexican Frontier*, 83-106.

26 Thomas A. Hereford to Esther S. Hereford May 1849 Santa Fe, New Mexico; Margaret S. Hereford to Esther S. Hereford 26 June 1849 El Paso, Texas, Box 1, HEH.

27 Margaret S. Hereford to Esther S. Hereford August 1848 Santa Fe, New Mexico, Box 1, HEH. Despite her Hispanic hosts friendly overtures, Margaret refused to attend any local galas since many rowdy types also participated in civic functions.

28 Ruth R. Olivera and Liliane Crete, *Life In Mexico Under Santa Anna 1822-1855* (Norman: University of Oklahoma Press, 1991), p. 106.

29 Thomas A. Hereford to unknown   November 1849 Chihuahua, Mexico, Box 1, HEH.

30 Margaret S. Hereford to Esther Sale Hereford 9 March 1850 Chihuahua, Mexico, Box 1, HEH. The Herefords favorable impressions may have been the exception rather than the rule. Disdain for Hispanic customs and culture were equally predominate among Anglo visitors throughout the Southwest and in Mexico. On the portrayal of Spanish women see, Antonia I. Castaneda, "Gender, Race, and Culture: Spanish- Mexican Women in the Historiography of Frontier California," *Frontiers: A Journal of Women's Studies* 11 (1990):8-20; Beverly Trulio, "Anglo-American Attitudes Toward New Mexican Women," *Journal of the West* 12 (April 1973):299-339; and also highlighted in Glenda Riley, "Western Women's History-A Look at Some of the Issues," *Montana: The Magazine of Western History* 41 (Spring 1991):66-70.

31 Ibid. A provocative study of female pioneers and native tribes is Glenda Riley, *Women and Indians on the Frontier, 1825-1915* (El Paso, Texas: Texas Western Press, 1987).

32 For a comparative look at overland travel to California, see Richard H. Dillon ed., *The Gila Trail, The Texas Argonauts and the California Gold Rush* (Norman: University of Oklahoma Press, 1960), and a visual perspective by John McDermott ed., *An Artist on the Overland Trail, The 1849 Diary and Sketches of James F. Wilkins* (San Marino: Huntington Library, 1968).

33 Thomas A. Hereford to Thomas S. Hereford Durango, Mexico 15 April 1850, and Thomas A. Hereford to Margaret S. Hereford 17 April 1850 Durango, Mexico, Box 1, HEH.

34 Margaret S. Hereford to Esther S. Hereford 9 March 1850 Chihuahua,

Mexico, Box 1, HEH.

35 Margaret S. Hereford to Esther Sale Hereford 20 April 1850 Mazatlan, Mexico, Box 1, HEH. On overland travel through Mexico, see Joseph Allen Stout, *The Liberators; Filibustering Expeditions into Mexico, 1848-1862 and the Last Thrust of Manifest Destiny* (Los Angeles: Westernlore Press, 1973), and Harlan Hague, *The Road to California: The Search for a Southern Overland Route, 1540-1848* (Glendale: A.H. Clark Co., 1978).

36 Ibid.

37 Margaret S. Hereford to Esther Sale Hereford 1 June 1850 San Francisco, Box 1, HEH.

38 Ibid. A recent entry on the social conditions at San Francisco, including the urban problems associated with arson, crime, and economic hardship is Kevin J. Mullen, *Let Justice Be Done: Crime and Politics in Early San Francisco* (Reno: University of Nevada Press, 1989). For consideration of the female role in The California gold rush, see Joann Levy, *They Saw The Elephant: Women in the California Gold Rush* (Hamden, CT: Archon Books, 1990), and primary source entries by Jeanne Hamilton Watson ed., *To The Land of Gold and Wickedness: The 1848-59 Diary of Lorena L. Hays* (St. Louis, MO: Patrice Press, 1988), and Janet Lecompte ed., *Emily, The Diary of a Hard-Worked Woman, by Emily French* (Lincoln: University of Nebraska Press, 1987).

39 Ibid. Broken hearts and lost dreams were realities shared by Margaret's contemporaries such as the wives of John C. Fremont and Thomas Larkin. See Pamela Herr, *Jessie Benton Fremont: A Biography* (New York: F. Watt, 1987, Pamela Herr and Mary Lee Spence, "I Really Had Something Like the Blues, Letters from Jessie Benton Fremont to Elizabeth Blair Lee, 1847-1883," *Montana, The Magazine of Western History* 41 (Spring 1991):17-31, and on Rachel Larken in Harlan Hague and David J. Langum, *Thomas O. Larkin, A Life of Patriotism and Profit in Old California* (Norman: University of Oklahoma Press, 1990), 199- 223.

40 Margaret S. Hereford to Mary Catherine [Hereford] Cooper 25 August 1850, San Jose, Box 1, HEH.

41 Margaret S. Hereford to Mary Catherine [Hereford] Cooper 13 October 1850, San Jose, Box 1, HEH.

42 Thomas A. Hereford to Margaret S. Hereford 16 June 1850 Petic, Mexico; Thomas A. Hereford to Margaret S. Hereford 3 July 1850 Guaymas, Mexico; Thomas A. Hereford to Margaret S. Hereford 25 August 1850, Santa Barbara, Box 1, HEH.

43 Thomas A. Hereford to Esther Sale Hereford 20 February 1851 Los Angeles, Box 2, HEH.

44 Col. J.J. Warner, Judge Benjamin Hayes, Dr. J.P. Widney, *An Historical Sketch of Los Angeles County California* (Los Angeles: Louis Lewin & Co., 1876), 78-80. Several fine secondary works provide a detailed

panorama of early Anglo settlement in Los Angeles, principle among them are W.W. Robinson, *Los Angeles, from the days of the Pueblo* (Menlo Park, CA: Lane Publishing Co., 1959), Andrew Rolle, *Los Angeles: From Pueblo to City of the Future* (San Francisco: Boyd & Fraser Publishing Co., 1981), and Ed Ainsworth, *Enchanted Pueblo, Story of the Rise of the Modern Metropolis around the Plaza de Los Angeles* (Los Angeles: Bank of America, N.T. & S.A., 1959). For bibliographical reference, see Doyce B. Nunis Jr. and Gloria Ricci Lothrop ed., *A Guide to the History of California* (New York: Greenwood Press, 1989), Doyce B. Nunis, Jr., *Los Angeles and Its Environs In The Twentieth Century* (Los Angeles: Ward Ritchie Press, 1973), and recent entries by Francis J. Weber, *California Bibliographies* (Los Angeles: Historical Society of Southern California, 1991), and William B. Secrest, Jr., "California on the Reference Shelf," *The Californians* 12 (1995): 52-57.

[45] John W. Robinson, *Los Angeles in Civil War Days, 1860-1865* (Los Angeles: Dawson's Book Shop, 1977), 28.

[46] Warner etal., *Historical Sketch*, 104.

[47] Thomas A. Hereford to Esther Sale Hereford 20 February 1851 Los Angeles, Box 2, HEH. We have only a vague sketch of this early period of the Herefords arrival in Los Angeles. Thomas and Margaret may have met Benjamin Wilson during their arrival at Los Angeles. Wilson managed and controlled the Bella Union Hotel, one of the few hostels located in the city during this period. The family probably rented a hotel room and developed an early acquaintance with their landlord. In point of fact, Robert S. Hereford succeeded as proprietor of the Bella Union in 1855. Warner etal., *Historical Sketch*, 82-83.

[48] Ibid.

[49] Thomas A. Hereford "To County Judge of Los Angeles County: Preemption Claim to Land in Wilmington" 23 June 1851, Box 2, HEH.

[50] Thomas A. Hereford "Will" 14 December 1851 Los Angeles, Box 2, HEH.

[51] Ibid.

[52] Margaret had domestic responsibilities while she stayed at Wilson's home. During a visit to San Francisco with the children, a friend of Wilson's provided a personal assessment of the governess. A.E. Russell was charmed by the widow Hereford, and "I was very happy indeed to meet her." A.E. Russell to Benjamin Davis Wilson 15 October 1852 San Francisco, Box 2, HEH.

[53] Joseph Lancaster Brent, Life in California, annotated by Francis Rosella [Kenner] Brent, (1900), 51, HEH.

[54] Benjamin Davis Wilson to Esther Sale Hereford 28 March 1853 Los Angeles, Box 2, HEH.

[55] For a biographical view of Wilson and his heirs, see Midge Sherwood, *Days of Vintage, Years of Vision*, (2 vols. San Marino, CA: Orizaba Publications, 1982, 1988); On Wilson the booster for early settlement,

see Remi A. Nadeau, *City-Makers* (Garden City, NY: Doubleday & Company, 1948); and John Walton Caughey, "Don Benito Wilson, an Average Southern Californian," *Huntington Library Quarterly* 2 (1939): 285-301.

CHAPTER FOUR

[1] This sketchy profile is drawn from the 1850 census, court case testimony of Evertson (referenced elsewhere), and a brief reference in Susanna Bryant Dakin, *A Scotch Piasano* (Berkeley: University of California Press, 1939), 156-157. Dakin however, indicates that Evertson was a Virginian, but his court testimony reveals that he was originally from South Carolina. See Court of Sessions, "Judah v. John R. Evertson," 5-13 September 1850, Special Collections, Seaver Center for Western History, Los Angeles County Museum.

[2] A few classic works deal with the 1850 Compromise, California statehood, and the controversy over slavery expansion. Principle among them are Allan Nevins, *Ordeal of the Union*, 2 vols. (New York: Scribners, 1947); Holman Hamilton, *Prologue to Conflict: The Crisis and Compromise of 1850* (New York: W.W. Norton & Co., 1964); and Edwin C. Rozwenc ed., *The Compromise of 1850* (Boston: D.C. Heath & Co., 1957).Historians have noted that Californians were divided over the statehood issue. Various alternative plans, ranging from state division along the North-South borders to forming a separate republic were proposed at Monterey. Some delegates believed that asking for admission was premature in 1850, while other members sympathetic with the slave states wished to delay the issue in the hopes of obtaining a more favorable slave state constituency in the future. See, Robert Glass Cleland, *A History of California: The American Period* (New York: The MacMillan Co., 1939), 247-261, and Warren A. Beck and David A Williams, *California: A History of the Golden State* (Garden City: Doubleday & Co., 1972).

[3] Court of Sessions. "People: Assault & Battery on Judah by John R. Evertson" #46, 12 September 1850, SCWH.

[4] Criminal Business Records. "Judah v. Evertson," 13 September 1850, 53, SCWH.

[5] A discussion of the California statehood question, see Patricia Gibson, "California and the Compromise of 1850," *Journal of the West* 8 (October 1969): 578-591, Ronald C. Woolsey, "A Southern Dilemma: Slavery Expansion and the California Statehood Issues in 1850 -A Reconsideration," *Southern California Quarterly* 65 (Summer 1983): 123- 144, and Ward M. McAfee, "California History Textbooks and the Coming of the Civil War: The Need for a Broader Perspective of California History," *Southern California Quarterly* 41 (1974): 159-174.

[6] Roy P. Basler, Marion Dolores Pratt, and Lloyd A. Dunlap, eds., *The Collected Works of Abraham Lincoln* (New Brunswick, NJ, 1953-1955) 2: 461-69. Also see Don E. Fehrenbacher, *Prelude to Greatness, Lincoln*

in the 1850s (California: Stanford University Press, 1962), 48, 70-95, and a comprehensive narrative on the period by David H. Donald, *Lincoln* (New York: Simon & Schuster, 1995).

[7] Congressional *Globe*, 31 Cong., 1 Sess. 244-247, 115-127.

[8] Ibid., 110.

[9] Ibid., 76.

[10] Ibid., 103.

[11] Ibid., 650.

[12] Charleston *Mercury*, 2 July 1850

[13] *Globe*, 31 Cong., 1 Sess., 1168.

[14] Ibid., 149.

[15] Ibid., 444.

[16] Ibid., 716

[17] Ibid., 199.

[18] Ibid., 384.

[19] Ibid., 466.

[20] Ibid., 153.

[21] J. Ross Browne, ed., *Constitutional Convention of 1849: (Debates and Reports* (Washington D.C.: J.T. Towers, 1850), 39.

[22] John Bassett Moore, ed., *The Works of James Buchanan* 12 vols. New York: Antiquarian Press Ltd., 1960) 8: 384-385.

[23] *Globe*, 31 Cong., 1 Sess., 668.

[24] Ibid., 652.

[25] Ibid., 154

[26] Ibid., 713.

[27] Ibid., 466.

[28] Ibid., 203.

[29] Mobile *Advertiser*, as cited in the *Baltimore American and Commercial Daily Advertiser*, 10 September 1850.

[30] John C. Rives, ed., *Abridgement of the Debates of Congress, 1789- 1856* (20 vols. New York: D. Appleton & Co., 1863) 15: 387.

[31] *Globe*, 31 Cong., 1 Sess., 648.

[32] W.W. Robinson, *Los Angeles, From The Days Of The Pueblo*, revised edition & introduction by Doyce B. Nunis Jr. (North Hollywood: California Historical Society, 1959, 1981), 113.

[33] Col. J.J. Warner, Judge Benjamin Hayes, Dr. J.P. Widney, *An Historical Sketch of Los Angeles County California* (Los Angeles: O.W. Smith, 1876, 1936), 82.

[34] The impact of Taylor's death upon the passage of the Omnibus Bill is detailed in Holman Hamilton, *Zachary Taylor: Soldier in the White House* (Indianapolis: Bobbs-Merrill Co., Inc., 1951). The breakdown of southern radical leadership and the Nashville Convention are noted in Hamilton, *Prologue to Conflict*, 102-109, and Rozwenc, ed., *The*

Compromise of 1850, 11-13.

35 Los Angeles Criminal Records, Judah v Evertson, 13 September 1850, 53, SCWH.

CHAPTER FIVE

1 John Walton Caughey, *Gold Is The Cornerstone* (Berkeley: University of California Press, 1948), 1.

2 New Orleans, *Daily Picayune* 6 May 1850.

3 Analysis of the Panama and overland routes to Gold Rush California can be found in Caughey, *Gold Is The Cornerstone*, 57-158; and John Walton Caughey ed., *Rushing for Gold* (Berkeley: University of California Press, 1949). Vivid primary accounts of the Panama trip can be found in John Edwin Pomfret ed., *California Gold Rush Voyages, 1848- 1849: Three Original Narratives* (San Marino, CA: Huntington Library, 1954); and W. Turrentine Jackson, *The California Gold Rush Diary of a German Sailor* (Berkeley, California: Howell-North Books, 1969).

4 Joseph Lancaster Brent, *Life in California* as annotated by Frances Rossella (Kenner) Brent, unpublished manuscript (1900), 1-3. Henry E. Huntington Library, San Marino, CA.

5 Although Mark Twain has been attributed with the words, but probably never said, "the coldest winter I ever spent, was a summer in San Francisco," Brent certainly would have taken credit given the chance.

6 Brent, *Life in California*, 2,10. Recent discussion of legal practices and cultural obstacles in frontier California, see David J. Langum, Langum, *Law and Community on the Mexican California Frontier, Anglo-American Expatriates and the Clash of Legal Traditions, 1821-1846* (Norman: University of Oklahoma Press, 1987), Gordon Morris Bakken, *Practicing Law in Frontier California* (Lincoln: University of Nebraska Press, 1991), and Bakken, *The Development of Law in Frontier California: Civil Law and Society, 1850-1890* (Wesport, CT: Greenwood Press, 1985). Updated bibliographic entries to law and the California frontier era is Henry E. Huntington Library and Art Gallery ed., *California Legal History manuscripts in the Huntington Library: A guide/by the Committee on History of Law in California of the State Bar of California* (San Marino, CA: Huntington Library, 1989).

7 Helen Hunt Jackson, *Ramona* (Boston: Little, Brown & Company, 1884, 1900) 1: 19-20.

8 Brent, *Life in California*, 3.

9 Ibid., 3, 7-8.

10 Ibid., 3.

11 Brent, *Life in California*, 2-3. United States census figures from 1850-1860.

12 Robert Glass Cleland, *Cattle on a Thousand Hills* (San Marino:The

Huntington Library, 1941), 163.

[13] Brent, *Life in California*, 5-7. Harris Newmark recalled that reputable lawyers were at a premium and, with low demand for their services, the profession did not provide "much of a living." See Harris Newmark, *Sixty Years in Southern California*, ed. by Maurice H. and Marco R. Newmark (Los Angeles: Zeitlin & Ver Brugge, 1916), 45.

[14] Brent was nearly broke when he arrived in Los Angeles. He borrowed $300 from the Wilson-Packard Company and gradually repaid the loan. During this period, the young Brent also worked as a common laborer, possibly on the Bell Block that was under construction at that time.

[15] Judson A. Grenier, *California Legacy, The James Alexander Watson-Maria Dolores Dominguez de Watson Family 1820-1980* (Los Angles: Watson Land Company, 1987), 100-102. Harris Newmark believed that Brent's legal expertise was a residual source of popularity to the community. See, Newmark, *Sixty Years*, 243.

[16] W.W. Robinson, *Lawyers of Los Angeles* (Los Angeles: Ward Ritchie Press, 1959), 34.

[17] Col. J.J. Warner, Judge Benjamin Hayes, Dr. J.P. Widney, *An Historical Sketch of Los Angeles County California* (Los Angeles: Louis Lewin & Co. 1876), 63-64.

[18] Robinson, *L.A. Lawyers*, 34.

[19] Ibid., 227; also in Newmark, *Sixty Years*, 47. W.W. Robinson makes the point, however, that Brent's library was "fairly representative, though inadequate." Robinson, *L.A. Lawyers*, 34.

[20] Newmark, *Sixty Years*, 105.

[21] The idealistic sentiments embodied in southerners such as Brent, James Watson, Benjamin Wilson, and Dr. John Griffin were, in the words of Judson Grenier, "would play a role in carrying Jacksonian Democracy to California." Grenier, *California Legacy*, 25.

[22] Brent, *Life in California*, 7.

[23] Ibid., 11-12, 41, 76. Brent's professional ties to the Hispanic community are referenced in Grenier, *California Legacy*, 76.

[24] Ibid., 8-10, 36-37.

[25] Ibid., 37-38.

[26] Ibid., 36-38. Not unlike Abel Stearns before him, Joseph Lancaster Brent expressed a romantic admiration of the the rancho era. This sentiment was expressed by contemporaries such as Benjamin Hayes, Horace Bell, and Harris Newmark. This conception, ironically, did not materialize into favorable public policy toward the Hispanic community.

[27] Robinson, *L.A. Lawyers*, 36-37.

[28] Brent, *Life in California*, 12.

[29] Warner etal., *Historical Sketch*, 64.

30 Brent, *Life in California*, 3.

31 Excellent secondary accounts of Democrat politics statewide are David A. Williams, *David C. Broderick; A Political Portrait* (San Marino: Huntington Library, 1969). The national crisis among Democrats is widely chronicled, including excellent studies by Roy F. Nichols, *The Disruption of American Democracy* (New York: Collier, 1948), Robert W. Johannsen, *Frontier Politics and the Sectional Conflict; The Pacific Northwest on the Eve of the Civil War* (Seattle: University of Washington Press, 1955), Eric Foner, *Politics and Ideology in the Age of the Civil War* (New York: Oxford University Press, 1980), and Dwight L. Dummond, *The Secession Movement, 1860-1861* (New York: The Macmillan Company, 1931); plus, selected studies by James L. Huston, *The Panic of 1857 and the Coming of the Civil War* (Baton Rouge: Louisiana State University Press, 1987, and Kenneth M. Stampp, *America in 1857: A Nation on the Brink* (New York: Oxford University Press, 1990).

32 Brent, *Life in California*, 23.

33 On Brent's influence and friendship in the pueblo, see Grenier, *California Legacy*, 25, 114-115.

34 Newmark, *Sixty Years*, 178. Also see Brent, *Life in California* 16-26.

35 Brent, *Life in California*, 23.

36 Newmark, *Sixty Years*, 47.

37 Brent, *Life in California*, 25-26.

38 Brent, *Life in California*, 29-30.

39 Ibid., 24-25, 40-41; reference on Scott in Robinson, *L.A. Lawyers*, 225.

40 Ibid., 42-43.

41 Local partisan politics is detailed in John W. Robinson, *Los Angeles in Civil War Days 1860-1865* (Los Angeles: Dawson's Book Shop, 1977), Ronald C. Woolsey, "Disunion or Dissent? A New Look At An Old Problem In Southern California Attitudes Toward The Civil War," *Southern California Quarterly* 66 (Fall 1984):185-205, and Robert J. Chandler, "Crushing Dissent: The Pacific Coast Tests Lincoln's Policy of Suppression, 1862," *Civil War History* 30 (September 1984): 235-254, and on political sentiment, see Ward M. McAfee, "California's House Divided," *Civil War History* 33 (June 1987): 115-130, and Ronald C.Woolsey, "The Politics of a Lost Cause: Seceshers and Democrats in Southern California During the Civil War," *California History* 69 (Winter 1990/91): 372-383.

42 Williams, *Broderick*, 214.

43 Brent, *Life in California*, 42-43.

44 Ibid., 39. In the words of Judson Grenier, the 1860 election "was the last to be dominated by the political machine of Joseph Lancaster Brent." Grenier, *California Legacy*, 172.

45 Ibid., 26-27.

46 Ibid., 65-67.

47 Pioneers Notes from the Diary of Judge Benjamin Hayes, 1849- 1875, edited by Marjorie T. Wolcott (Los Angeles: McBride Printing Co. 1919), 251.

48 Brent, Life in California, 64-65.

49 James McPherson, Battle Cry of Freedom, The Civil War Era (New York: Oxford University Press, 1988), 239-240. For a detailed discussion of the libertarian spirit behind the Confederate movement, see Emory M. Thomas, The Confederacy as a Revolutionary Experience (Englewood Cliffs, NJ, Prentice-Hall, 1971), Thomas, The Confederate Nation, 1861-1865 (New York: Harper & Row, 1979), and E. Merton Coulter, The Confederate States of America 1861-1865 (Baton Rouge: Louisiana State University Press, 1950).

50 Brent, Life in California, 58-59, 62, 65-67.

51 On local Southern sympathy see, Helen B. Walters, "Confederates in Southern California," Historical Society of Southern California Quarterly 35 (March 1953): 41-54, Benjamin Franklin Gilbert, "The Confederate Minority in Caifornia," California Historical Society Quarterly 20 (June 1941): 154-170, William F. King, "El Monte, an American Town in Southern California, 1851-1866," Southern California Quarterly 53 (December 1971): 303-316; and on overt Confederate participation, see Harry Innes Thornton, Jr., "Recollection of the War by a Confederate Officer From California," and Clarence C. Clendenen, "A Confederate Spy in California: A Curious Incident of the Civil War," Southern California Quarterly 45 (June 1963):195-234, and Clendenen, "Dan Showalter -California Secessionist," California Historical Society Quarterly 40 (December 1961): 309-325.

52 Brent to Benjamin Davis Wilson, 17 June 1868, Wilson Collection, HEH.

CHAPTER SIX

1 The composite profile of Barton's life is reconstructed from various primary sources, including Col. J.J. Warner, Judge Benjamin Hayes, Dr. J.P. Widney, An Historical Sketch of Los Angeles County, California (Los Angeles: Louis Lewin & Co., 1876), 58, 95-96; Joseph Lancaster Brent, Life in California annotated by Francis Rossella [Kenner] Brent (1900), Henry E. Huntington Library; Maurice H. & Marco R. Newmark eds., Sixty Years in Southern California, 1853-1913: Containing the Reminiscences of Harris Newmark(Los Angeles: Zeitlin & Ver Brugge, 1916, 4th ed., 1970), 208; Horace Bell, Reminiscences of a Ranger(Santa Barbara: Wallace Hebberd, 1927), and Bell, On The Old West Coast (New York: Grosset & Dunlap, 1930).

2 On the Bidwell-Bartleson party and, beginning in the 1840s, the flow of settlers moving west to build permanent settlements rather than to

come only as traders and trappers, see introduction and comments by Doyce B. Nunis, Jr. ed., *The Bidwell-Bartleson Party, 1841 California Emigrant Adventure* (Santa Cruz: Western Tanager Press, 1991), 1-25.

[3] Ed Ainsworth, *Enchanted Pueblo* (Los Angeles: Bank of America, N.T. $ S.A., 1959), 31.

[4] Warner, *An Historical Sketch*, 115, 86-87, and Newmark eds., *Sixty Years*, 61, 118.

[5] Warner, *An Historical Sketch*, 84.

[6] Los Angeles *Star*, 10 July 1852.

[7] Los Angeles, Court of Sessions, "People vs. Joseph Caddick and Charles Norris" 12 July 1852, Seaver Center for Western History, Los Angeles County Museum.

[8] Ibid., "People vs. J.S.K. Ogier" 7 September 1854.

[9] Los Angeles *Star*, 16 July 1853.

[10] Warner, Hayes, & Widney, *An Historical Sketch*, 80-81.

[11] Newmark, *Sixty Years*, 207.

[12] Interview with Guadalupe Gallo Valenquela in Frank F. Latta, *Joaquin Murrieta and His Horse Gangs* (Santa Cruz: Bear State Books, 1980), 86-87.

[13] Brent, *Life in California*, 33.

[14] Marjorie T. Wolcott, ed., *Pioneer Notes from the Diary of Judge Benjamin Hayes, 1849-1875* (Los Angeles: McBride Printing Company, 1929), 108.

[15] Ibid.

[16] Bell, *Reminiscences of a Ranger*, 403.

[17] Los Angeles, District Court, "People vs. Vicente Guerrero & an Unknown Frenchman," 14 August 1856, SCWH. Tensions during the summer of 1856 ran high because of the San Francisco Vigilance Committee and the statewide search for renegades associated with that phenomenon. See Ronald C. Woolsey, "L.A. Law: 1856 Vigilante Wars," *True West* 41 (December 1994): 19-25.

[18] Los Angeles, Court of Sessions, Box 3 of 6, SCWH.

[19] David J. Weber, *Foreigners in Their Native Land: Historical Roots of the Mexican-Americans* (Albuquerque: University of New Mexico Press, 1973), 174.

[20] "People vs. Diego Nieta", 21 November 1856, SCWH.

[21] Henry Rice Myles to Benjamin Davis Wilson, 28 January 1857, Box 6, HEH.

[22] John Forster to Cave Johnson Couts, 27 January 1857, Box 13, HEH.

[23] Henry Rice Miles to Benjamin Davis Wilson, 28 January 1857, Box 6, HEH.

[24] Harris Newmark, *Sixty Years*, 204.

[25] Sacramento *Daily Bee*, 8 February 1857.

[26] Miles to Wilson 28 January 1857, Box 6, HEH.

[27] Newmark, *Sixty Years*, 205-206; Los Angeles *Star*, 31 January & 14 February 1857.

[28] For a classic description of the chase and capture of the Flores gang, see Robert Glass Cleland, *From Wilderness to Empire* (New York: Alfred A. Knopf, 1944), 291-293.

[29] Newmark eds., *Sixty Years*, 208.

[30] Ibid., 210.

[31] Bell, *Reminiscences*, 401.

[32] Los Angeles *Star*, 21 February 1857.

[33] On California prison conditions see Clare V. McKanna, Jr., "Crime and Punishment: The Hispanic Experience in San Quentin, 1851- 1880," *Southern California Quarterly* 72 (Spring 1990): 1-18.

[34] Bell, *Reminiscences*, 403.

[35] Testimony on the Flores raid can be found in Los Angeles, District Court. "The People vs. Leonardo Lopez, et al; alias Luciano Tapia," preliminary hearing 14 December 1857, SCWH.

[36] Richard Allan Griswold del Castillo,"La Raza Hispano Americana: The Emergence of an Urban Culture Among the Spanish Speaking of Los Angeles 1850-1880," Ph.D. dissertation, University of California at Los Angeles, 1974, 196.

Many scholars argue that an indifferent legal system, xenophobic sentiment, and poor economic times led to cultural frictions and the rise of "Robin Hood" style bandits. David Johnson highlights the inequities of the justice system, noting that "from 1849 to 1902 non-whites, primarily Hispanics, composed a dramatically disproportionate percentage of those who experienced the wrath of the people."David A. Johnson, "Vigilance and the Law: The Moral Authority of Popular Justice in the Far West" *American Quarterly* 33 (Winter 1981): 573. Supporting views can be found in Ricardo Romo, *East Los Angeles, History of a Barrio* (Austin: University of Texas Press, 1983), Richard Griswold del Castillo, *The Los Angeles Barrio, 1850-1890: A Social History* (Berkeley: University of California Press, 1979), and Albert Camarillo, *Chicanos in a Changing Society: From Mexican Pueblos to American Barrios in Santa Barbara and Southern California, 1849-1930* (MA: Harvard University Press, 1979).

On vigilantism in general, see the classic study by Richard Maxwell Brown ed., *Strain of Violence: Historical Studies of American Violence and Vigilantism* (New York: Oxford University Press, 1975), and recent overview of literature on the subject in Ronald C. Woolsey, "An Outlaw as Outcast: Juan Flores, The Social Bandit Revisited," *The Californians* 11 (April 1994): 44-50.

[37] El *Clamor Publico*, 30 January 1857.

[38] Bell, *Reminiscences*, 406. An excellent analysis of Californio participation in the caputure of renegade gangs, see Robert Willis Blew, "Californios and American Institutions: A Study of Reactions to Social

and Political Institutions," Ph.D dissertation, University of Southern California, 1973, 171-184, and Blew, "Vigilantism in Los Angeles 1835-1874," *Southern California Quarterly* 54 (Spring 1972): 11- 12.

39 John Forster to John Strother Griffin, 30 January 1857, SG Box 29, HEH.

40 Los Angeles *Star*, 7 February 1857.

41 Historians are divided on the extent and nature of "social banditry" as bandido motivation. John Boessenecker asserts that revisionist scholars "would have one believe that the Old West's prisons were filled with persecuted ethnic minorities, innocent of the offenses they were charged with." For Boessenecker, "such scenarios did occur, but they were the exception and not the rule." See Boessenecker, *Badge and Buckshot: Lawlessness in Old California* (Norman & London: University of Oklahoma Press, 1988), 3.

William Secrest also supports Boessenecker's main contention that the vast majority of Hispanics were "honest and industrious citizens and any impression to the contrary is wrong!" Secrest, *Lawmen and Desperadoes, A Compendium of Noted, Early California Peace Officers, Badmen and Outlaws 1850-1900* (Spokane, WA: Arthur H. Clark Co., 1994), 15.

42 Bell, *Reminiscences*, 409.

43 *El Clamor Publico*, 21 February 1857; Griswold del Castillo, "La Raza Hispano Americana," 197.

44 Ylsio Guarro [spelling?], Jesus Lopez, Pedro Botello, and Ramon Nunez were four of the forty-six jurors that judged the Luciano Tapia case in December, 1857. Tapia was the only bandit tried in district court since the vigilante fevor had passed by the time of his capture. Los Angeles. First District Court. "The People v. Luciano Tapia" 17 December 1857, no. 337, SCWH.

45 Forster to Griffin, 30 January 1857, SG Box 29, HEH.

46 Cameron E. Thom to Benjamin D. Wilson, 10 February 1857, Box 6, HEH.

47 *El Clamor Publico*, 18 February 1857.

48 "People v. Tapia" 17 December 1857, SCWH.

49 Los Angeles *Star*, 20 February 1858.

CHAPTER SEVEN

1 Remi Nadeau, *City Makers: The Men Who Transformed Los Angeles from Village to Metropolis During the First Great Boom, 1861-1876* Garden City, NY: Doubleday and Company, 1948), 15.

2 Kevin Starr, *Inventing the Dream: California Through the Progessive Era* (Oxford University Press, 1985), 31. Few works, surprisingly, are exclusive of these pioneers. Benjamin Hayes is frequently cited in secondary form in the *Southern California Quarterly* and *California Historical Society Quarterly*. The lone study on Horace Bell is Benjamin

S. Harrison, *Fortune Favors the Brave, The Life and Times of Horace Bell Pioneer Californian* (Los Angeles: Ward Ritchie Press, 1953), and monographs by Abraham Hoffman, "Horace Bell: Southern California's Pioneer with the Pungent Pen," *The Californians* 8 (March-April 1991): 22-31, and Ronald C. Woolsey, "Pioneer Views and Frontier Themes: Benjamin Hayes, Horace Bell, and the Southern California Experience," *Southern California Quarterly* 72 (Fall 1990): 255-274.

3 Benjamin Hayes to Cave Johnson Couts, 12 January 1863, Cave Johnson Couts Collection, Henry E. Huntington Memorial Library, San Marino, CA.

4 Hayes to Couts, 10 December 1862, HEH. Benjamin Hayes assigned an open letter that urged Governor Peter F. Burnett to form a local government in anticipation of a "stream of emigration" due to mining activity. Other signatories included Augustin Olvera, County Judge; George T. Burrill, Sheriff; and Antonio F. Coronel, Assessor. See Granville Arthur Waldron, "Courthouses of Los Angeles," *Historical Society of Southern California Quarterly* 41 (December 1959): 350-351.

5 Hayes to Couts, 15 January 1863, HEH. Southern California courts exercised a wide range of informal procedures, restraint, and liency in the interpretation of justice. A general description of this subject can be found in Marco R. Newmark, "Early Los Angeles Bench and Bar," *Historical Society of Southern California Quarterly* 41 (December 1959): 350-351.

6 Horace Bell, *On The Old West Coast* (New York: Grosset and Dunlap, 1930), 267, 166.

7 Horace Bell, *Reminiscences of a Ranger* (Santa Barbara: Wallace Hebberd, 1927), 156.

8 Bell, *Reminiscences*, 214-215.

9 Bell, *On The Old West Coast*, 230.

10 Ibid., 160.

11 Ibid., 242.

12 Ibid., 259.

13 On a broader theme, a recent entry that argues for further definition of the laborer as a "distinct group" in the Westward Movement is Carlos Schwantes, "The Concept of the Wageworkers' Frontier: A Framework for Future Research," *Western Historical Quarterly* 18 (January 1987): 39-55.

14 Bell to Caroline (Bell) Rush, 10 February 1872; also reference similar sentiments in Bell's correspondences of 9 May 1869, 18 March 1873, 7 April 1873, HEH.

15 Marjorie T. Wolcott, ed., *Pioneer Notes from the Diary of Judge Benjamin Hayes*, 1849-1875 (Los Angeles: McBride Printing Company, 1929), 101, 133.

16 Bell, *On The Old West Coast*, 157, 244, 286.

[17] Bell, *Reminiscences*, 294, 300-301.

[18] Specific studies that catalogue the decline of the Hispanic during this period are Leonard Pitt, *The Decline of the Californios: A Social History of the Spanish-Speaking Californians, 1846-1890* (Berkeley: University of California Press, 1966); Richard Griswold del Castillo, *The Los Angeles Barrio, 1850-1890* (Berkeley: University of California Press, 1979); and Ronald C. Woolsey, "Rites of Passage? Anglo and Mexican-American Contrasts in a Time of Change: Los Angeles 1860-1870," *Southern California Quarterly* 69 (Summer 1987): 81-101.

[19] Bell, *Reminiscences*, 239.

[20] Ibid., 295-296.

[21] Ibid.

[22] Ray Allen Billington and Albert Camarillo, eds., *The American Southwest, Image and Reality* (Los Angeles: University of California Press, 1977), 13.

[23] Thomas Workman Temple II, "Our Heritage from the Days of the Dons," *Historical Society of Southern California Quarterly* 40 (March 1958): 58. Hayes' first wife, formerly Emily Martha Chauncey, died in 1857. He later married Dona Adeleida Serrano in a Catholic ceremony at San Diego in 1866. See Wolcott, ed., *Pioneer Notes*, IX-X.

[24] Ibid., 74, 10 February 1850 entry.

[25] Ibid., 91, 24 January 1853 entry.

[26] Ibid., 91-92.

[27] Bell, *Reminiscences*, 200.

[28] Harrison, *Fortune Favors the Brave*, 37.

[29] W.W. Robinson, Los Angeles from the *Days of the Pueblo, A Brief History and Guide to the Plaza Area* revised with an introduction by Doyce B. Nunis Jr. (Los Angeles: California Historical Society, 1959, 1981), 66.

[30] Ronald C. Woolsey, "Crime and Punishment: Los Angeles County, 1850-1856," *Southern California Quarterly* 61 (Spring 1979): 79-97.

[31] Bell, *On The Old West Coast*, 166.

[32] Bell, *Reminiscences*, 239, 279.

[33] Benjamin Hayes to Cave Johnson Couts, 3 December 1862, HEH.

[34] Hayes to Couts, 26 & 30 November 1862, HEH. After a second hearing, Carrillo was released and murdered not long afterwards. Marjorie Wolcott noted than an organization existed determined to hang him [Carrillo] and were probably responsible for his death. Wolcott ed., *Pioneer Notes*, 176.

[35] Hayes to Couts, 8 December 1862, HEH.

[36] Temple II, "Our Heritage from the Days of the Dons," 76.

[37] Hayes to Couts, 17 February 1864, HEH.

[38] Bell, *Reminiscences*, 410, 482-483.

[39] Los Angeles Court of Sessions, Special Hearing by Judge Benjamin Hayes, Case No. 272, 22 July 1856, SCWH.

[40] Wolcott ed., *Pioneer Notes*, 171, entry of 28 September 1857.

[41] Bell to Caroline [Bell] Rush, 10 February 1872, HEH.

[42] Hayes to Cave Johnson Couts, 6 July 1865, HEH.

[43] Wolcott, ed., *Pioneer Notes*, 92, letter of Hayes to B.M. Hughes, 24 January 1853.

[44] Ibid., diary entry of 14 September 1857.

CHAPTER EIGHT

[1] Background information on Henry Hamilton can be found in John W. Robinson, "A California Copperhead: Henry Hamilton and the Los Angeles Star," *Arizona and the West* 23 (Autumn 1981) 213-230. For a discussion of Hamilton's stewardship at the *Star* see, William B. Rice, *The Los Angeles Star, 1851-1864: The Beginnings of Journalism in Southern California* (Berkeley: University of Califronia Press, 1947); and Edward C. Kemble, *A History of California Newspapers, 1846-1858* (Los Gatos, CA: Talisman Press, 1962).

[2] Los Angeles *Star*, 5 December 1857.

[3] Ibid., 6 February & 10 October 1857, 3 December 1859.

[4] Rice, *The Los Angeles Star*, 121.

[5] *Los Angeles Star,* 14 June 1856.

[6] For a general overview of Kewen's life see, John W. Robinson, "Colonel Edward John Cage Kewen: Los Angeles Fire-Eating Orator of the Civil War Era," *Southern California Quarterly* 61 (Summer 1979): 159- 181; and Oscar T. Shuck, *Representative and Leading Men of the Pacific* (San Francisco: Bacon & Company, 1870), 341-346.

[7] *Los Angeles Star*, 10 August 1859.

[8] Shuck, *Representative and Leading Men of the Pacific*, 341-343.

[9] Edward John Cage Kewen, "Speech...at the American Mass Meeting, 8 August 1855," (Sacramento 1855), Special Collections, Henry E. Huntington Library, San Marino, CA.

[10] On Kewen's daily activities and lifestyle in Southern California see, Robert Glass Cleland, *El Molino Viejo* (Los Angeles: Ward Ritchie Press, 1950), 20-37.

[11] Los Angeles *Star*, 8 August 1859.

[12] Ibid., 17 January 1857, 11 December 1858, & 11 June 1859.

[13] Robinson, "Kewen: Fire-Eating Orator," 166-167.

[14] Los Angeles *Star*, 20 April 1861.

[15] *Journal of the House of Assembly of California*, 12 Session (Sacramento: C.T. Botts, 1861), 194, 309. D.B. Kurtz (San Diego) also supported the resolution. The measure however, was defeated in the assembly by a 41-28 margin.

[16] Los Angeles *Star*, 4 May 1861.

[17] Ibid., 2 February 1861.

----

[18] On dissident activity in Southern California, see William F. King, "El Monte, An American Town in Southern California, 1851-1866," *Southern California Quarterly* 53 (Secember 1971):322-323, Helen B. Walters, "Confederates in Southern California," *Historical Society of Southern California Quarterly* 35 (March 1953): 45, and Ronald C. Woolsey, "The Politics of a Lost Cause: 'Seceshers' and Democrats in Southern California During the Civil War," *California History* 69 (Winter 1990/91): 372-383.

[19] Octavius Decatur Gass to Abel Stearns, 18 September 1861, Abel Stearns Papers, HEH.

[20] Marjorie T. Wolcott ed., *Pioneer Notes from the Diary of Judge Benjamin Hayes*, 1849-1875 (Los Angeles: McBride Printing Co., 1929), 251.

[21] Walters, "Confederates in Southern California," 45.

[22] San Francisco *Daily Evening Bulletin*, 11 July 1861.

[23] Mrs. W.A. Franklin to Dr. George P. Hammond, 8 July 1957, Journal of Alexander Grayson Bowman, Special Collections, Brancroft Library, University of California, Berkeley.

[24] Joseph Lancaster Brent, *Life in California*, annotated by Frances Rossella (Kenner) Brent (1900), 63-65, HEH.

[25] Ibid. Also see Woolsey, "Politics of a Lost Cause," 376-377.

[26] *War of the Rebellion*, 50: 733. Specific troop movements along the border and in Arizona are documented in Arthur A. Wright, *The Civil War in the Southwest* (Denver: Big Mountain Press, 1964), Leo P. Kibby, "California Soldiers in the Civil War," *California Historical Society Quarterly* 40 (December 1961): 343-350; Aurora Hunt, *The Army of the Pacific* (Glendale: The Arthur H. Clark Co., 1951); and Leo E. Oliva, "The Santa Fe Trail in Wartime: Expansion and Preservation of the Union," *Journal of the West* 28 (April 1989): 53-58.

[27] Judson A. Grenier, *California Legacy, The James Alexander Watson-Maria Dolores Dominguez de Watson Family 1820-1980* (Los Angeles: Watson Land Company, 1987), 246, 265-66.

[28] Los Angeles *Star*, 22 February 1862. The Confederacy toyed with the idea of a southwest campaign into Southern California, but the Richmond government never acted on these proposals due to the urgency of the war effort in the East. See H. H. Watford, "The Far-Western Wing of the Rebellion, 1861-1865," *California Historical Society Quarterly* 34 (June 1955): 125-148, and Aurora Hunt, *The Army of the Pacific* (Glendale, CA: The Arthur H. Clark Co., 1951).

[29] James Henry Carleton to Christopher Carson, 12 October 1862, Carleton Portfolio, BL.

[30] Los Angeles *Star*, 23 May 1863.

[31] Edward J.C. Kewen to Cave Johnson Couts, 5 July 1862, HEH. Kewen urged Cave Johnson Couts to attend the state Democrat convention scheduled for August 6 in Sacramento.

[32] Kewen to Couts, 21 January 1863, HEH. The problems of fraud and contested elections are discussed in Robert J. Chandler, "Crushing Dissent: The Pacific Coast Tests Lincoln's Policy of Suppression, 1862," Civil War History 30 (September 1984): 235-254, & Woolsey, "Disunion or Dissent?" 185-206.

[33] Los Angeles Star, 5 January 1861.

[34] Ibid., 12 February 1862.

[35] Peter Heywood Wang, "The Mythical Confederate Plot in Southern California," San Bernardino County Museum Quarterly 16 (Summer 1969): 11-12.

[36] Maurice H. and Marco R. Newmark eds., Sixty Years in Southern California 1853-1913, Containing the Reminiscences of Harris Newmark (Los Angeles: Zeitlin & Ver Brugge, 1916, 4th ed., 1970), 323. Resentment toward Union occupation was a point of controversy from the early stages of the war and became a principle issue in the state legislature. See Harry Innes Thornton, Jr., "Recollection of the War by a Confederate Officer from California," Southern California Quarterly, 45 (September 1963): 202.

[37] Los Angeles Semi-Weekly News, 30 August 1861.

[38] Wolcott ed., Hayes Diary, 261-262.

[39] Statistical data found in the Los Angeles Star, 7 & 21 September 1861; Los Angeles Semi-Weekly News, 11 September 1861.

[40] The 1861 election is discussed in Woolsey, "Politics of a Lost Cause," 378, & "Disunion or Dissent?," 187.

[41] On the immediate impact of Stanford's election see, Hubert H. Bancroft, Works, (50 vols., San Francisco: The History Company, 1884-1890), 7: 290-292.

[42] Los Angeles Star, 28 September 1861.

[43] Wolcott, Hayes Diary, 258.

[44] Augustus Ensworth to Cave Johnson Couts, 9 October 1862, HEH.

[45] Los Angeles Star, 28 September 1861.

[46] John W. Davidson to Major D.C. Buell, 13 August, 1861 in the War of the Rebellion, 50: 568.

[47] Ibid., Kimball H. Dimmick to General E.V. Sumner, 8 August 1861.

[48] Los Angeles, Court of Sessions "Russell T. Hayes vs. E.J. Kewen," (No. 618, 28 October 1862), Special Collections, Seaver Center for Western History, Los Angeles County Museum. Although Kewen won the election, he was arrested a few months later for treason. After a brief period in jail, he took his seat in the state legislature. See Schuck, Representative and Leading Men of the Pacific, 341-345.

[49] Ibid., F.P. Ramirez vs. Henry Hamilton" (No. 639, 23 September 1863), SCWH.

[50] Statewide politics during the period is best discussed in several unpublished works. Principle among them are William Penn Moody, "The Civil

War and Reconstruction in California Politics" (Ph.D. dissertation, University of California, Los Angeles, 1950; Robert Chandler, "The Press and Civil Liberties in California During the Civil War, 1861-1865" (Ph.D. dissertation, University of California, Riverside, 1978); Albert Lucien Lewis, "Los Angeles in the Civil War Decades, 1850-1868" (Ph.D. dissertation, University of Southern California, 1970). On the impact of the slavery issue in partisan politics see, Gerald Stanley, "Racism and the Early republican Party: The 1856 Election in California," *Pacific Historical Review* 43 (May 1974): 171-187 and "Slavery and the Origins of the Republican party in California," *Southern California Historical Quarterly* 60 (Spring 1978): 1-16; Robert J. Chandler, "Crushing Dissent: The Pacific Coast Tests Lincoln's Policy of Suppression, 1862," *Civil War History* 30 (September 1984): 235-254; and John W. Robinson, *Los Angeles in Civil War Days 1860-1865* (Los Angeles: Dawson's Book Shop, 1977).

[51] John G. Downey to Benjamin D. Wilson, 3 April 1864, HEH.

[52] John Forster to Cave Johnson Couts, 22 June 1863, HEH.

[53] Forster to Couts, 9 October 1862, HEH.

[54] Jose Guadalupe Estudillo to Cave Johnson Couts, 12 February 1864, HEH.

[55] Cornelius Cole, *Memoirs* (New York: McLoughlin Brothers, 1908), 158.

[56] Los Angeles *Star*, 3 October 1863.

[57] Willie Blount Couts to Cave Johnson Couts, 9 November 1863, HEH. Profiles on California miners can be found in John W. Caughey, *History of the Pacific Coast of North America* (New York: Prentice-Hall Inc., 1938), 353-55.

[58] Chandler, "The Press and Civil Liberties," 451-452; and Robinson, *Civil War Days*, 139-140.Los Angeles *Star*, 3 & 24 October 1863.

[59] Edward John Cage Kewen to Cave Johnson Couts, 5 July 1862, HEH. Kewen urged Couts to attend the state Democratic Convention scheduled for August 6 in Sacramento.

[60] Ibid., John G. Downey to Pablo de la Guerra, 8 October 1860, HEH. Another Democratic leader, James Watson, had the same conviction as Downey regarding Lincoln's election. He, too, lost a Federal position as tax collector after the Republican victory. See Grenier, *California Legacy*, 161-162.

[61] "Political Statement to the People of the First Judicial District," 21 October 1863 in Benjamin Hayes, Scrapbooks, BL.

[62] Edward John Cage Kewen, "Speech Delivered at the Assembly Hall" (Sacramento, 1863), BL. Statewide, the party divided between "peace" and "war" Democrats. Ultimately, as Robert Chandler observed, "both...opposed the war, recognized the Confederacy as an independent nation, and almost preferred not to save the Union." Chandler, "The Press and Civil Liberties," 274.

63 Robinson, *Civil War Days*, 146-149;

64 Rice, *The Los Angeles Star*, 252-254.

65 John S. Griffin to Cave Johnson Couts, 27 October 1864, HEH.

66 John Forster to Cave Johnson Couts, 14 October 1864, HEH.

67 John Griffin to Cave Johnson Couts, 27 October 1864, HEH.

68 The 1864 election totals can be found in Bancroft, *Works*, 24: 311; Robinson, *Civil War Days*, 151.

69 Benjamin Wilson to Joseph Lancaster Brent, 21 September 1865, HEH.

70 Los Angeles *Semi-Weekly News*, 26 September 1865. Economic themes and post-war adjustment are addressed in Midge Sherwood, *Days of Vintage, Years of Vision* (2 vols., San Marino, Ca.: Orizaba Publications, 1982-1988), 1: 29-47; and Grenier, *California Legacy*, 203-204.

71 Edward John Cage Kewen, *Idealina: And Other Poems* (San Francisco: Cooke, Kenny & Co., 1853), 10.

CHAPTER NINE

1 Events in the early life of Charles Louis Ducommun can be found in interviews with Charles Ducommun, family recollections, and notes of Z. Lenide Ducommun. See, "History of Charles Louis Ducommun Dit Tinon," unpublished manuscript by C.A. Ducommun, #6 Box 5 (March 1930); C. Ducommun, "Charles Louis Ducommun and the Golden Island,", unpublished manuscript, n.d., #5 Box 5; and Ducommun since 1849, unpublished booklet, n.d., #7 Box 5, at the Seaver Center for Western History, Los Angeles County Museum.

2 Ralph Moody, *The Old Trails West* (New York: Thomas Y. Crowell Company, 1963), 29.

3 Ibid., 28-33, 93. Moody notes that "during the gold-rush years, sixty thousand people, and more than double that number of beef cattle and sheep, entered California by way of the Gila Trail." For a general understanding of trail history during this era, see classic works by Roscoe and Margaret Conkling, *Butterfield Overland Mail 1857-1869* (Arthur H. Clark Company, 1947), Leroy and Ann Hafen, *The Old Spanish Trail* (Arthur H. Clark Company, 1955), Benjamin Harris, *Gila Trail* (Norman, OK: University of Oklahoma Press, 1960), Bernard De Voto, *The Course of the Empire* (Houghton Mifflin Company, 1952), and George R. Stewart, *The California Trail* (New York: McGraw-Hill Book Company, Inc., 1962).

4 Nearly two centuries earlier, Eusebio Kino recognized the the threat of Indians along the trail. He noted that the "common sorrow" in the settlements was the "continued invasions, robberies, and murders by so many hostile Hocomes, Apaches, and Xanos [native tribes along the Gila Trail]." See, Herbert Eugene Bolton, *Kino's Historical Memoir of Pimeria Alta, 1683-1711* (Cleveland: The Arthur H. Clark Co., 1919), 171.

[5] John Walton Caughey, *Gold Is A Cornerstone* (Berkeley: University of California Press, 1948), 145.

[6] William G. Robbins, "Western History: A Dialectic on the Modern Condition," *Western Historical Quarterly* 20 (November 1989): 436.

[7] Harris Newmark, *Sixty Years in Southern California 1853-1913* (Boston & New York: Houghton Mifflin Company, 1930), 68.

[8] Robert V. Hine, *Community on the American Frontier, Separate But Not Alone* (Norman: University of Oklahoma Press, 1980), 157.

[9] Sarah Bixby Smith, *Adobe Days*, with a forward by Gloria Ricci Lothrop (Lincoln: University of Nebraska Press, 1931, 1987), 102.

[10] Newmark, *Sixty Years*, 69.

[11] "Ducommun and the Golden Island," Ducommun Collection #5, Box 5, 25-26, SCWH.

[12] Business transactions, deeds, and warranties are found in the Ducommun collection at the Seaver Center for Western History. See, Warranty Deed B.D. Wilson to C.L. Ducommun 25 November 1853; Deed of Trust, Joseph Bernstein to Charles Ducommun 13 January 1855; Deed of Trust, John Barre to Charles L. Ducommun 14 May 1857; and Deed of Trust George Torrya and Antonio Torrya to Charles L. Ducommun 31 March 1858. All documents in Box 4, SCWH.

[13] Col. J.J. Warner, Benjamin Hayes, J.P. Widney, *An Historical Sketch of Los Angeles County California* (Los Angeles: Louis Lewin & Co., 1876), 82-83.

[14] Boyle Workman, *The City That Grew* (Los Angeles: Southland Publishing Co., 1936), 127.

[15] Newmark, *Sixty Years*, 69.

[16] Los Angeles *Star* as quoted in Ducommun, "Ducommun and the Golden Island," #5, Box 5, 29, SCWH.

[17] Ibid., 28.

[18] "Ducommun and The Golden Island," Ducommun Collection #5 Box 5, 28, SCWH. Ducommun participated in a few important cases of the 1850s. He testified in the pursuit and investigation of Ned McGowan, an alleged conspirator in the murder of newspaper editor, J. King of William. The San Francisco Vigilante Committee had pursued McGowan throughout the state, and Ducommun testified of hearing that he was in hiding at the San Fernando Mission under the protection of Andres Pico and Jack Powers. Ducommun also participated in the jury trial of Luciano Tapia, the last of the Flores gang to be captured, tried, and hanged. See testimony and court records in District Court, "People v. Jack Powers & Andres Pico: Ducommun testimony, 14 July 1856, and "People v. Tapia" 17 December 1857, SCWH.

[19] Ibid., #6 Box 5.

[20] Ibid.

[21] Workman, *The City That Grew*, 57-104.

22 Wilson to Joseph Lancaster Brent, 10 April 1868. Banning's railroad connection from San Pedro to Los Angeles was important to the farming boom of the late 1860s. See, Remi Nadeau, *From Mission to Modern City* (Los Angeles: Longmans, Green and Company, 1960), 64-65.

23 Chimawabo Consolidated Copper and Silver Mining Company, Stock Certificate No. 128, 6 October 1863, (50 shares @ $50 per share), Folder #3, Box 6, SCWH.

24 Ibid.; Pioneer Oil Company, Stock Certificate No. 20, 12 October 1865, Folder #2, Box 6. Also mentioned in Workman, *The City That Grew*, 255-256, and Newmark, Sixty Years, 346.

25 Robert Glass Cleland, *The March of Industry* (Los Angeles: Powell Publishing Co., 1929), 171.

26 Newmark, *Sixty Years*, 346.

27 Newmark, *Sixty Years*, 423.

28 Robert Glass Cleland, *Isaias W. Hellman and the Farmers and Merchants Bank* (San Marino, The Huntington Library, 1965, 1980), 25, 28, 32, 43-47.

29 "History of Charles Louis Ducommun Dit Tinon," Ducommun Collection #6 Box 5, SCWH.

30 Ibid., # 7 Box 5.

31 Ibid., #5 Box 5, pp. 31-36.

CHAPTER TEN

1 S. A. Gilpin, "Difficulties of the Indian Problem," *University of New Mexico* 2 (July 1887): 14.

2 San Jacinto Valley *Register*, 1939, Special Edition, "Origin of the Ramona Play Idea Early Efforts to Produce" by Jeanne Foreman. On the commercial and promotional impact of *Ramona* in Southern California, see Ramona Pageant, *California's Greatest Outdoor Play: Ramona, Souvenir Program and Directory of Landmarks* (Little, Bronw, & Co., 1939); Charles R. Le Menager, *Ramona and Round About, A History Of San Diego County's Little Known Back Country* (Ramona,Ca.: Eagle Peak Publishing, 1989); and Lulu R. O'Neal, *The History of Ramona, California and Environs* (Ramona: CA: Ballena Press, 1975).

3 Kevin Starr, *Inventing The Dream, California Through the Progressive Era* (Oxford: Oxford University Press, 1985), 292. Loretta Young also starred in a later movie version of *Ramona*. For an interesting visual discussion of the myth and film, see the Los Angeles History Project Series, *Ramona: A Story of Passion & Protest*, produced for KCET Channel 28 by Wilkman Productions; also, a brief overview by Nancy Wilkman, "Helen Hunt Jackson's Ramona," *The Southern Californian* 7 (Spring 1995): 4

4 H.D. Barrows, "Antonio Coronel," *Annual Publication of Historical Society of Southern California and Pioneer Register* 5 (1901): 78.

5 Antonio Coronel, Speech, unknown dates, #239, 242-243, Coronel Collection, Seaver Center for Western History, Los Angeles County Museum.

6 Ibid., 80-81. Also see, *An Illustrated History of Southern California* (Chicago: The Lewis Publishing Company, 1890), 759.

7 Susan Coultrap-McQuin, *Doing Literary Business, American Women Writers in the Nineteenth Century* (Chapel Hill: University of North Carolina Press, 1990), 148.

8 Evelyn I. Banning, *Helen Hunt Jackson* (New York: Vanguard Press, 1973), 195-197.

9 Rosemary Whitaker, "Helen Hunt Jackson," *Western History Writer Series* 78 (1987): 28.

10 Antonio [Franco] Coronel to J. Adams 11 April 1889, Antonio [Franco] Coronel Letters, Henry E. Huntington Library, San Marino, CA.

11 Jeanne C. [Smith] Carr, "Recollections of Helen Hunt Jackson," unpublished manuscript (1895 est.), HEH.

12 Ruth Odell, *Helen Hunt Jackson* (New York: D. Appleton-Century Company, 1939), 177. In fact, Mrs. Coronel's close relationship with Jackson is alluded to years later, when Charles C. Painter recalled that Mrs. Coronel "will be more fully convinced than ever before, that the sainted spirit of Helen Hunt Jackson, still moves on the minds and hearts of some who have been dealing with this question." Painter to Antonio F. Coronel, 28 January 1891, SCWH.

13 Valerie S. Mathes, *Helen Hunt Jackson and Her Indian Reform Legacy* (Texas: University of Texas Press, 1990), 45.

14 Henry Y. Sandham to Antonio Coronel, 7 October 1882, SCWH.

15 Carr, "Recollections."

16 Edward Roberts, "Ramona's Home, A Visit To The Camulos Ranch, And to Scenes Described by H. H." in Helen Hunt Jackson, *Ramona* (Cambridge: Roberts Brothers, 1884), 1-7. In a larger context, for a fine overview of selected essays on the impact of Spanish culture on Southern California, see Doyce B. Nunis, Jr. ed., *Southern California's Spanish Heritage: An Anthology* (Los Angeles: Historical Society of Southern California, 1992).

17 O'Neal, *The History of Ramona*, 25.

18 Carlyle Channing Davis & William A. Alderson, *The True Story of Ramona, Its Facts and Fictions, Inspiration and Purpose* (New York: Dodge Publishing Company, 1914), 27-32.

19 Charles C. Painter to Antonio Coronel, 15 June 1886, HEH.

20 Coronel to Painter, 22 May 1886, HEH.

21 Coronel discussed Indian relocation with Jackson. See Coronel to Jackson December 1882 & 1 August 1883, Coronel Collection, SCWH. Native American Women Rights activists were inspired by

Jackson's writings, and her influence in shaping government policy was evident during the 1880s. See, Valerie Sherer Mathes, "The California Mission Indian Commission of 1891, The Legacy of Helen Hunt Jackson," *California History* (Winter 1993/94): 338-360

[22] Coronel, Speech, unknown date, #244, SCWH.

[23] Helen Hunt Jackson, *Ramona*, with an introduction by Michael Dorris (New York: New American Library, 1884, 1988), 12.

[24] Coronel to Adams, 11 April 1889, HEH.

[25] Ibid., comment & translation by George Butler Griffen, 9 November 1890.

[26] *Illustrated History*, 759.

[27] Jackson, *Ramona*, 22-26.

[28] *Ilustrated History*, 759.

[29] Jackson, *Ramona*, 66.

[30] Los Angeles *Star*, 24 May 1851. Also discussed in Ronald C. Woolsey, "Crime and Punishment: Los Angeles County, 1850-1856, *Southern California Quarterly* 41 (Spring 1979): 83-85.

[31] Los Angeles *Star*, 21 February 1852.

[32] Ibid., 28 August 1852.

[33] Ibid., 16 October 1852.

[34] Jackson, *Ramona*, 74.

[35] Ibid., 18, 78. The character of Padre Salvierderra was patterned after a priest Jackson had met while she was at Mission Santa Barbara in 1882. See Kevin Starr, *Material Dreams, Southern California Through the 1920s* (Oxford: University of Oxford Press, 1990), 251-252.

[36] Channing & Alderson, *The True Story of Ramona*, 28.

[37] Unsigned Letter,"Indian Woman's Rights," *Ramona Days* 2 (April 1888): 11-12, Special Collections, Huntington Library.

[38] Los Angeles, Court of Sessions, *People v. Juan de dios de Garcia*, testimony of Jesus Parado, 10 September 1850, SCWH.

[39] *People v. Fernando Vacquites*, testimony of Samuel C. Won, 11 July 1850,SCWH.

[40] Wilbur R. Jacobs,"On The Trail Of Debris: Some Environmental Encounters In American History," lecture given at California State University, Los Angeles, 13 July 1994. Professor Jacobs notes provided to the author.

[41] Jackson, *Ramona*, 267.

[42] Ramona Pageant, *Greatest Play*, overview, n.p., HEH.

[43] E. M. Jordan to Horatio Nelson Rust, 14 December 1903, Rust Papers, HEH.

[44] Ramona Pageant, *Greatest Play*, overview, n.p.

[45] Ibid.

[46] Jackson, *Ramona*, 362

CONCLUSION

[1] Col. J.J. Warner, Judge Benjamin Hayes, and Dr. J.P. Widney, *An Historical Sketch of Los Angeles County California* (Los Angeles: Louis Lewin & Co., 1876), 62.

[2] Midge Sherwood, *Days of Vintage Years of Vision*, (2 vols. San Marino: Orizaba Press, 1987) 2:361.

[3] Margaret Wilson to Joseph Lancaster Brent, 10 April 1866, Benjamin Wilson Collection, Henry E. Huntington Library, San Marino, CA.

[4] Benjamin Harrison, *Fortunes Favor the Brave, The Life and Times of Horace Bell Pioneer Californian* (Los Angeles: Ward Ritchie Press, 1953), 278.

[5] Warner etal., *Historical Sketch*, 85.

[6] Los Angeles *Herald*, 29 November 1879.

[7] Los Angeles *Times*, 5 April 1896.

[8] Helen Hunt Jackson to Horatio Nelson Rust, 29 April 1885, HEH.

[9] Jackson to Antonio Coronel, 30 July 1885 Coronel Collection, Seaver Center for Western History, Los Angeles County Museum.

[10] Frank S. Thayer ed., *In Memoriam, Helen Hunt Jackson* (Denver, CO: Frank S. Thayer, 1886).

[11] H.D. Barrows, "Antonio Coronel," *Annual Publication of Historical Society of Southern California & Pioneer Register* 5 (1900): 78. An excellent overview of Coronel's life and writings is Doyce B. Nunis, Jr. ed., *Tales of Mexican California by Antonio Coronel* (Santa Barbara, CA, 1994).

Bibliography

I. Unpublished Works

A. Special Collections, Letters, Papers

1. California State Library, California Room, Sacramento
   California History Photography Collections

2. Hubert Howe Bancroft Library, University of CA, Berkeley
   Alexander Grayson Bowman Journal
   James Henry Carleton Portfolio
   Benjamin Hayes Scrapbooks
   Los Angeles Star Scrapbook
   Edward John Cage Kewen Letters, Speeches

3. Henry E. Huntington Library, San Marino, California
   Abel Stearns Collection
   Horace Bell Papers
   Joseph Lancaster Brent Collection
   California Historical Documents Collection
   Antonio Coronel Letters
   Cave Johnson Couts Collection
   John G. Downey Papers
   Hugo Reid Letters
   Horatio Nelson Rust Letters
   Benjamin Davis Wilson Papers
   General Photography Collection

4. Seaver Center for Western History. Los Angeles County Museum
   Criminal Court Records
   Antonio Coronel Collection
   Charles Louis Ducommun Papers
   General Collection of Photographs
   Hugo Reid Collection

B. Newspapers
Baltimore *American*
Contra Costa *Gazette*
Charleston *Mercury*
El *Clamor Publico*
Los Angeles *Herald*
Los Angeles *News*
Los Angeles *Semi-Weekly News*
Los Angeles *Star*
Los Angeles *Times*
Mobile *Advertiser*
Oroville *Butte Record*
Sacramento *Daily Bee*
Sacramento *Daily Union*
San Francisco *Daily Evening Bulletin*
San Jacinto *Register*
Southern Californian
New Orleans *Daily Picayune*

C. Dissertations, Lectures, Manuscripts

Blew, Robert Willis. "California and American Institutions: A Study of Reactions to Social and Political Institutions." Ph.D. dissertation, 1973. University of Southern California.

Brent, Joseph Lancaster. *Life in California*, annotated by Frances Rossella [Kenner] Brent, unpublished manuscript (1900). Huntington Library, San Marino, CA.

Carr, Jeanne C. [Smith]. *"Recollections of Helen Hunt Jackson."* unpublished manuscript (1895 est.) Huntington Library, San Marino, CA.

Chandler, Robert. *"The Press and Civil Liberties in California during the Civil War, 1861-1865."* Ph.D. dissertation, 1978, University of California, Riverside.

Griswold del Castillo, Richard. *"La Raza Hispano Americana: The Emergence of an Urban Culture Among the Spanish Speaking of Los Angeles 1850-1880."* Ph.D. dissertation, 1974, University of California, Los Angeles.

Hough, John Cushing. *"Abel Stearns, 1848-1871."* Ph.D. dissertation, 1961. University of California, Los Angeles.

Jacobs, Wilbur R. *"On The Trail of Debris: Some Environmental Encounters in American History."* Lecture given at California State University Los Angeles, notes in author's possession, 13 July 1994.

Kiefer, Melissa D. *"Female Heroes on the Overland Trails."* B.A. Thesis, 1989, Scripps College, Claremont.

Lewis, Albert Lucien. *"Los Angeles in the Civil War Decades, 1850- 1868."* Ph.D. dissertation, 1970, University of Southern California.

Moody, William Penn. *"The Civil War and Reconstruction in California Politics."* Ph.D. dissertation, 1950, University of California, Los Angeles.

Tays, George. *"Revolutionary California: The Political History of California During the Mexican Period 1822-1846."* Ph.D. dissertation, University of California, Berkeley, 1955.

II. Published Primary Sources

Basler, Roy P., Pratt, Marion Dolores, and Dunlap, Lloyd A., ed. *The Collected Works of Abraham Lincoln.* 8 vols. New Jersey: Rutgers University Press, 1953-1955.

Bell, Horace. *On the Old West Coast: Being Further Reminiscences of a Ranger.* edited by Lanier Bartlett. New York: Grossett & Dunlap, 1930.

————. *Reminiscences of a Ranger.* Santa Barbara: Wallace Hebberd, 1927.

Brown, J. Ross ed. *Constitutional Convention of 1849: Debates and Reports.* Washington D.C.: J.T. Towers, 1850.

Congressional Globe. 31 Congress, 1 Session. 1850. Washington, D.C.: Government Printing Office, 1851.

Davis, William Heath. *Seventy-Five Years in California, A History of Events and Life in California: Personal Political and Military.* San Francisco: John Howell, 1889, 1967.

Hammond, George P., ed. *The Larkin Papers.* 10 vols. Berkeley: University of California Press, 1955.

Heizer, Robert F. ed. *The Indians of Los Angeles County, Hugo Reid's Letters of 1852.* Los Angeles: Southwest Museum, 1968.

Jackson, Helen Hunt. *Ramona.* Iintroduction by Michael Dorris. New York: New American Library, 1884, 1988.

————. *Journal of the House of Assembly of California.* 12 Session, Sacramento: C.T. Botts, 1861.

Kewen, Edward John Cage. *Idealina: And Other Poems.* San Francisco: Cooke, Kenny & Co., 1853.

Larkin, Thomas O. *The Affair at Monterey, October 20 & 21, 1842.* Introduction by Doyce B. Nunis Jr. Los Angeles: The Zamorano Club, 1964.

Lecompte, Janet ed. Emily French, *The Diary of a Hard-Worked Woman.* Lincoln: University of Nebraska Press, 1987.

Moore, John Bassett, ed. *The Works of James Buchanan.* 12 vols. New York: Antiquarian Press Ltd., 1960.

Newmark, Maurice H. and Marco R., eds. *Sixty Years in Southern California 1853-1913, containing the Reminiscences of Harris Newmark.* 4th ed. Los Angeles, Zeitlin & Ver Brugge, 1916, 1970.

Nunis Jr., Doyce B., ed. *The Bidwell-Bartleson Party, 1841 California Emigrant Adventure.* Santa Cruz: Western Tanager Press, 1991.

———— ed. *Tales of Mexican California by Antonio Coronel.* Santa Barbara, CA: Bellerophon Books, 1994.

Parkman, Francis. *The Oregon Trail.* New York: The Library of America, 1847, 1991.

Pomfret, John Edsin, ed. *California Gold Rush Voyages, 1848-1849: Three Original Narratives.* San Marino: Huntington Library, 1954.

Reid, Hugo. *The Indians of Southern California.* Forward by Arthur M. Ellis. Los Angeles: privately printed, 1926.

Rives, John C. ed. *Abridgement of the Debates of Congress, 1789- 1856.* 20 vols. New York: D. Appleton & Co., 1863.

Robinson, Alfred. *Life in California, and Friar Geronimo Boscana, Chinigchinich.* Introduction by Andrew Rolle. Santa Barbara: Peregrine Publishers, Inc., 1970.

Royce, Josiah. *California, From the Conquest in 1846 to the Second Vigilance Committee in San Francisco.* Boston: Houghton Mifflin Co., 1886.

Smith, Sarah Bixby. *Adobe Days.* Forward by Gloria Ricci Lothrop. Lincoln: University of Nebraska Press, 1931, 1987.

The War of the Rebellion: A Compilation of the Official Records of the Union and Confederate Armies. Series 1, 50 vol. Washington D.C.: Government Printing Office, 1897.

Weber, David J. *The Californios versus Jedediah Smith 1826-1827, A New Cache of Documents.* Spokane, WA.: Arthur H. Clark Co., 1990.

————. *Northern Mexico on the Eve of the United States Invasion, Rare Imprints Concerning California, Arizona, New Mexico, and Texas, 1821-1846.* reprint ed. New York: Arno Press, 1976.

Wolcott, Marjorie T., ed. *Pioneer Notes from the Diary of Judge Benjamin Hayes, 1849-1875.* Los Angeles: McBride Printing Company, 1929.

III. Published Secondary Sources

A. Books

Ainsworth, Ed. *Enchanted Pueblo.* Los Angeles: Bank of America, N.T. & S.A., 1959.

Allen, Martha Mitten. *Traveling West: 19th Century Women on the Overland Routes.* El Paso: Texas Western Press, 1987.

An Illustrated History of Southern California. Chicago: The Lewis Publishing Company, 1890.

Bakken, Gordon Morris. *The Development of Law in Frontier California: Civil Law and Society, 1850-1890.* Wesport, CT: Greenwood Press, 1985.

————. *Practicing Law in Frontier California.* Lincoln: University of

Nebraska Press, 1991. Bancroft, Hubert Howe, Works, 50 vols.
San Francisco: The History Co., Publisher, 1880-1890.

Banning, Evelyn I. *Helen Hunt Jackson*. New York: Vanguard Press, 1973.

Barrera, Mario. *Race and Class in the Southwest: A Theory of Racial Inequality*. Notre Dame: University of Notre Dame Press, 1989.

Beck, Warren A. and William, David A. *California: A History of the Golden State*. Garden City, NY: Doubleday & Co., 1972.

Billington, Ray Allen, and Camarillo, Albert, eds. *The American Southwest, Image and Reality*. Los Angeles: University of California Press, 1977.

————. *The Far Western Frontier 1830-1860*. New York: Harper & Brothers, 1956.

————. *The Frontier and American Culture*. Sacramento: California Library Association, 1965.

Boessenecker, John. *Badge and Buckshot: Lawlessness in Old California*. Norman: University of Oklahoma Press, 1988.

Bolton, Herbert Eugene. *Kino's Historical Memoir of Pimeria Alta, 1683-1711*. Cleveland: The Arthur H. Clark Co., 1919.

Brown, Richard Maxwell, ed. *Strain of Violence: Historical Studies of America Violence and Vigilantism*. New York: Oxford University Press, 1975.

Huntington Library ed. *Manuscripts in the Huntington Library: A guide by the committee on history and law in California of the state bar of California*. San Marino: Huntington Library, 1989.

Camarillo, Albert. *Chicanos in a Changing Society: From Mexican Pueblos to American Barrios in Santa Barbara and Southern California, 1849-1930*. Cambridge, MA: Harvard University Press, 1979.

Caughey, John W. *Gold Is The Cornerstone*. Berkeley: University of California Press, 1948.

————. *History of the Pacific Coast of North America*. New York: Prentice Hall Inc., 1938.

———— ed. *Rushing for Gold*. Berkeley: University of California Press, 1949.

Churchill, Charles B. *Adventurers and Prophets, American Autobiographies in Mexican California, 1828-1847*. (Spokane, WA: Arthur H. Clark Co.,1995).

Cleland, Robert Glass. *A History of California: The American Period*. New York: The MacMillan Co., 1939.

————. *Cattle on a Thousand Hills*. San Marino: Huntington Library, 1941.

————. *El Molino Viejo*. Los Angeles: Ward Ritchie Press, 1950.

————. *From Wilderness to Empire*. New York: Alfred A. Knopf, 1994.

————. *Isaias W. Hellman and the Farmers and Merchants Bank.* San Marino: Huntington Library, 1965.

————. *The March of Industry. Los Angeles*: Powell Publishing Co., 1929.

Clinton, Catherine. *The Other Civil War: American Women in the Nineteenth Century*. New York: Hill and Wang, 1984.

————. *The Plantation Mistress: Woman's World in the Old South*. New York: Pantheon Books, 1982.

Conkling, Roscoe and Margaret. *Butterfield Overland Mail 1857-1869.* Glendale, CA: Arthur H. Clark Company, 1947.

Connor, Seymour V. and Skaggs, Jim M. *Broadcloth and Britches: The Santa Fe Trade*. College Station: Texas A & M University Press, 1977.

Coulter, E. Merton. *The Confederate States of America, 1861-1865.* Baton Rouge: Louisana State University Press, 1950.

Coultrap-Mcquin, Susan. *Doing Literary Business, American Women Writers in the Nineteenth Century*. Chapel Hill: University of North Carolina Press, 1990.

Dakin, Susanna Bryant. *A Scotch Paisano*. Berkeley: University of California Press, 1939.

Davis, Carlyle Channing & Alderson, William A. *The True Story of Ramona, Its Facts and Fictions, Inspiration and Purpose*. New York: Dodge Publishing Company, 1914.

Davis, W. W .H. *El Gringo, or New Mexico and Her People*. New York: Harper & Brothers, 1857.

Deutsch, Sarah. *No Separate Refuge: Culture, Class, and Gender on an Anglo-Hispanic Frontier in the American Southwest, 1880-1940*. New York: Oxford University Press, 1987.

De Voto, Bernard. *The Course of the Empire*. New York: Houghton Mifflin Company, 1952.

Dillon, Richard H., ed. *The Gila Trail, The Texas Argonauts and the California Gold Rush*. Norman: University of Oklahoma Press, 1960.

Donald, David H. *Lincoln*. New York, NY: Simon and Schuster, 1995).

Drumm, Stella M., ed. *Down the Santa Fe Trail and Into Mexico: The Diary of Susan Shelby Magoffin, 1846-1847*. New Haven, CT: Yale University Press, 1926.

Dubois, Ellen Carol and Ruiz, Vicki L., eds. *Unequal Sisters: A Multicultural Reader in U. S. Women's History*. New York: Routledge, 1990.

Dummond, Dwight L. *The Secession Movement, 1860-1861*. New York: Macmillan Company, 1931.

Fehrenbacher, Don E. *Prelude to Greatness, Lincoln in the 1850s*. Stanford, CA: Stanford University Press, 1962.

Foner, Eric ed. *Nat Turner*. Englewood Cliffs, NJ: Prentice Hall, 1971.

————. *Politics and Ideology in the Age of the Civil War*. New York: Oxford University Press, 1980.

Foote, Cheryl J. *Women of the New Mexico Frontier, 1846-1912*. Boulder: University of Colorado Press, 1990.

Geiger, Maynard, O. F. M. *Franciscan Missionaries in Hispanic California, 1769-1848*. San Marino: Huntington Library, 1969.

Genovese, Eugene. *Political Economy of Slavery: Studies in the Economy & Society of the Slave South*. Middletown, CT: Wesleyan University Press, 1967, 1989.

Gibson, Arrell Morgan. *Yankees in Paradis: The Pacific Basin Frontier.* Albuquerque: University of New Mexico Press, 1993.

Goetzmann, William H. *Army Exploration in the American West*. Austin: Texas A & M University Press, 1959, 1991.

————. *Exploration and Empire: The Explorer and the Scientist in the Winning of the American West*. New York: Knopf, 1966.

————. *The West of the Imagination*. New York: Norton, 1986.

Grenier, Judson A. *California Legacy: The Watson Family*. Los Angeles: Watson Land Co., 1987.

Griswold del Castillo, Richard. *The Los Angeles Barrio, 1850-1890*. Berkeley: University of California Press, 1979.

Hafen, Leroy and Ann. *The Old Spanish Trail*. Glendale, CA: Arthur H. Clark Company, 1955.

Hague, Harlan. *The Road to California: The Search for a Southern Overland Route, 1540-1848*. Glendale, CA: Arthur H. Clark Co., 1978.

Hague, Harlan and Langum, David J., Thomas O. Larkin. *A Life of Patriotism and Profit in Old California*. Norman: University of Oklahoma Press, 1990.

Hamilton, Holman. *Prologue to Conflict: The Crisis and Compromise of 1850*. New York: W.W. Norton & Co., 1964.

————. *Zachary Taylor: Soldier in the White House*. Indianapolis: Bobbs-Merrill Co., 1951.

Harris, Benjamin. *Gila Trail*. Norman: University of Oklahoma Press, 1960.

Harrison, Benjamin S. *Fortune Favors the Brave, the Life and Times of Horace Bell Pioneer California*. Los Angeles: Ward Ritchie Press, 1953.

Hawgood, John A., ed. *First and Last Consul, Thomas Oliver Larkin and the Americanization of California*. San Marino: Huntington Library, 1962.

Heizer, Robert F. and Almquist, Alan F. *The Other Californians: Prejudice and Discrimination Under Spain, Mexico, and the United States to 1920*. Los Angeles: University of California Press, 1971.

Herr, Pamela. *Jessie Benton Fremont: A Biography*. New York: Watt Publishing, 1987.

Hine, Robert V. *Community on the American Frontier, Separate But Not Alone.* Norman: University of Oklahoma Press, 1980.

Hunt, Aurora. *The Army of the Pacific.* Glendale: CA: The Arthur H. Clark Co., 1951.

Hutchinson, C. Alan. *Frontier Settlement in Mexican California, The Hijar-Padres Colony, and Its Origins 1769-1835.* New Haven, CT: Yale University Press, 1969.

Hurtado,l Albert L. *Indian Survival on the California Frontier.* New Haven, CT: Yale University Press, 1988.

Huston, James L. *The Panic of 1857 and the Coming of the Civil War.* Baton Rouge: Louisiana State University Press, 1987.

Jackson, W. Turrentine. *The California Gold Rush Diary of a German Sailor.* Berkeley: Howell-North Books, 1969.

Jensen, Joan M. and Miller, Darlis, eds. *New Mexico Women: Intercultural Perspectives.* Albuquerque: University of New Mexico Press, 1986.

Johannsen, Robert W. *Frontier Conflicts and the Sectional Conflict: The Pacific Northwest on the Eve of the Civil War.* Seattle: University of Washington Press, 1955.

Kemble, Edward C. *A History of California Newspapers, 1846-1858.* Los Gatos, CA: Talisman Press, 1962.

Lamar, Howard. *The Far Southwest 1846-1912, A Territorial History.* New York: Norton, 1966.

Langum, David J. *Law and Community on the Mexican California Frontier, Anglo-American Expatriates and the Clash of Legal Traditions, 1821-1846.* Norman: University of Oklahoma Press, 1987.

Latta, Frank F. *Joaquin Murrieta and His Horse Gangs.* Santa Cruz: Bear State Books, 1980.

Lavender, David. *Bent's Fort.* Garden City, NY: Doubleday & Co., 1945.
————. *California: Land of New Beginning.* New York: Harper & Row, 1972.

Le Menager, Charles R. *Ramona and Round About, A History of San Diego County's Little Known Back Country.* Ramona, CA.: Engle Peak Publishing, 1989.

Levy, Joann. *They Saw the Elephant: Women in the California Gold Rush.* Hamden, CT: Archon Books, 1990.

Limerick, Patricia Nelson. *The Legacy of Conquest: The Unbroken Past of the American West.* New York: Norton Publishers, 1987.

Mathes, Valerie S. *Helen Hunt Jackson and Her Indian Reform Legacy.* Austin: University of Texas Press, 1990.

McDermott, John, ed. *An Artist on the Overland Trail, The 1849 Diary and Sketches of James F. Wilkins.* San Marino, CA: Huntington Library, 1968.

McKitrick, Eric, ed. *Slavery Defended: The Views of the Old South.* Englewood Cliffs, NJ: Prentice Hall, 1963.

McPherson, James. *Battle Cry of Freedom, The Civil War Era.* New York: Oxford University Press, 1988.

Montejano, David. *Anglos and Mexicans in the Making of Texas, 1836- 1986.* Austin: University of Texas Press, 1987.

Moody, Ralph. *The Old Trails West*. New York: Thomas Y. Crowell Co., 1963.

Mullen, Kevin J. *Let Justice Be Done: Crime and Politics in Early San Francisco*. Reno: University of Nevada Press, 1989.

Nadeau, Remi. *City Makers: The Men Who Transformed Los Angeles from Village to Metropolis During the First Grreat Boom, 1861-1876*. Garden City, NY: Doubleday and Company, 1948.

————. *From Mission to Modern City*. Los Angeles: Longmans, Green and Company, 1960.

Nevins, Allan. *Ordeal of the Union*. 2 vols. New York: Scribners, 1947.

Nichols, Roy F. *The Disruption of American Democracy*. New York: Collier Publishing, 1948.

Nunis, Jr., Doyce B. and Lothrop, Gloria Ricci, eds. *A Guide to the History of California*. Westport, CT: Greenwood Press, 1989.

Nunis, Jr., Doyce B. *Los Angeles and Its Environs In The Twentieth Century*. Los Angeles: Ward Ritchie Press, 1973.

————. *Southern California's Spanish Heritage: An Anthology*. Los Angeles: Historical Society of Southern California, 1992.

O'Neal, Lulu R. *The History of Ramona, California and Environs*. Ramona, CA: Ballena Press, 1975.

Odell, Ruth. *Helen Hunt Jackson*. New York: D. Appleton-Century Company, 1939.

Olivera, Ruth R. and Crete, Liliane. *Life in Mexico Under Santa Anna 1822-1855*. Norman: University of Oklahoma Press, 1991.

Pascoe, Peggy. *Relations of Rescue: The Search for Female Moral Authority in the American West*. New York: Oxford University Press, 1990.

Phillips, George Harwood. *Chiefs and Challengers, Indian Resistance and Cooperation in Southern California*. Berkeley and Los Angeles: University of California Press, 1975.

————. *Indians and Intruders in Central California, 1769-1849*. Norman: University of Oklahoma Press, 1993.

Pitt, Leonard. *The Decline of the Californios: A Social History of the Spanish-speaking California, 1846-1890*. Berkeley and Los Angeles: University of California Press, 1966.

Ramona Pageant. *California's Great Outdoor Play: Ramona*. Souvenir Program and Directory of Landmarks. Boston: Little, Brown & Co., 1939.

Rice, Richard B. Bullough, William A. and Orsi, Richard J. *The Elusive Eden: A New History of California*. New York: Alfred A. Knopf, 1988.

Rice, William B. *The Los Angeles Star, 1851-1864: The Beginnings of Journalism in Southern California*. Berkeley: University of California Press, 1947.

Riley, Glenda. *The Female Frontier: A Comparative View of Women on the Prairie and the Plains*. Lawrence: University of Kansas Press, 1988.

———. *Woman and Indians on the Frontier, 1825-1915*. El Paso: Texas Western Press, 1978.

Robinson, John W. *Los Angeles in Civil War Days 1860-1865*. Los Angeles: Dawson's Book Shop, 1977.

Robinson, W. W. *Lawyers of Los Angeles*. Los Angeles: War Ritchie Press, 1959.

———. *Los Angeles from the Days of the Pueblo, A Brief History and Guide to the Plaza Area*. Introduction by Doyce B. Nunis, Jr. Los Angeles: California Historical Society, 1959, 1981.

———. *Woman of California: Susana Bryant Dakin*. Bancroft Library: The California Arboretum Foundation Inc., 1967.

Rolle, Andrew. *John C. Fremont: Character as Destiny*. Norman: University of Oklahoma Press, 1991.

———. *Los Angeles: From Pueblo to City of the Future*. San Francisco: Boyd & Fraser Publishing Co., 1981.

Romo, Ricardo. *East Los Angeles, History of a Barrio*. Austin: University of Texas Press, 1983.

Rozwenc, Edwin C. *The Compromise of 1850*. Boston: D.C. Heath & Co., 1957.

Schlissel, Lillian. *Woman Diaries of the Westward Journey*. New York: Schoken Books, 1982.

Secrest, William B. *Lawmen & Desperadoes, A Compendium of Noted, Early California Peace Officers, Badmen and Outlaws 1850-1900*. Seattle, WA: Arthur H. Clark Company, 1994.

Sherwood, Midge. *Days of Vintage, Years of Vision*. 2 vols. San Marino, CA.: Orizaba Publications, 1982, 1988.

———. *San Marino: From Ranch to City*. San Marino, San Marino Historical Society, 1977.

Shuck, Oscar T. *Representative and Leading Men in the Pacific*. San Francisco: Bacon & Company, 1870.

Stampp, Kenneth M. *America in 1857: A Nation on the Brink*. New York: Oxford University Press, 1990.

———. *The Peculiar Institution: Slaver in the Ante-Bellum South*. New York: Knopf, 1956.

Starr, Kevin. *Inventing the Dream: California Through the Progressive Era*. New York: Oxford University Press, 1985.

————. *Material Dreams, Southern California Through the 1920s.* New York: Oxford University Press, 1990.

Stewart, George R. *The California Trail, An Epic With Many Heroes.* New York: McGraw-Hill Book Co., 1962.

Stout, Joseph Allen. *The Liberators: Filibustering Expeditions into Mexico, 1848-1862 and the Last Thrust of Manifest Destiny.* Los Angeles: Westernlore Press, 1973.

Thayer, Frank S., ed. *In Memoriam, Helen Hunt Jackson.* Denver: Frank S. Thayer, 1886.

Thomas, Emory M. *The Confederacy as a Revolutionary Experience.* Englewood Cliffs, NJ: Prentice Hall, 1971.

————. *The Confederate Nation, 1861-1865.* New York: Harper & Row, 1979.

Vickery, Oliver. *Harbor Heritage, Tales of the Harbor Area of Los Angeles, California.* Mountain View, CA: Morgan Press, 1979.

Warner, Col J.J., Hayes, Benjamin, Widney, J.P. *An Historical Sketch of Los Angeles County California.* Los Angeles: Louis Lewin & Co., 1876.

Watson, Jeanne Hamilton, ed. *To the Land of Gold and Wickedness: The 1848-59 Diary of Lorena L. Hays.* St Louis, MO: Patrice Press, 1988.

Weber, David J. *Foreigners in Their Native Land: Historical Roots of the Mexican Americans.* Albuquerque: University of New Mexico Press, 1973.

————. *The Mexican Frontier 1821-1846, The American Southwest Under Mexico.* Albuquerque: University of New Mexico Press, 1971.

————. *The Taos Trappers, The Fur Trade in the Far Southwest, 1540-1846.* Norman: University of Oklahoma Presws, 1971.

Weber, Francis J. *California Bibliographies.* Los Angeles: Historical Society of Southern California, 1991.

Williams, David A. *David C. Broderick; A Political Portrait.* San Marino: Huntington Library, 1969.

Workman, Boyle. *The City That Grew.* Los Angeles: Southland Publishing Company, 1935.

Wright, Arthur A. *The Civil War in the Southwest.* Denver: Big Mountain Press, 1964.

Wright, Doris Marion. *A Yankee in Mexican California, Abel Stearns 1798-1848.* Santa Barbara: Wallace Hebbard, 1977.

B. Articles

Barrows, H.D. "Abel Stearns." *Annual Pubication of Historical Society of Southern California & Pioneer Register* 4 (1899): 197-199.

————. "Antonio Coronel." *Annual Publication of Historical Society of Southern California & Pioneer Register* 5 (1901): 78-84.

Beck, Nicholas. "The Vanishing Californians: Education of Indians in the Nineteenth Century." *Southern California Quarterly* 69 (Spring 1987): 33-50.

Blew, Robert W.. "Vigilantism in Los Angeles, 1835-1874." *Southern California Quarterly* 54 (Spring 1972): 11-30.

Brumgardt, John R. and Putney, William David. "San Salvador: New Mexican Settlement in Alta California." *Southern California Quarterly* 59 (Winter 1977): 353-364.

Burgess, Sherwood D. "Lumbering in Hispanic California." *California Historical Society Quarterly* 41 (September 1962): 237- 248.

Castaneda, Antonio I. "Gender, Race, and Culture: Spanish Mexican Women in the Historiography of Frontier California." *Journal of Women's Studies* 11 (1990): 8-20.

Castillo, Edward D. "The Assassination of Padres Andres Auintana by the Indians of Mission Santa Cruz in 1812: The Narration of Lorenzo Asiara." *California History* 64 (Fall 1989): 117-213.

Caughey, John Walton. "Don Benito Wilson, An Average Southern Californian." *Huntington Library Quarterly* 2 (1939): 285-301.

Chandler, Robert J. "Crushing Dissent: The Pacific Coast Tests Lincoln's Policy of Suppression, 1862." *Civil War History* 30 (September 1984): 235-254.

Churchill, Charles B. "Hawaiian, American, Californio: The Acculturation of William Heath Davis." *Southern California Quarterly* 76 (Winter 1994): 341-376.

Clendenen, Clarence C. "A Confederate Spy in California: A Curious Incident of the Civil War." *Southern California Quarterly* 45 (June 1963): 195-234.

————. "Dan Showalter -California Secessionist." *California Historical Society Quarterly* 40 (December 1961): 309- 325.

Fernandez, Ferdinand F.,"Except a California Indian: A Study in Legal Discrimination." *Southern California Quarterly* 50 (June 1968): 161-176.

Gates, Paul W. "The Land Business of Thomas O. Larkin." *California Historical Quarterly* 57 (Winter 1975): 323-344.

Gibson, Patricia. "California and the Compromise of 1850." *Journal of the West* 8 (1969): 578-591.

Gilbert, Benjamin Franklin. "The Confederate Minority in California." *California Historical Society Quarterly* 20 (June 1941): 154-170.

Guest, Francis F. "An Inquiry into the Role of the Discipline in California Mission Library." *Southern California Quarterly* 68 (Spring 1989): 1-68.

Guinn, J.M. "Historic Seaports of Los Angeles." *San Pedro Historical Society Shoreline* 8 (February 1981): 7-10.

Herr, Pamela and Spence, Mary Lee. "I Really Had Something Like The Blues, Letters from Jessie Benton Fremont to Elizabeth Blair Lee, 1847-1883." *Montana, The Magazine of Western History* 41 (Spring 1991): 17-31.

Hoffman, Abraham. "Horace Bell: Southern California's Pioneer with the Pugent Pen." *The Californians* 8 (March/April 1991): 22-31.

Hurtado, Albert L.. "California Indian Demography, Sherburne F. Cook, and the Revision of American History." *Pacific Historical Review* 75 (August 1989): 323-344.

Hutchinson, William H. "Westward: The Vision and the Purpose." *The Pacific Historian* 27 (Summer 1983): 22-30.

Jensen, Joan M. and Miller, Darlis A.. "The Gentle Tamers Revisited: New Approaches to the History of Women in American West." *Pacific Historical Review* 49 (May 1980): 173-213.

Johnson, David A. "Vigilance and the Law: The Moral Authority of Popular Justice in the Far West." *American Quarterly* 33 (Winter 1981): 558-586.

Kibby, Leo P. "California Soldiers in the Civil War." *California Historical Society Quarterly* 40 (December 1961): 343-350.

King, William F. "El Monte, an American town in Southern California, 1851-1966." *Southern California Quarterly* 53 (December 1971): 303-323.

Lothrop, Gloria Ricci. "Rancheras on the Land: Women and Property Rights in Hispanic California." *Southern California Quarterly* 76 (Spring 1994): 59-84.

McAfee, Ward M. "California History Textbooks and the Coming of the Civil War: The Need for a Broader Perspective of California History." *Southern California Quarterly* 41 (1974): 159-174.

McAfee, Ward M. "California's House Divided." *Civil War History* 33 (June 1987): 115-130.

McKanna, Clare V. Jr. "Crime and Punishment: The Hispanic Experience in San Quentin, 1851-1880." *Southern California Quarterly* 69 (Spring 1990): 1-18.

Mathes, Valerie Sherer. "The California Mission Indian Commission of 1891: The Legacy of Helen Hunt Jackson." *California History* 72 (Winter 1993/94): 338-360.

Meighan, Clement W. "Indians and California Missions." *Southern California Quarterly* 66 (Fall 1987): 187-202.

Miranda, Gloria E. "Racial and Cultural Dimension of Gente de Razon Status in Spanish and Mexican California." *Southern California Quarterly* 67 (Fall 1988): 265-278.

Nelson, Howard J. "The Two Pueblos of Los Angeles: Agricultural Village and Embryo Town." *Southern California Quarterly* 59 (Spring 1977): 1-12.

Neri, Michael C. "A Journalistic Portrait of the Spanish-Speaking People of California, 1868-1925." *Southern California Quarterly* 55 (Summer 1973): 193-208.

———. "Jose Gonzalez Rubio: A Biographical Sketch." *Southern California Quarterly* 70 (Summer 1991): 107-124.

Newmark, Marco R. "Early Los Angeles Bench and Bar." *Historical Society of Southern California Quarterly* 34 (December 1952): 327- 346.

Nunis, Doyce Jr., and Castillo, Edward D. "California Mission Indians: Two Perspectives." *California History* 70 (Summer 1991): 206-215.

Oliva, Leo E. "The Santa Fe Trail in Wartime: Expansion and Preservation of the Union." *Journal of the West* 28 (April 1989): 53-58.

Riley, Glenda. "Western Womens History -A Look at Some of the Issues." *Montana, The Magazine of Western History* 41 (Spring 1991): 66-70.

Robbins, William G. "Western History: A Dialectic on the Modern Condition." *Western Historical Quarterly* 20 (November 1989): 429- 449.

Robinson, John W. "A California Copperhead: Henry Hamilton and the Los Angeles *Star*." *Arizona and the West* 23 (Autumn 1981): 213-230.

———. "Colonel Edward John Cage Kewen: Los Angeles Fire-eating Orator of the Civil War." *Southern California Quarterly* 61 (Summer 1979): 159-181.

Robinson W. W. "The Indians of Los Angeles and What Became of Them." *Historical Society of Southern California Quarterly* 17 (December 1938): 156-172.

Romer, Margaret. "The Story of Los Angeles." *Journal of the West* 2 (April 1963): 166-192.

Schwantes, Carlos. "The Concept of the Wageworkers' Frontier: A Framework for Future Research." *Western Historical Quarterly* 18 (January 1987): 39-55.

Secrest, William B. Jr. "California on the Reference Shelf." *The Californians* 12 (1995): 52-57.

Stamps, Pearl Pauline. "Abel Stearns: California Pioneer." *Grizzly Bear* 39 (May 1926): 1-2, 4, 12; (June 1926): 54, 59; (July 1926): 4, 52-53, 61-62; (August 1926): 8, 57.

Stanley, Gerald. "Racism and the Early Republican Party: The 1856 Election in California." *Pacific Historical Review* 43 (May 1974): 171-187.

———. "Slavery and the Origins of the Republican Party in California." *Southern California Quarterly* 60 (Spring 1978): 1- 16.

Temple II, Thomas Workman. "Our Heritage from the Days of the Dons." *Historical Society of Southern California Quarterly* 40 (March 1958): 70-76.

Thornton, Harry Innes, Jr. "Recollection of the War by a Confederate Officer from California." *Southern California Quarterly* 45 June 1963): 195-234.

Trulio, Bererly. "Anglo-American Attitudes Toward New Mexican Women." *Journal of the West* 12 (April 1973): 299-339.

Unsigned Letter. "Indian Womens Rights." *Ramona Days* 2 (April 1888): 11-12.

Waldron, Granville Arthur. "Courthouses of Los Angeles County." *Historical Society of Southern California Quarterly* 41 (December 1959): 345-374.

Walters, Helen B. "Confederates in Southern California." *Historical Society of Southern California Quarterly* 35 (March 1953): 41-54.

Wang, Peter Heywood. "The Mythical Confederate Plot in Southern California." *San Bernardino County Museum Quarterly* 16 (Summer 1969): 1-16.

Watford, H.H. "The Far Western Wing of the Rebellion, 1861-1865." *California Historical Society Quarterly* 34 (June 1955): 125-148.

Whitaker, Rosemary. "Helen Hunt Jackson." *Western History Writer Series* 78 (1987): 1-50.

Wilkman, Nancy. "Helen Hunt Jackson's Ramona." *The Southern Californian* 7 (Spring 1995): 4.

Woolsey, Ronald C. "A Capitalist in a Foreign Land: Abel Stearns in Southern California Before the Conquest." *Southern California Quarterly* 75 (Summer 1993): 101-118.

————. "A Southern Dilemma: Slavery Expansion and the California Statehood Issues in 1850 -A Reconsideration." *Southern California Quarterly* 65 (Summer 1983): 123-144.

————. "An Outlaw as Outcast: Juan Flores, The Social Bandit Revisited." *The Californians* 11 (1994): 44-50.

————. "Conflicting Cultures, Law and Order in Frontier Southern California." *The Californians* 8 (Jan/Feb 1991): 38-47.

————. "Crime and Punishment: Los Angeles County, 1850-1856." *Southern California Quarterly* 61 (Spring 1979): 79-98.

————. "Disunion or Dissent? A New Look at an Old Problem in Southern California Attitudes Toward the Civil War." *Southern California Quarterly* 66 (Fall 1984): 185-204.

————. "Hugo Reid and the Southern California Indians Revisited." *The Branding Iron* 186 (Winter 1991/92): 10-14.

————. "L.A. Law: 1856 Vigilante Wars." *True West* 41 (December 1994): 19-25.

————. "Pioneer Views and Frontier Themes: Benjamin Hayes, Horace Bell, and the Southern California Experience." *Southern California Quarterly* 72 (Fall 1990): 255-274.

————. "Politics of a Lost Cause: Seceshers and Democrats in Southern California During the Civil War." *California History* 69 (Winter 1990/91): 372-383.

————. "Rites of Passage? Anglo and Mexican-American Contrasts in a Time of Change: Los Angeles 1860-1870." *Southern California Quarterly* 69 (Summer 1987): 81-101.

Worster, Donald, Armitage, Susan, Malone, Michael P., Weber, David J., Limerick, Patricia Nelson. "The Legacy of Conquest, by Patricia Nelson Limerick: A Panel of Appriasal." *Western Historical Quarterly* 20 (August 1989): 303-322.

Index